The Sorrow, the Sacrifice, and the Triumph

The Apparitions, Visions, and Prophecies of Christina Gallagher

THOMAS W. PETRISKO

A TOUCHSTONE BOOK
Published by Simon & Schuster
New York London Toronto
Sydney Tokyo Singapore

TOUCHSTONE
Rockefeller Center
1230 Avenue of the Americas
New York, NY 10020

Designed by DEIRDRE C. AMTHOR

Manufactured in the United States of America

7 9 10 8 6

Library of Congress Cataloging-in-Publication Data
Petrisko, Thomas W.
The sorrow, the sacrifice, and the triumph : the apparitions, visions, and prophecies of Christina Gallagher / Thomas W. Petrisko.
p. cm.
Includes bibliographical references and index.
1. Mary, Blessed Virgin, Saint—Apparitions and miracles—Ireland. 2. Gallagher, Christina. I. Title.
BT652.I73P48 1995
248.2'9—dc20 95-35753
CIP

ISBN 0-684-80388-7

2

4/18/00

Dear Perry—

May Our Mother Mary and Our Redeemer, Jesus, speak to you through the words on these pages.

With love and gratitude for all the words you have used in speaking to me.

Sue

Our Blessed Lady
appears to
Christina Gallagher
under the title
Our Lady Queen of Peace

This book is dedicated to my mother, Mary Petrisko,
and to my Heavenly Mother Mary,
Our Lady Queen of Peace.
I thank God, from the depth of my soul,
for such grace in my life.

I must boast, not that it is profitable, but I will go on to visions and revelations of the Lord. I know someone in Christ who, fourteen years ago—whether in the body or out of the body I do not know, God knows—was caught up to the third heaven. And I know that this person—whether in the body or out of the body, I do not know, God knows—was caught up into Paradise and heard ineffable things which no one may utter. About this person I will boast, but about myself I will not boast, except about my weaknesses. Although if I should wish to boast, would not be foolish, for I would be telling the truth. But I refrain, so that no one may think more of me than what he sees in me or hears from me (because of the abundance of the revelations). Therefore, that I might not become too elated, a thorn in the flesh was given to me, an angel of Satan, to beat me, to keep me from being too elated. Three times I begged the Lord about this, that it might leave me, but he said to me, "My grace is sufficient for you, for strength is made perfect in weakness." I will rather boast most gladly of my weaknesses, in order that the strength of Christ may dwell with me. Therefore, I am content with weaknesses, insults, hardships, persecutions, and constraints for the sake of Christ; for when I am weak, then I am strong.

(2 Cor. 12:1–10)

ACKNOWLEDGMENTS

This book could not have been written without the patience and understanding of my wife, Emily, and my daughters Maria and Sarah. Their sacrifices were great; may God reward them.

I am also indebted to many other people who helped and supported me. It goes without saying that Christina Gallagher and her spiritual director, Father Gerard McGinnity, gave all of themselves to perfect this work. Likewise, without Mrs. Marita Wojdak, this book may not have come to fulfillment. Her assistance was immeasurable as was the assistance of Mrs. Karen Seisek, who contributed in many ways to the finalizing of this book.

I am also grateful to Dr. Frank Novasack, Jr., Therese Swango, Carole McElwain, Robert Petrisko, Joan Smith, Amy Resch, and Catherine Dailey, all who advised, assisted, or prayed for the success of this work.

Finally, a special thank-you to my confreres, who helped by their encouragement or advice: Jan and Ed Connell, Stan Karminski, Bud McFarlane; my editors at Simon & Schuster: Sheila Curry, Rebecca Cabaza, and Philip Metcalf; Sister Agnes McCormick, Father Robert Hermmann, Father John Koza, Father John

O'Shea, and Father Richard Foley; Ms. Noreen Brubeck, whose company, Mediaright Productions, assisted in the editing of the manuscript; and Mr. R. Vincent, whose wonderful account of the experiences of Christina Gallagher, *Please Come Back to Me and My Son,* was drawn upon heavily.

CONTENTS

PREFACE

The account you are about to read is the story of a visionary, a mystic, a stigmatist, and a victim soul. It is the story of a woman who, through the will and grace of God, has received an incredible number of special graces that God wishes her to share with all mankind.

What Christina Gallagher has to give to the world and the Church through her life is more than just rare, because her experiences exceed those of some of the most well known mystics to date. She is not just a chosen soul, but a soul whose graces are given at a chosen time in history. Thus, her revelations are not just for souls at this time, but for the world at this time.

I traveled to Ireland in February of 1992 to meet with Mrs. Gallagher. From that encounter and from everything I was able to review, this account has been written. May its contents greatly contribute to the awareness of the infinite love and mercy God wishes to give souls.

THOMAS W. PETRISKO
April 3, 1995

THE SORROW, THE SACRIFICE, AND THE TRIUMPH

Foreword

What initially attracted me was the House of Prayer for Priests. According to reports, it had been set up by Christina Gallagher, acting on Our Lady's instructions, to provide a spiritual haven for priests and thus help toward their sanctification.

I was to discover that much prayer is now actually done by priests in that holy house dedicated to the Queen of Peace, where the Blessed Sacrament is exposed daily. In addition, much prayer is done *for* priests by ever-increasing numbers of lay visitors from near and far.

Anyhow, I decided that this spiritual powerhouse on Ireland's beautiful west coast was well worth a visit. Fellow priests will be particularly interested to hear how I fared.

Proof Beyond Doubt

I had never met Christina Gallagher, though from what I had read and heard I was inclined to accept her as genuine. But what in the event completely convinced me of this was the extraordinary insight she displayed into my interior life, including my spiritual track record to date: that is, my memory bank of triumphs and failures over the years in the Lord's service.

In other words, this remarkable Irishwoman demonstrated beyond any doubt that she possessed a sort of X-ray vision into my private world of conscience and moral striving. She could read the secrets of my heart. She could witness within me that hidden arena where, as is the case with everyone, warfare is waged nonstop between good and evil, truth and falsehood, light and darkness.

Thus aware that other priests had a similar experience, I was nonetheless bowled over when Christina Gallagher proceeded to discern with clinical precision the weaknesses and strengths of my world within.

Her Special Charism

All this took place in the course of an interview I had requested of her as part of my three-day retreat. Let me immediately add that Christina conducts such interviews in a manner that is unfailingly discreet, respectful, and pleasant. You realize that she is simply carrying out the task for which God has endowed her with such a special charism.

The charism in question evidently functions in conjunction with two of the Holy Spirit's sevenfold gifts. The first is knowledge; Christina knows intimately the secrets of minds and hearts. The second gift is counsel; she offers priests advice that is wonderfully wise, consoling, inspiring, and upbuilding.

The end result of my experience with this amazing mystic was deep peace of soul; which, as we learn from Saint Ignatius, is unfailingly a sign of God's presence in any given spiritual process and procedure.

Her Urgent Message

Having been so impressed and helped by the Irish visionary, I now take all the more pleasure in commending this excellent book on her by Dr. Thomas Petrisko. He brings into clear focus not only Christina's profound prayer life and mystical suffering but the urgency of her message and mission for today's Church and world.

Certainly this book deserves to find its way into many, many hands, especially priestly ones. *Indeed, let me suggest that laypeople make a gift of it to some priests(s) they know.* For it is undoubtedly we men of little faith—we, the Lord's anointed, His ministerial priests —who stand to benefit most from any form of contact with the supercharged, clear-sighted faith that animates everything Christina is and does.

Her meaning and role come at a providentially opportune time. For the turmoil within today's Church has rightly been diagnosed as basically a crisis of faith. Largely responsible for this state of affairs is the liberal theology already so deeply entrenched in many of our seminaries and theological faculties, which is rapidly spreading its poison among the laity and undermining their faith.

Tonic for Faith

Faith really means two things. The first is our awareness of supernatural realities. Faith's second meaning concerns its contents, that is, *what* we believe. Both these aspects of our faith receive an invigorating tonic from any form of contact with Christina Gallagher's world.

Her own awareness of supernatural realities is so keen and habitual that it practically merges with her perception of the material world. Thus, for her, God's supernatural kingdom is as real and matter-of-fact as driving a car or spreading butter on bread. As for the invisible presence in that divine kingdom—everyone from Our Lord and His Mother down to her guardian angel and the special saints she is on close terms with—these are like familiar houseguests.

With regard to faith's contents, Christina Gallagher is a beacon of light and orthodoxy. For the messages she receives from Heaven touch upon a good number of the Church's traditional teachings, including those under attack by latter-day heretics parading themselves as progressive-minded Catholic liberals.

The Eucharist; the sacramental priesthood; the efficacy and value of Confession; the dark mystery of sin both original and actual; the dignity and authority of Peter's successor; the filial obedience we owe to the Church's Magisterium; the reality of Heaven, Hell, and Purgatory; the unique role of Mary in God's plan of salvation and dispensation of grace; the existence and activity of angels and devils; the marvelous interconnectedness between the saints in Heaven, the souls in purgatory, and us wayfaring pilgrims on earth—these are among the doctrines that feature in Christina's communications with the supernatural world.

Her Underlying Task

This humble Mayo housewife and mother is a prophetic figure for our times. She speaks about the warning and the divine wrath to come, and exhorts us to repent, to pray, to do penance, and to trust profoundly in God's mercy.

What is surely Christina's underlying God-given task is to mobilize the Church Militant and spur it on to victory over the powers of darkness. Through her the Mother of God is pleading for priests, above all, to be burning and shining lights amid "the darkness that overshadows both the Church and the world." Fallen angels rage upon the earth and many souls are being lost in "the abyss of death eternal."

Dr. Thomas Petrisko and his publishers are to be thanked for presenting us with this stimulating study of a major modern mystic and apostle.

Richard Foley, S. J.
London, England
August 15, 1994

PART I

A Chosen Soul from a Chosen Land

CHAPTER ONE

From Genesis to the Triumph

I WILL PUT ENMITY BETWEEN THEE AND THE WOMAN, AND THY SEED AND HER SEED. SHE SHALL CRUSH THY HEAD AND THOU SHALT LIE IN WAIT FOR HER HEEL.

—GEN. 3:15

It's always a surprise where the Virgin Mary appears. Whether it be distant mountaintops or hidden grottos, the first question people wonder aloud is always "Why here?" For Christina Gallagher and the people of County Mayo, it was no different those first winter days of 1988.

County Mayo is in the beautiful windswept countryside in the western part of Ireland known for the Atlantic rains that storm inland across Connemara where the Twelve Pins Mountains shoulder one another toward the sea.[1] Yes, it's a wet place. But on clear days, there is a breathtaking view of the summit of Croagh Padraig in the distant western horizon, where for forty days in the year 435, Saint Patrick fasted, prayed, and beseeched Heaven to convert the faithful of beautiful Erin to an "Isle of Saints."

But although Our Lady Queen of Peace would come to make

many visits to Christina in County Mayo, it was in Dublin that Our Lady first appeared to her. Indeed, the Virgin Mary's first apparition was totally unexpected.

While visiting a grotto in County Sligo, Ireland, in the fall of 1985, she had unexpectedly witnessed with her eyes the Head of Jesus crowned with thorns. Unknown to her, it was this apparition that would actually begin the series of miraculous events in her life, events she could not have imagined.

Besides encounters with the Virgin Mary and apparitions of Christ, the simple Irish homemaker was soon being shown extraordinary, mystical, and heavenly sights. From awesome glimpses of the Face of the Eternal Father in Heaven to terrorizing experiences with the Prince of Darkness in her own home, her breathtaking accounts are numbing. Within a short time, a considerable number of messages for the Church and the world were conveyed to Christina. She was to be, God indicated, a "fearless witness" to a misguided and "sinful generation."

Yet as incredible as all of this was, we must remember Christina Gallagher's spiritual experiences are designed primarily as incisive reminders of God's will for His people. They uphold for us the truth of our faith and the glorious eternal life with God that awaits believers. Indeed, they embody the message of the Gospel, the same message of hope, love, and peace Jesus spelled out to the world almost two thousand years ago.

Likewise, her apparitions and revelations are strikingly similar to past accounts of such great Catholic mystics as Theresa Neumann, Saint Anne Catherine Emmerich, Saint Bridget of Sweden, and the Venerable Mary of Agreda. More than that, the revelations given to Christina Gallagher reveal powerful images of the hidden world of God's Kingdom, the world of the spirit. Riveting in description, some of her mystical experiences are more powerful than we are capable of absorbing. They deliberately convey the serious responsibility one has for the salvation of the soul.

"It's our soul that is at risk, and mankind doesn't want to listen," Christina repeats over and over.

By this emphasis on the soul, Christina confirms her desire to remove obsessive concerns with earthly chastisements. These are concerns which distract many listeners from the core of the Virgin Mary's message. These concerns with impending earthly uncertainty, Our Lady insists, are not as important as the salvation of the soul. The Virgin Mary has come to bring *souls* back to God, not just to warn of a coming tribulation. As the Blessed Mother confirmed to Christina the destiny of those who fail to convert, "They will never rise from the death of the soul."

But as implausible as it seems, this serious message, Christina admits, is not getting through. People go their merry way. Everyday, the world staggers forward like a wounded animal, in the power of darkness, greed, and sensuality, renouncing God's invitation. It refuses completely, or chooses to hear little of what God has to say. Instead, many reply, "We will not serve."

So, like the children at Fatima, Christina now confronts people with exactly what she has seen—some of which is not very pleasant. When humanity ignores the protection of the soul, says Christina, an irreversible fate is sealed. Failure to protect one's soul, she says, will inevitably lead them to Hell.

Today, few believe that Hell, the world of the damned, exists. Considered to be an imaginary world, the secular media only refers to it when it's extremely hot or cold outside or when describing the chances of a snowball's survival there. People damn one another, not realizing that by their very own actions, they are at risk of this inescapable death sentence.

Yet talk of its existence and horror awakens some people. Like mystics over the centuries, Christina's vivid account of Hell gives fresh testimony to its reality and its eternal inhabitants. She has seen their sealed fate, their endless agony. She has watched the unrepentant as they swim in fire, an unquenchable fire that disfigures and torments its captives.

Adding to this nightmare, Christina has been shown sights of individuals headed for this fate. But this was necessary for a reason. It is through her voluntary suffering for these souls that God wishes to save them. This is perhaps how God has come to use Christina the most. As a victim soul, she suffers the wounds of Jesus Christ in her body. Bravely, she offers this physical, emotional, and mental anguish for the salvation of many who would otherwise be lost for eternity.

Once, on her way to give a talk in the south of Ireland, the Virgin Mary showed her thousands of people who, according to Our Lady, "had lost all love for God in their hearts." In a second sight, she saw thousands who were well on their way to Hell. It was not a pretty sight. As the Blessed Mother wept, she besought Christina to offer her life and death for these souls. Christina complied, whereupon the Blessed Mother led Christina in a prayer of self-offering of mind, will, heart, soul, and body to God. Later Jesus told her these souls would be saved. Thus, it is in this way as a victim soul in union with the suffering of Christ that Christina has come to find the most meaning in her mission.[2]

But her mystical experiences don't end there. God's plan through Christina continues to unfold. Although the Virgin Mary's apparitions to Christina began in 1988, apparitions, mystical experiences, and heavenly messages continue with no end indicated. It is a generous outpouring of revelations, revelations that deal with urgent conversion of heart and events to come. In His plan, God has revealed to Christina a variety of the supernatural. From vivid scenes out of the Old and New Testaments to symbolic apparitions of the coming era of peace, she has seen a lot. In the past two years alone, more and more of the most celebrated saints and departed faithful servants of the Catholic Faith, have appeared to her. Moses the Lawgiver, Elijah the Prophet, Saint John the Evangelist, Blessed Michael the Archangel, Padre Pio, Saint Philomena, The Little Flower, Saint Catherine of Siena, Saint Teresa of Avila, Saint Anthony, Saint Joseph, Bishop Sheen, and Sister Faustina are among those she now intimately refers to as "her friends," friends that now enjoy the beatific vision.

These friends appear to play a role in a baffling, yet integrated plan of private revelation God wishes to give the world through Christina Gallagher. By their mere presence these chosen ones subtly bring the events and teachings of the past back to life while concurring with God's plan for the fulfillment of the future. As messengers and advisers they give us a dimension to God's plan that is important and vital.

By means of the saints, God demonstrates through Christina that the Church, Triumphant in Heaven, is wholeheartedly involved in the fulfillment of the times. As the Queen of Peace revealed to her, "The Martyrs of Ireland are constantly interceding before God, with a holy restlessness."

Yet all this intercession holds great purpose. For a war now rages—an awesome invisible war of the principalities—and all Heaven shudders at what is to come while the earth remains unmoved. Christina has already learned, in part, what the future holds.

From these experiences, Christina gives us a sweeping picture of our times. It is no less a picture of the end times—a picture the Virgin Mary presented many times before and continues to present now. And while it is the Virgin Mary who brings us this news, it actually is the completion of a design which included the Blessed Mother from the beginning.

Indeed, visionaries throughout the world point to the Virgin Mary as the woman in the Book of Genesis (Gen. 3:15) who crushes the head of the serpent. It's been her role from the beginning. Confirmed at Lourdes as having no mark on her from Satan, the Mother of All now comes as Mother of Jesus, *Queen of Peace,* through the power of the Holy Spirit to warn the world of its destiny.

Yes, the victory is hers. The Blessed Mother is the New Eve. And now the time has arrived for the world to know.

Ever true to the vast review of His work through Christina, God once more confirmed this fact by a powerful sight that accompanied an important message. She received this apparition and message along with a monumental announcement, while she was in the Philippines.

During her first night in the Philippines, the young Irish mystic was awakened at 3:00 A.M. Immediately she knew she was to pray. Engrossed in prayer, the Lord showed her an awesome sight of the sky transformed and illuminated by a spectacular bright red light.

Out of the red sky, in great splendor and beauty, appeared the Blessed Virgin Mary. Our Lady was standing on a globe, deep in prayer, with hands joined.

Suddenly, Christina noticed a large black snake raise its head daringly toward the Virgin Mary's foot. Although she didn't acknowledge the serpent directly, the Blessed Mother, like the woman in the Book of Genesis, calmly raised her right foot and crushed its head. As the serpent's body squirmed and shuddered over a vast area, Christina could see the Filipino people momentarily frightened. But quickly Our Lady laid to rest their worries as she extended her mantle in a huge gesture and covered them protectively with it.

As Christina watched in awe, the voice of the Risen Savior was heard.

> You, My people, are truly Mine. Through your suffering, My Mercy will save you and many who are blind. I am beholden unto you My Heart and I send to you My Mother. You will realize the value of your suffering and the power of your Mother's love and intercession. You, My people, I will save from the beast's devouring anger. My people, do not sin in impurity of body. I, Jesus, your Lord, and My Beloved Mother are with you and love you. Go in My Peace and serve your Lord God.

The Lord's reference to the blind was of tremendous significance, because only a few days before a miraculous healing of a blind man occurred as Christina recited a special prayer at one of her speaking engagements in the Philippines.

NOTE: A commentary on the above message by Father McGinnity, Christina Gallagher's spiritual director:

> This word "beholden" means "obliged" or "indebted" and Jesus seems to mean "I owe you My protection, because you truly belong to Me and are faithful to Me, even though you

suffer so much." He has an "utang na loob" (the Filipino expression used).

This word "Beast," which is used in The Apocalypse to describe the Devil's power, refers to Freemasonry, according to Our Lady's explanations of The Apocalypse to Father Gobbi. There, she points out that whereas the Red Dragon represents atheistic Communism and its outright denial of God, the Black Beast of Masonry believes in God, but works secretly against the Almighty by structures which deceptively try to undermine the Church. These structures offer worldly success and power and try to attract people by money and pleasure to abandon God's law, the Commandments. The hidden work of the Beast is to destroy Christ's Kingdom on earth with the spread of the Kingdom of darkness and sin.

Since receiving the message, news from the Philippines about proposals to forcefully introduce "population control" brings to light a deeper level of meaning in this message. Artificial contraception as a means of population control is opposed to the Church's teaching of God's law. The contraceptive mentality has been proven to lead to the practice of abortion all over the world. The Filipino people respect unborn life. The smiling children, although poor, and their struggling but generous parents who accept humbly God's gift of new life are obviously most pleasing to Jesus, Our Lord, God, but Jesus says the Beast is "angry." The Devil resents this openness to God, to His Divine Law, and to His Gift of Life. His "anger" is, in Jesus' words to Christina, a "devouring anger." In other words, like a bullying beast, he is intent on killing and destroying life. (Many artificial contraceptives are also abortifacients: they actually work by expelling the new baby immediately after it is conceived.) However, the hopeful message of Jesus shows that His Merciful Heart will send His Mother to protect that country.

Before departing the Philippines, Jesus again spoke to Christina. Although steeped in mystery, it was a far-reaching disclosure and one of significance. And from it, Christina's experience of the prophecy from the Book of Genesis began to make even more sense. "Because you have come, I am able to implement My plan. The Triumph of My Mother's Immaculate Heart will begin here and spread throughout the whole world."

The subsequent refusal of the Filipino people to cooperate with the government proposals to limit and destroy human life powerfully proves Our Lord's prophecy through Christina.

Just months later, Christ's words to her seemed to usher in a monumental event in Russia. It was a mystical event of such magnitude, such importance, that Church historians after the Triumph may write about it forever. It was an event many say is likely connected with the Second Coming of Christ.

Yet we cannot get ahead of ourselves. That would be a mistake. We must remember that before Christ's return, the Tribulation, the Triumph, and the Era of Peace will come.

And by September 1993 the Lord indicated to Christina that a crucial moment was near. It was now time, Jesus told her, for the Angel of the Passover to appear. Yes, the same angel from the Old Testament who had visited once before.

Described as the Angel of Death, or a Destroyer, the Book of Exodus speaks woefully of the night of his visitation to the Egyptians. Like the Lord's announcement of the Immaculate Heart's Triumph beginning in the Philippines, here was an equally prodigious disclosure. The Angel of the Passover was close at hand.

But before we go any further, let us first go back. Let us see how all this began for Christina. Let us examine all she has been gifted with. In Christina Gallagher, God has buried a treasure for our salvation.

All we have to do, through humility and faith, is unearth it.

CHAPTER TWO

"I Am the Virgin Mary, Queen of Peace"

BUT WHO AM I THAT THE MOTHER OF MY LORD SHOULD COME TO ME?

—LUKE 1:43

It all began in 1985.

One evening while Christina Gallagher was in prayer at a grotto, a powerful force somehow turned her head and she found herself a witness to the apparition of a living, suffering Head of Jesus Christ.

To this day, she cannot forget the sight of Christ's Head turned upwards in agony, crowned with very black thorns.

His hair was dark brown and His eyes bulged and then closed. His face was shrunken, especially below the cheekbones, and His beard damaged and uneven. A glow of light surrounded His Head and His Face was besmeared with blood. He was clearly suffering.

In her agony of soul, a deep contrition fell upon her. And a painful thought occurred to her that it was her own sins that were crucifying the Lord. It was a profound intuition, one that left her trembling. "I knew Jesus bore my sins," she said. Deep within herself, she begged for His forgiveness.

On another occasion, Christina watched a statue of Our Lady disappear and be replaced with an apparition of the Blessed Mother. Our Lady drew back her mantle and beneath it Christina could see the living, suffering, crucified Christ as the Virgin Mary herself disappeared.

When queried, Christina thought His countenance was strikingly similar to the reversed image of Christ's face on the Shroud of Turin. That's all she could compare it to.

Days later, she remained in shock. But something else was beginning to happen to her. These heartrending events had touched her deeply and so powerfully; especially Christ's Crucifixion. The face, the blood, and agony ate at her heart. She couldn't forget it. The vivid reality of the Lord hanging near death on the cross burned into her soul and affected her life forever.

Indeed, her life began to change. God commenced His work in her and she responded to His grace. Prayer and the Church became staples in her life. She spoke to others about "trust in God" and His "ever-near presence." She began to enjoy praying the Rosary. Daily Mass and Communion, fifteen decades of the Rosary, confession, and fasting—it was a new person emerging from the old. Her surrender to God's Will was absolute. But it wasn't until three years later that Christina Gallagher's mission would become clear.

On Thursday, January 21, 1988, while visiting relatives in Dublin, Ireland, the Queen of Peace miraculously appeared before her very eyes. Christina was totally taken into a deep peace and love that was not of this world. She looked up and beheld a beautiful lady with big, blue eyes, hovering slightly above the floor. Surrounded in luminous white light, the glowing figure looked directly at Christina, piercing her soul with her eyes.

Stunned, she was consumed with a deep love and peace. It was an awesome sight. "Our Holy Mother was radiantly beautiful," says Christina, "with light coming from within her body. I could see her feet and hands. I could see Our Lady clearly."

The Blessed Mother was holding her hands in a praying position. She then opened them to reveal a clear glass globe with smoke swirling inside it. Later, Our Lady told her the globe was the world, but never mentioned the smoke. Perhaps it was the smoke of Satan, which Our Lady once told Christina was issuing from the earth because the people were not responding to her call. The Virgin Mary invited Christina under her mantle and then said, "I am leaving you now." Our Lady made the Sign of the Cross, blessing them, and then began to fade and was consumed into a light which also faded.

They were left speechless. What had happened?

An indescribable elation gripped both of them. The other person present, though seeing nothing, was deeply moved and felt "a presence." As their tears flowed, they tried to somehow grasp what had just occurred, but they couldn't. It wasn't to be captured and it was gone like the wind. Saturated in joy, it was clear Heaven had just paid them a visit.

But the joy didn't last. Those in whom Christina confided advised her to keep quiet. Her reality was questioned. Perhaps she was losing her mind, they said. People warned her of hallucinations. If not for the unexplainable love and peace she felt, Christina claims she would have "questioned her mental state."

That same night, she journeyed by train back to County Mayo. Although filled with excitement and wonder, she was equally consumed with questions. After examining it all, she became perturbed.

Crazy? Hallucinations? Her mind raced with thoughts and feelings that left her drained. What should she do? Should she tell anyone else? The hardest part though was that the heavenly lady hadn't told her anything, not even her name. And yet she felt she loved this lady so much, and the peace she experienced contradicted the idea she was somehow ill. It was agonizing. When first told about Christina's apparitions, her husband and mother responded with blank stares and silence. And although her mother simply inquired if she was "all right," the whole thing began to take its toll.

A week later, the beautiful lady returned. Accompanying her this time was a lovely young girl whom Christina discovered was Saint Bernadette of Lourdes.

Again, the Virgin Mary's visit was unexpected. Christina said, "Our Lady was transparent from a distance. As she came closer and her form filled completely, I could see that the light which appeared to glow over her heart was actually a Eucharistic Host."

As the Virgin Mary materialized, so did the overwhelming feeling of peace. The apparition occurred in Christina's kitchen at her home in Gortnadreha, a small village of only a dozen or so families. And again, the heavenly lady was quiet. No words were spoken.

The Holy Eucharist was glowing brightly above Our Lady's breast. Saint Bernadette remained kneeling, transfixed upon it. According to Christina, the youthful saint had dark hair, a round face, and joined hands. She wore a brown dress and a gray headpiece. Motionless, Saint Bernadette remained in reverence and awe throughout the apparition.

Once again Our Lady spoke no words, but left Christina immersed in peace and love.

The following day, the beautiful woman appeared again. Our Lady immediately spoke to Christina. With a soft melodic voice, the Blessed Mother announced, "Be not afraid, I am the Virgin Mary, Queen of Peace, and I come in peace." Our Lady's appearance this time was different, too. She wore a cream-colored mantle with a gold seam around the edge. The heavenly garb radiantly glowed as light poured out everywhere. It was Thursday, February 4, 1988.

Without hesitation, the Queen of Peace moved to comfort Christina, who confessed to be overwhelmed with awe. The Virgin Mary's love quickly soothed her fears of the unbelievers.

> My child, why are you so troubled? I have told you I come in peace. Do not fear what has not come to pass. . . . When you have fears about so many things, you cannot allow peace to live in your heart. . . . My Son and I have been trying to open your heart for some time to get you ready for this, but you did not know. You fought us with such strength. Please, my child, do not keep on fighting us, be-

cause the same strength will help us to win souls. I want you to pray more, as much as you can. I know you have your family to think about, but my Son and I are giving you the graces you need, through your prayers. So I say to you, rid yourself of fear. I know you do not understand all, but you will. You have accepted in your heart how to pray, but you must know I want you to pray more and more. Do not waste time, my child.

True to her mission, the Queen of Peace immediately began to teach and guide Christina. Christina's work was to begin. Time was short. Our Lady requested of her the full fifteen decades of the Rosary, advising:

"I say to all the people who find it difficult to accept my messages and those of my Son, pray the Rosary from your heart, all three mysteries, for nine days. Offer up these prayers to my Son's heart and to the Holy Spirit for enlightenment. If you do that you will understand. I bless you, my child, Father, Son, and Holy Spirit."

From that day forward, the Virgin Mary didn't waste time or words. With her first exhortation the Blessed Mother delivered through Christina Gallagher a powerful piece of advice to help unbelievers.

It was clear there was no more time to give excuses for not believing, because excuses someday would not be enough. If one wanted to find the truth, the formula was now given. With just a little faith and prayer, the Queen of Heaven was showing the way to the Light.

A light, the Virgin Mary insisted, the Irish people avoid no longer, because they were to be its beacon.

CHAPTER THREE

"My Son Has Chosen Christina"

"How do you know me?" Nathaniel asked him. "Before Philip called you," Jesus answered, "I saw you under the fig tree."

—John 1:48

Right from the beginning, her apparitions were different.

Unlike the visionaries at Fatima and Lourdes, Christina Gallagher was not a child when the Queen of Peace appeared to her. Nor was she religious, like a number of adult mystics over the centuries. And adding to what appears to be a litany of contradictions, Christina was also married and the mother of two children.

Yet these weren't contradictions at all. Visionaries are often very different from each other, often different in many ways. There is no standard, no prototype, no "perfect" visionary.

Although frequently it is emphasized that Our Blessed Mother chooses children, no documented facts support this assumption. The Church-approved apparitions at Lourdes, LaSalette, Beauraing, and Banneux were indeed to children, but many apparitions have been to men and women of all ages and backgrounds.

But that's not news. Our Blessed Mother says these souls are the ones God has prepared and waited for. His plan is always one of perfect patience and respect for the free will of His children. Indeed, God is in no hurry. He seldom tips His hand. With a seed planted long before, one often sees the fruits of humility, charity, and simplicity in His chosen ones regardless of age, sex, education, or faith. He chooses souls He knows He can work in, souls such as Christina Gallagher.

In fact, Christina humbly admitted even her faith was weak, confessing, "The Rosary was only a rhyme for me."

But God knew all along how special this soul was to Him as He does with all His chosen ones. He had planted His seed. She was His—right from the start.

In a brief message Christina received for a friend, the Queen of Peace revealed Heaven's way of thinking: "My Son has chosen Christina, because she has an open heart to Him and me, and yet knows little."

Not surprisingly, Christina has been compared to Saint Bernadette Soubirous. Both were poor and weak; it was a natural comparison. Like Bernadette, her failures and shortcomings were visible to all, just as God planned. They were gifts from Him, great gifts.

Brigid Christina (Ferguson) Gallagher was born on June 4, 1953, in Calladashan, Knockmore, County Mayo, Ireland, a small village of about ten families, two miles from her present home in Gortnadreha. Named after Saint Brigid of Ireland, she has always gone by her middle name, Christina.

At about five feet tall, she looks and definitely sounds Irish. Her brogue is strong and clear, a textbook accent. Though fairly light-skinned, she has dark eyes and dark brown hair that is short and stylish. When she smiles her eyes seem to glimmer a momentary sigh of relief, perhaps from the pain she endures through the redemptive suffering she fully embraces.

Like other Irish girls, Christina was married young—when she was just eighteen. Her husband, Patrick, whom she refers to as "Paddy," is forty-nine and a plumber by trade. They've been married twenty-four years and have two children.

Her mother recently passed away and her father is alive. Although at first puzzled about it all, they were supportive.

The Fergusons lived in a small cottage with just two bedrooms. Christina shared a room with her older brother Joseph and older sister Marie. Despite the tight fit, their faith made it work. Nightly the family Rosary was prayed while kneeling against a wooden bench in the kitchen. Monthly confession was also the rule.

Each Sunday the Ferguson family walked the two miles to Christ the King Church. This included Christina's mother, Martha, who suffered from chronic tuberculosis. Again, their faith carried the load. Christina remembers no complaints. "We were always glad and happy for what we had." This is an intrinsic quality in people from County Mayo. For they are people known for their positive outlook in the midst of their constant hardships. When her mother lingered near death, it was Christina's stubborn faith as a youth that prompted her to implore God's Mercy for her mother's life and also for herself. She was only fourteen. God's ears were not closed, as her mother regained her health.

Some time later, Christina's other prayer was answered. By accident she noticed one day she was somehow able to read and write. She thought it was a mistake. But it was another gift from God in her life. Yet to this day, she remains an unaffected, quiet, sincere individual who at times is embarrassed by all the attention these spiritual matters have brought upon her. Graced with a natural humility, Christina leaves those who inquire with a sense that she has always been kind of heart and easygoing.

Perhaps it is again that warm smile, a smile according to one theologian that "neither Stigmata nor other sufferings has interfered with."[1]

As author Michael H. Brown wrote, "She is today one of the most famous mystics in the world."[2] Yet regardless of this fame, Christina likes to be Christina—no one new, no one else. She likes people and enjoys talking to them. She is even known for her sense of humor.

World famous mystic or not, she prefers remaining at home. It is here she finds her peace. The limelight is not for her. She disdains attention and reminds people that the Blessed Mother has warned that aggressive conduct by a visionary is a sign that warrants careful discernment.

Indeed, Christina upholds she is still a homemaker above all else. A homemaker like any other. Cooking, ironing, cleaning, and housework—that's the routine. After morning prayers, she's out the door. With her own household affairs in order, she's off to do the shopping; no lights, no cameras, no questions. This is how she likes it. Nothing fancy, nothing out of the ordinary.

But the worldwide excursions are out of the ordinary. Christina now speaks at many Marian conferences and finds it difficult. The long flights to America, Europe, or Asia are grueling, even overwhelming. Yet there's no getting around them.

Like other *chosen souls,* she endures the mental discomfort and the physical duress. She must. Sometimes this can be hard, because Christina must not only travel, but also say what God wants to have said. Some of which, to make matters more difficult, people do not necessarily want to hear. Sin, Satan, Conversion, Chastisement, and Hell are not exactly words of endearment to many.

But often the Holy Spirit takes over while Christina is speaking and her words become even more powerful and uplifting, leaving even her a bit surprised. As she wrote to her spiritual director, "I was talking all about God in such a way it was shocking to me."

But not shocking to God. The Most Holy Trinity is powerfully at work within this special soul. She has developed a legion of followers who love her and her messages dearly. And although it takes its toll, the life of a chosen soul has had its rewards.

Today Christina is "inwardly stronger." She is confident—confident in God, confident in His strength. He can do all, she can do nothing. She is all weakness, He is all strength. This newly recognized confidence reminds one of Saint Teresa of Avila, who appeared to Christina and in whom Christina recognized the virtue of resolute firmness. Christina says she can relate to Saint Teresa of

Avila, who at first seemed a hard and tough nun. However, she later discovered Saint Teresa was actually quite gentle, yet strong-willed and determined. She always called upon the infinite power and authority of God. "Saint Teresa is someone," says Christina, "who would walk through walls for God."

Although Christina had no prior knowledge of Saint Teresa's life, a small prayer written by the saint hundreds of years ago for her novices succinctly demonstrates the accuracy of Christina's description of her:

> O King of Glory, Lord of Lords, Emperor of Emperors, Saint of Saints, Power above all the Powers, Knowledge above all the Knowledges, Wisdom itself; You Lord are Truth itself, Riches themselves, do You never cease forever to reign![3]

In 1992, the Eternal Father and Jesus spoke to Christina. It was a monumental disclosure. From this conversation she learned she was specially *chosen*. In fact, her calling is crucial. For Jesus and the Eternal Father told her it will affect an entire generation of God's people.

Like most mystics, her full role in God's plan is one of deep mystery, one known only to God. But it doesn't matter. She doesn't understand it all, and doesn't try. Instead, she centers on her own unworthiness. "I am not worthy of any of these things—not even the cross. I am worthy of nothing. God is everything."

Reflecting on the many tragedies in the world today, including AIDS victims and mothers contemplating abortion, Christina points out that she realizes she could easily be the worst of sinners. "I could be a great sinner," says Christina, "but for the grace of God in my life." And clearly that is the lesson for us all.

But the grace in Christina's life is very special and unique. It's a grace that has allowed her to experience what the Queen of Peace spoke of as a "pure conversion," a conversion that's powerful and lasting.

Only this pure conversion didn't come as easily as it sounds. In fact, it didn't come easily at all. With what God planned to do through this chosen Irish soul, there had to come a price, a steep price: A price that's paid by carrying the cross, a heavy cross.

And for Christina Gallagher, the time soon arrived for her to pick up her cross and begin to carry it.

CHAPTER FOUR

A Pure Conversion

WONDER NOT, THAT I SAID TO THEE, YOU MUST BE BORN AGAIN.
—JOHN 3:7

From the beginning, the apparitions to Christina Gallagher were never meant, like those at Lourdes or Fatima, to be public gatherings, never meant to be big events. They were intended to be private, and they were.

They were also without precise schedule. God's plan with Christina was somewhat different from other well-known apparitions, somewhat different from other chosen souls. But again, this was not so unique.

Over the past two centuries, the special importance attached to some Marian apparitions can be explained in part by the fact that many of these apparitions were both "serial" and "public."[1] A public apparition is simply one in which people gather in public around the seers during their experiences.[2] They come to observe. They come to pray. They come to believe. While those gathered may witness a sign, such as the miracle of the sun, or light phenomena, generally speaking they do not see or expect to see the Virgin

Mary themselves. Although, in rare cases, this occurs.[3] Many apparitions are neither public nor serial, as was the case with most of Christina Gallagher's apparitions.

After the third apparition, the Virgin Mary appeared on an irregular basis. These apparitions occurred not only in her home, but also in a local church, at a nearby grotto, and at a few other places. It was a strictly local affair. Most often, they occurred in Christina's living room or kitchen at various times of the day.

Although on occasions there were others present, Christina says that most often she did not desire observers. This was, she says, "to prevent sensationalism of the apparitions." It was not to be a show. At a local grotto, small groups of up to twenty-five people, never more, would sometimes gather in the field for an apparition. This was the way it was to be. This was the way God planned it.

Because of the difficulties Christina experienced from people skeptical of her reported apparitions, Sister Joseph Mary from Sligo referred her to a priest, Father Gerard McGinnity of Armagh, Ireland, for spiritual direction. Father McGinnity had been Dean at Ireland's National Seminary and was now on the staff of Saint Patrick's Grammar School in Armagh, Ireland. This site was chosen by Saint Patrick himself for his Metropolitan See after the admonishment of an angel.

Indeed, Father McGinnity was Heaven sent, a true soldier of Christ, a firm believer in the Church and its teachings. Assured by the Virgin Mary, the Irish theologian's help quickly proved to be a blessing, one that could not have come any sooner, because Heaven was moving strongly in her life. And the Devil was taking no breaks.

The humble Irish priest understood much, but what he couldn't help Christina understand was the actions of others. This she had to discover for herself. It was a difficult period in her life.

Time and time again she was mocked, disbelieved, and ridiculed, often pushing her to the point of tears. The press twisted stories and faked interviews. Outside her home, reporters waited for as many as three days, just to snap pictures or ask bizarre questions.

She was just what they were looking for. They accused her of predicting it was the end of the world and twisted a message concerning the year 1992 in order to generate sensationalism. They doctored photographs to make her look like a fool. It was, indeed, a painful time of great confusion. Even to this day, she is grieved when the messages are distorted. The personal attacks are one thing, but she must defend the message. To set the record straight, she insists people know the truth. "I never got anything about the end of the world," said Christina. "The only references I ever got were when Our Blessed Mother said that from 1992 onward, we would see more calamities and more disasters worldwide. And Our Blessed Mother said all kinds of terrible things would happen in the world and they would multiply from then on. The three specific dates which were given to me in advance were related to the Antichrist raising himself up to power through the Maastricht Treaty."

In so many words, this was really no different from what other seers were saying. From the signs of the times, even Catholic priests and Protestant ministers were saying that much. Yet it didn't help. The damage had been done, and Satan was working to corrupt the messages. Like many visionaries, the persecutions added to the weight of Christina's cross as she struggled to fulfill what God sought from her. But this was also a time of tremendous spiritual growth for Christina, a period of transition and grace, which she later understood was of the utmost necessity in her conversion. A conversion that, as already suggested, was a total or pure conversion.

The Queen of Peace often spoke to Christina of this grace of a pure conversion, which Our Lady explained meant "through the pure grace of God, they are converted in full." It's a special gift, a gift few can say they have received. Slowly, Christina learned to pray for her tormentors, the disbelievers, the cynics, the reporters, even the ones she ironically overheard in church nudging each other and whispering how sad it was that she had gone crazy.

Following Our Blessed Mother's advice, she offered everything to God and God showed her that humiliation was another precious gift from Him. Jesus specifically advised her that when she suffers from persecution, especially from people who refuse to believe or reject the messages, this suffering should be handed over instantly to Him, "before it has time to cause any resentment." "This type of suffering," says Christina, "is particularly powerful to convert the hearts of the actual persecutors." "And is," reminds Father McGinnity, "a good lesson for all of us."

Indeed, this advice proved valuable. It was a gold mine. For besides her apparitions, Christina soon began to report many other mystical experiences.

CHAPTER FIVE

The World of the Supernatural

THROUGH THE HANDS OF THE APOSTLES, MANY SIGNS AND WONDERS OCCURRED AMONG THE PEOPLE.

—ACTS 5:12

Apparitions, locutions, speaking in tongues, prophecies, strange odors, reading souls, bilocating; so many mystical things began to happen to Christina Gallagher that even her spiritual director was amazed.

According to Father McGinnity, all of these combined spiritual gifts were exceeding the textbook histories of many saints and renown seers. It was a virtual explosion of mysticism within a previously ordinary soul's life. What in the world was going on? From visits to Heaven, Hell, and Purgatory to experiences of Christ towering in the sky, God continued His work in the life of Christina.

Yet these types of experiences had occurred previously to others. From many scholarly works, they had been defined and categorized. Without trying to explain every single gift given to Christina, it is important, before proceeding, to examine the various types of mystical experiences she has received from God. This will prepare a more solid foundation for understanding her many revelations.

Specifically, the major supernatural experiences of Christina Gallagher fall into different categories of divine intellectual phenomena. Mystical theology teaches that there are three different kinds of mystical experiences or revelations which chosen souls can receive from God. Not surprisingly, Christina receives them all. In practical terms, these were spiritual gifts from God to help her in the battle she was being called to join. Here is a brief summary of the types of mystical experiences she has received.

The first and most recognized type of phenomenon Christina experiences is a sensible manifestation wherein she perceives the supernatural with her own physical senses. This action occurs primarily through her eyes and ears. Simply put, she sees the presence of the manifestation or apparition with her eyes. When the apparition speaks, she hears it with her ears. Some visionaries even touch and embrace the Virgin Mary or Jesus. Christina has touched the Baby Jesus with both hands and, on another occasion, touched and caressed the face of the Risen Christ. In Los Angeles, He touched her face and the skin of her face quivered at the touch of His fingers. She still gets that sensation from time to time, usually as a consolation in times of difficulty. Christina's apparitions of the Virgin Mary fall into this category. So does the 1985 apparition she had of Christ on the Cross at a local grotto. She has also seen Satan with her eyes.

The second category of divine phenomenon Christina experiences could be described as "seeing with the eyes of the soul."

Often "chosen souls" express an understanding of something without having had any previous exposure to it. Sometimes these take on a prophetic nature. At other times, it's as if the mystic has the ability to read a person's soul or mind. Padre Pio was known for this gift, as was Saint John Vianney, the Curé of Ars.

Father McGinnity wrote of this unique gift of Christina's. "I found she was receiving gifts you might read about in the lives of the saints, but with which you never came face-to-face. She has been given extraordinary spiritual gifts, such as the gift of knowledge, whereby she would find herself reading souls and telling people about their inner lives and their sins, when so directed by God. Yet I am also impressed by her good humor, common sense, honesty, and sincerity. She is a person of great love."

Father McGinnity goes on, "For example, a priest would visit her and she might be impelled to tell him his past life. Within a few minutes, he would be overcome, start weeping, and go away completely converted and preach Our Lady's messages. Or a person would come and she would find herself impelled to tell him that he needed to go to Confession. If he remained noncommittal, she would tell him his sins, and even see him committing the sins. That is an extraordinary gift, seldom given, even to mystics."

On one special occasion, says Father McGinnity, the relatives of a victim of a car bomb in Northern Ireland inquired of Christina if she could discern the man's fate. In prayer, she was able to see this deceased soul and describe him, his clothing, his personality, and even his murderers. She also told them where his soul was. Almost embarrassed by this knowledge at times, Christina sometimes rushes to apologize when it blurts out, often confessing, "I don't know how these things are given to me."

Her other intellectual gifts include speaking in tongues and the ability to suddenly erupt into beautifully worded spontaneous hymns.

Occasionally, she has received the gift of song praising the Blessed Trinity in Latin, Greek, and several other languages. Puzzled at first by what she was uttering, it took a priest to identify the different languages, some of which Christina had never heard before.

Some of her experiences are at the same time sensible and intellectual. While hard to explain, this has happened before.

The best example is Saint Paul's experience on the road to Damascus. The apostle beheld with his eyes blinding light; he saw the personal traits of Ananias, who would come to help heal his eyes; and his mind understood God's will in the instant conversion he experienced. So without ever hearing Christ, Paul immediately began to preach the Gospel of Jesus with as much knowledge and authority as the original apostles and disciples.

Finally, Christina, the Irish mystic, also received inner locutions. By definition, locutions are supernatural words that are manifestations of the Divine Thought conveyed to the exterior or interior senses, or directly to the intelligence. Locutions, like apparitions, can be auricular (heard) or intellectual. Presently God or the Virgin Mary speak to Christina frequently in this fashion.

From bilocation experiences (being in two places at the same time) to a strong perfumelike fragrance that exudes from Christina's body and remains for a long while, Christina Gallagher's mystical experiences continue.

In all these revelations we see how Christina Gallagher not only is able to give us direct messages from the Virgin Mary and Jesus, but is also able to convey to us profound understandings of the divine life, along with the afterlife worlds of Heaven, Hell, and Purgatory.

Obviously, you can't go to school to learn this; they don't teach it. But it's all real.

These are all mystical experiences which God wants His people to believe exist as much as the messages they embody. Even Albert Einstein, the renown scientist, accepted the existence of the world of the mystical. Einstein wrote, "The most beautiful and profound emotion we can experience is the sensation of the mystical."

Since 1988, Christina Gallagher has experienced the supernatural world. She has experienced it with total openness. She knows these mystical dimensions exist, in the same way she knows our world is real, sometimes even more so.

But all of this was not given to her for her own private spiritual agenda. No, it was given to her for all of us. It was given so that we, like her, can prepare for the battle. As this County Mayo woman is called to fight in this battle, so, too, are we. It is the ultimate battle for souls.

And by late 1990, both Saint Catherine of Siena and the Queen of Peace were sent by God to officially confirm to Christina that the final phase of this spiritual Armageddon had now begun.

CHAPTER SIX

From Russia with Love

THEN ANOTHER SIGN APPEARED IN THE SKY; IT WAS A HUGE DRAGON, FLAMING RED, . . .

—REV. 12:3

The events surrounding Christina Gallagher moved quickly as the Virgin Mary concluded her communiqué through the apparitions, for all intents and purposes, by the end of 1988.

Trained for the harvest of souls, Christina was then, as it were, sent out to the fields to begin her mission. The Virgin Mary's message was clear—an urgent call to salvation and the announcement that the dawning of the Triumph of her Immaculate Heart was close at hand. She had come for everyone, for their souls, she insisted.

The world, the Queen of Peace disclosed to Christina, was now flooded in the Mercy of Jesus Christ. Preparations were under way for the advent of a new era. However, Our Lady repeated her warning that Satan's anger had exploded and time was running out. The final moments of these times, the Blessed Mother repeated, would be like none the world had ever seen.

In 1988 alone, Christina received twenty-five major messages from the Blessed Mother. They were for herself, the people of Ireland, and the world. They were for anyone who would listen. While instructional and informative, Heaven's directions were highly concise and very specific.

Although Christina received few apparitions in 1989 and 1990, her supernatural experiences continued. This period was marked by an increase in extraordinary mystical experiences of Jesus and His Kingdom, the Kingdom the Lord was now inviting Christina to witness. During this same time, Christina was called to a life of greater suffering, terrible suffering. Mental, emotional, physical, and spiritual anguish filled her. But this was a life she would grow to embrace. Her body began to reveal the visible wounds of Jesus Christ, leaving her totally consumed with suffering.

During this period, Christina received messages concerning the world, the Pope, and Satan. The messages revealed plenty. They were poignant and profound, echoing recent as well as age-old predictions of a time of turmoil for the Church and the world. In addition, startling prophetic experiences began to accompany these messages.

By 1989, God's plan to enlist the aid of much of Heaven in His work with Christina also began to unfold. More saints appeared to Christina.

In an apparition in 1990, she witnessed hundreds of these celestial beings dressed in white as angels hovered above. Saint Catherine of Siena, Padre Pio, Saint Thérèse of Lisieux, Saint Martin de Porres, and Saint John the Evangelist were among them, as God introduced her to some of His most chosen souls. This experience revealed the powerful intercession taking place for her and the world, as Heaven and earth united to fight the enemy through *love.* Overwhelmed, Christina described this spectacle:

This morning Saint Catherine of Siena came to me. She talked. She was dressed in a most lovely white dress with gold-colored trim around the edge. As she moved her head I could see the veil shimmer in gold color. Oh, she is lovely. She was soft-spoken. She said to me "Pray for the Pope every day and priests, bishops, and cardinals and for my sister nuns." Then her eyes filled with tears. I asked her why she was unhappy, but she did not reply. I then asked her why she should speak to me now and not before. She told me that she was not permitted to speak but that she had come before to let me know she was with me. She said we are in the time of battle, but only at the early stage. Then I said, "In Jesus' name are you Catherine?" She smiled and said "Yes." She told me many of the good souls accompany the Virgin Mary and that they suffer because they are permitted to come to the world, and they could see the evil, but that God's protection was with them. Then she said, "Look."

I could see hundreds of people in white; real people I did know—Saint Thérèse, Padre Pio, Saint Martin de Porres. Some I did not know. For some reason Catherine said, "This is John the Evangelist." He did not speak; just looked at me. Then many angels were above the crowd, who must have been saints, and they were singing "Ave Maria." I asked Catherine about the war. She turned away as if looking at something or someone. Then she turned toward me again and said, "My sister, do not be troubled. Some will tell you to do this and others tell you to do that. Do only as your heart inspires. Let God lead you. When a person says to do something, pray and ask God to guide your heart. He will." Then she said, "You have been judged by many. Forgive, then God will forgive. Pray that you won't be put to the test." I said, "Catherine, and what is it when people don't understand me? Am I not being put to the test?" She smiled and said, "Yes. The test I mean is that you will have the strength to persevere. God gives you all you need but if you don't know how to receive it then you want to give up. You had been like that a short time ago. We were interceding for you. My sister, God's love is beyond all things. Mary, the true Virgin and Mother of Jesus, is with you at all times. Be at peace, my sister."

Through 1995, Christina continued to have apparitions on rare occasions and many mystical experiences of Jesus and the Blessed Mother often now accompanied by more alarming messages for urgent world conversion. The Virgin Mary's message to her children was direct, "Please come back to me and my Son!"

And there were also apparitions during times of duress.

During this period, many physical and spiritual healings were also reported. More and more fruits of the apparitions became visible. More than a million Matrix Medals were being mailed throughout the world. (See page 230.) Within almost no time at all, the Matrix Medals were distributed as fast as they were made. Heartwarming stories of miracles were proclaimed publicly. God did not hesitate to prove this work was His.

In October 1992, a special event of historical significance occurred. An army of God's faithful invaded Russia, Satan's stronghold for so long. And again, Christina Gallagher was destined to be there.

While in Moscow on the last leg of a historic pilgrimage, Christina received a prophetic message concerning this great spiritual event and the approaching Triumph of Our Blessed Mother's Immaculate Heart in the world.

The joyful Virgin Mary proclaimed the glorious sunrise of God's great light upon the world was just beyond the horizon:

> My beloved Daughter, my Immaculate Heart rejoices in your response to the call of your Mother's Heart. Long have I tried to sow the rich seed of grace in the hearts of my children in Russia. The desire of your Mother's Heart is for conversion, love, peace, and unity to grow in the hearts of all my children. Russia is a priceless jewel that has lost its sparkle. I desire this jewel to sparkle once more to bring joy to the Heart of my Divine Son Jesus. I desire to lavish rich graces upon my children and bless them abundantly with my love.

I bless you and all who have responded to the call of your Mother and I bless all my children in Russia, who have remained faithful to the Good News of Christ. They are true disciples of my Divine Son Jesus. Blessed are the peacemakers and all who strive for peace. With peace there is unity and hope. All comes through love and Christ Jesus is love. I bless you all, dear children. Continue to respond to the graces I give you. In the name of the Father, Son, and Holy Spirit.

This eventful pilgrimage, by almost one thousand faithful from throughout the world, was characterized by many blessed events.

CHAPTER SEVEN

Beautiful Beyond Imagination

THEN MARY SAID, "MY BEING PROCLAIMS THE GREATNESS OF THE LORD, . . ."

—LUKE 1:46

The Light.

It's always the flashes of light that visionaries speak of first, though they find no words adequate to describe it. No words can.

Like the blast of horns that herald a royal entrance, this brilliant light is often the definitive signal of the Virgin Mary's impending arrival. Described as whiter than white, its pureness and intensity are said to be blinding, yet overwhelmingly inviting.

"It's a heavenly light more resplendent than light itself," recounted Saint Catherine Labouré at Rue Du Bac, Paris in 1831.[1] "It's like a moonlight," wrote the Ukrainian visionary Josyp Terelya. "But it wasn't moonlight . . . it seemed to be a living, breathing illumination."[2]

Often, visionaries seek to cower away or shield their eyes from this incredible light; some even tear from its intensity. Yet its silver-white rays gently become bearable and even grab and pull its captives toward it, locking them into a magnetic state of wonder and enchantment. A state that immediately becomes almost painful to leave.

A mystical union begins to unfold. Within seconds, great joy saturates the visionary's mind into an ecstatic awe. These chosen ones often behold, within the center of this hypnotic light, a vague vaporous image like a hologram beginning to materialize and take shape. It is the shape of a woman—a woman like they have never seen before, a glowing woman from Heaven.

At Lourdes (1858), Our Lady's white radiance of surrounding light was clearly described by Bernadette as a "bright light glowing like the sun's reflection off water on a brilliant day."[3] At Beauraing (1932), the five children visionaries at first thought this blinding glow was "a reflection from car lights."[4] While at Guadalupe (1531), Juan Diego reported that the emblazoned Virgin Mary was standing in the sun because of the overpowering brilliance of the golden beams that surrounded her person from top to bottom. Ironically, the sun was not even above the horizon.[5]

Most chosen souls chronicle the Blessed Virgin as encased in this light as it forms a luminous globelike bubble around her, thus fulfilling with great accuracy the vision Saint John the Evangelist wrote about in the Book of Revelation which describes "a woman clothed with the sun." (Rev. 12:1) But every description falls short, because the appearance of the all-pure and shining one is without comparison or complete description.

Radiantly attractive, Our Lady's appearance in such dazzling light truly betrays, they say, her "irresistible purity." An appearance that is deliberately designed to reflect the Mother of God as the purest of all human beings who ever lived: so pure that from her glowing radiance, we are reminded that Our Lady conceived and brought forth the Second Person of the Most Holy Trinity into the world through a virgin birth; so pure we are reminded why Mary of Agreda wrote that God exceeded the sum of all His creation when He made the Virgin Mary.[6]

Christina Gallagher could not agree more. She knows and her words confide it. Without contemplation, the Irish mystic describes Our Lady Queen of Peace as being filled with brilliant light, light that seems to radiate from her. "A light," says Christina, "that simultaneously shines on her and from her." Light which forms, she insists, "a luminous glow that appears to come from inside her."

Usually clothed in an immaculate white dress and blue mantle, the Blessed Mother's garments are depicted by Christina to be of a special fabric and texture, very unique in appearance and embroiderings. "A garment of light," she says. Sometimes Our Lady wears a crown, similar to the Fatima crown, dipped in the center with a globe of the world surmounted by the cross.

Because of the Blessed Mother's obedience to the will of God, to bring forth the Redeemer of the world in her virginal womb, God crowned her Queen of Heaven and earth and Mother of the Redemption. Through the redeeming source of her Son, Our Lady was made the Mediatrix of All Graces and Advocate for all her children before the Heart of her Son. (Our Lady explained this as the meaning of this crown to Christina.) Christina has seen the Virgin Mary with many different crowns but this is the one Our Lady explained to her.

Christina tells us that:

> Our Holy Mother appears to be about nineteen or twenty in age, with eyes that are like deep pools of blue and her face is beautiful beyond imagination.
>
> Our Holy Mother is more beautiful than any person I have ever seen. No statue or picture can show her beauty. Our Holy Mother is radiantly happy. She moves slowly and reverently and brings with her an indescribably heavenly peace. She always smiles. She pours that love through me. If Our Holy Mother is speaking about something you may see her going from the smiles to sadness, to tears, and even to tears of blood. But Our Lady always smiles, no matter what. I have even seen Our Lady smile through the tears.
>
> The peace when I would see Our Holy Mother or the peace when Our Holy Mother comes, even inwardly, is as if

> everything is stilled beyond description. I have never found this stillness anywhere in the world or at any other time in my life, only through the apparitions. Our Holy Mother's love is beyond description. It's as if you are the only person existing to her at that moment. You're so loved and you're so in love with Our Blessed Mother.

Magnetized and awed by the appearance, presence, and words of the Queen of Peace, Christina often becomes consumed, during and after an apparition, by the overwhelming love and peace Our Lady brings with her. This heavenly consummation is sometimes to the point of "wanting to depart for Heaven with her."

Indeed, the elation Christina experiences, compounded with her intense suffering, often leaves her lost, in her mind and in this world, for want of words. This causes her confusion as to whether she can wait much longer for her heavenly departure.

For visionaries, it's another form of suffering, another gift from God. Saint Paul shared the same predicament in this reflection:

> Life to me, of course, is Christ, but then death would be a positive gain.
>
> (Phil. 1:21)

Almost overwhelmed, Christina candidly admits she often finds herself pleading with the Virgin Mary during an apparition: "Holy Mother, please don't leave me here, take me with you now." Christina goes on: "My experience was as if I was a little child being left alone without my mother on a desert island. Our Holy Mother was as if she was the only true mother I loved (despite the fact that I intensely loved my earthly mother), and I wanted to go with her. But Our Blessed Mother always gave me the same reply, 'My child, when your work is complete, I will come for you.' " But this was no consolation to Christina.

Christina observed, "So I realized that I wanted the easy way out—by asking to go with Our Lady—because what God desires is that I wait here, and share His joys and His Cross, a combination of both."

In further consolation, she remembers Jesus once confided to her, "I want to share all with you."

CHAPTER EIGHT

Through the Eyes of a Prophet

AND THE LORD TOOK ME FROM FOLLOWING THE FLOCK, AND THE LORD SAID TO ME, "GO PROPHESY TO MY PEOPLE, ISRAEL."

—AMOS 7:15

As a chosen soul Christina Gallagher embraces experiences few people who have ever lived can relate to in a personal way. She's seen Jesus. She's seen the Blessed Mother. She's seen angels, Heaven, Purgatory, Hell, and even Lucifer. With the eyes of her soul, she has gazed in wonder, in awe, upon the face of the Eternal Father. Yet she is very much alive and on earth like the rest of us.

"When invisible realities become visible, it is neither the beatific vision nor absolute knowledge . . . ," wrote one of the world's foremost Mariologists. "It is rather a limited communication in sign, made for reasons of teaching, addressed to a particular time, place, and audience. Those who receive this communication are not, for all that, removed from this earthly situation and their subjectivity," he said.[1]

Indeed, visionaries are not removed from their subjectivity. It surrounds them. It holds them here. Yet who can they really relate to except chosen souls like themselves? How do they cope if so few really understand?

Few visionaries have visionary friends. There are no clubs and interaction is limited. Because close associates and relatives are often unable to empathize, many of their feelings and thoughts become buried and lost in their souls. Thus, it is not an easy life, nor a life to be envied.

Yet as time goes by, these chosen souls simply surrender their frustrations and inability to be understood. They concern themselves with one thing only, pleasing their Lord and Master, their beloved Jesus. As Christina wrote to her spiritual director:

I do not understand, and somehow I don't care to understand, any more. I feel so useless and I have no desire to be in talks, talks, talks. All I desire is to live and accept my sufferings and rejections, and to be in union in my heart with Jesus. I am not sure if that is what my dear Jesus desires, nor do I know why my heart felt such pain and sorrow.

Today is Sunday but as I write this long letter (it is 1:30 in the morning), I see just now, with my soul, Jesus looking at me as I have done many times before. He had the white dress with the red wrap. He holds in His hand a big gold staff; at His feet a Lamb. Many Angels surround Jesus. Now it looks as if Jesus is showing me great darkness (that darkness that I once told you about on the horizon) but it is engulfing what looks like the world, churches, many people falling, lightning flashing. Jesus is raising His hands and the wounds in His hands are like light, and now His feet too. He is telling me—write, write what I see. I feel afraid.

Now, that big angel is there again. He is the Angel of Wrath. Jesus is holding some sort of paper rolled up. He is now opening it. He is showing me a red stamp or seal. There is blood on the stamp or seal. Mountains are falling covering houses and people. It is like looking at a film, but I feel my soul quiver. Now all is turning to smoke. The Pope is now weighed down with great trials. I can feel this, like sorrow. Lord, please take it away. Now there is a clock, and inscribed on its face "time is running out." I will get on with this later.

Tonight is Monday night. Please God and our Holy Mother, when all this thing of sacrifice becomes clear, if it is God's will, I will write it down or speak it on the tape. Now, Father, why would God be permitting me to see these scenes if it were all in the Bible already? I don't understand many things.

(Christina Gallagher)

In Part II of this book, Christina reveals what it is like not only to see the Queen of Peace and Jesus but also to talk to them; and not just them, but also the Eternal Father, Blessed Michael the Archangel, Saint Patrick, Saint Catherine of Siena, Saint Teresa of Avila—even Satan.

She takes us inside. She gives what we want, a feeling for all of this, because we need to understand. We need to have information. We need to relate, and Christina's experiences are just what we're looking for.

From intimate glimpses into the afterlife worlds of Heaven, Hell, and Purgatory to apparitions of a mysterious face of a man known only to her as Antichrist, it's an invitation to a banquet of mysticism. Who could say no?

Christina gives us a unique personal look at her numerous spiritual experiences. In many chapters, a direct dialogue of questions and answers brings to the forefront an insightful look at who and what she has seen and heard. Christina sees through the eyes of a prophet, and through her own words she allows us to penetrate her experiences. She deeply wants us to relate to her, not for her sake, but for ours—for the sake of our souls.

As you listen to her words, feel their truth. For Christina's accounts are remarkably similar to others, especially her description of Our Lord and Our Lady.

From describing the brilliant white light that precedes the Queen of Peace to the deep feeling of peace and love she brings, Christina's words add to the rich universal treasure of information, which chosen souls give us about the Mother of God.

Likewise, this little soul's accounts of the Savior coincide with others who have written of their experiences with Jesus. We especially notice in Christina's words striking similarities to the accounts given by other victim souls. All of whom, like Christina, knew Jesus in union with His sufferings. All of whom, like Christina, knew Jesus' love, His mercy, and His hunger for souls.

All of whom, like Christina, knew Jesus.

PART II

Taken into the Intimacy of the Life of God

CHAPTER NINE

A Mother and Her Child

WOMAN, BEHOLD THY SON.

—JOHN 19:26

There have been hundreds of books written about the apparitions of the Blessed Virgin Mary, many of them with great skill and detail, under the guidance of the Holy Spirit. They are blessed realities that are part of God's plan as much as the apparitions. Still, nothing seems to have a greater influence than accounts given in the visionaries' own words, especially in personal interviews. It is then that their feelings reveal their experiences in the greatest detail.

Christina Gallagher knows the Mother of God like her real mother. In this chapter, in her own words, this unfolds in even clearer terms. It is a detailed account of the relationship and love between our Heavenly Mother and one of her children. It's a revelation that brings great joy; through Christina's words we can rest assured that the Virgin Mary, our spiritual mother in Heaven, loves us no less.

Through Christina's own words, we find the best understanding of those early days of the apparitions and what this chosen young woman was undergoing in her life.

Q. Could you see Our Lady's entire body?
A. Yes.
Q. Could you see the Blessed Mother's feet?
A. Yes, but only once.
Q. Did she wear a crown?
A. The third time Our Holy Mother appeared she had a crown on.
Q. Was it a crown of stars?
A. No, it was just bright gold, similar to the Fatima crown, but it was dipped in the center with a globe of the world surmounted by a cross.
Q. Could you see Our Lady's hair?
A. A number of times I could not see Our Holy Mother's hair, because the mantle always covered it. People were asking what color of hair Our Lady had, and I couldn't tell them. One particular time, at a grotto, when Our Blessed Mother came in an apparition, she had a veil on her head. This time, for some apparent reason the veil began to fall backward as if it was falling off Our Lady's head. This revealed all Our Holy Mother's hair and I could clearly see it. Her hair was dark brown to black in color.
Q. How long was Our Lady's hair?
A. Our Blessed Mother's hair fell to below her shoulders. On some occasions, I've seen Our Lady's hair revealed as if it was in loose strands. On other occasions, Our Holy Mother's hair seemed to be more curly or wavy, but dark in color.
Q. How has Our Lady appeared? How was she dressed?
A. Our Holy Mother wore a blue mantle and a white dress the majority of the time. Other times Our Lady appeared in all white. One time stands out. On an Easter Sunday, it was as if her dress and mantle were of white light, in sequins of gold. When Our Blessed Mother would move, it would be a combination of gold and silver, because of the reflections of the light.

Now, there is always a radiance from Our Holy Mother's body as if she gives out this light. The light seems to come through Our Lady's clothes as if there was enormous light shining from inside her.

Q. Has Our Lady ever appeared dressed in black?

A. Yes, she has. That was on her birthday and I don't recall the date, but I remember it was Our Lady's birthday. I wasn't expecting to see Our Blessed Mother and then she suddenly appeared. Our Holy Mother had a black mantle with white satin on the inside and she was crying. I found this very strange because afterward I heard it was her birthday. The Blessed Mother was crying for her children.

Q. On the third occasion when Our Lady appeared to you she called herself the *Queen of Peace*. Why did she refer to herself as the Queen of Peace? Has she talked to you about this?

A. Our Lady Mother said, "Be not afraid, I am the Virgin Mary, Queen of Peace and I come in peace." In the first apparitions of Our Blessed Lady, I experienced tremendous peace and love. People were saying to me, don't let anybody hear you saying these things about seeing this Lady because that's called hallucinations. I couldn't understand it. If this was what a person describes as "going mad," and if I was going mad, then how could I be so peaceful and so full of love? That's how I felt in my heart. When Our Blessed Mother came to me the third time, she was wearing a crown on her head and was dressed in cream. Our Holy Mother told me not to be afraid, that she was the Virgin Mary, Queen of Peace. In other words, the Queen of Peace hadn't come to cause destruction or hurt me because of what people were saying about me. Our Holy Mother is a mother of peace and in that sense, wherever she is, peace comes with her.

Q. Tell us about your locutions. Can you describe what a locution is according to your experiences?

A. It's when Our Blessed Mother or Jesus speaks within me.

Q. Your spiritual director has informed me that on two occasions you experienced bilocation. Can you tell us about this?

A. On two occasions, I was used by God through bilocation. On one occasion I was taken to the cell of a dying nun. The nun was alone lying on a bed that was very plain (like a doctor's examination couch). She greatly feared death. This surprised me. I spoke to her of the love of God. On the second occasion, I was sent to a primitive tribe. It was night. I didn't know what country it was, but the people were all black. The strange thing is they weren't speaking English, but I knew what they were saying as clearly as if they were speaking English. They weren't Catholic. There was a witch doctor. He tried to make sure I was not some evil spirit. I assured them I was not an evil spirit, that I was a messenger from God. I told them of God and Our Holy Mother. This witch doctor man wasn't sure of me. But in the situation one of them said, "Are you an Angel?" I said, "Do you know about angels?" Then they were all baffled because the young girl who said this to me didn't know what she had said or why, because she didn't know of angels.

Q. You mentioned the peace, love, and joy you experience when Our Lady comes. Tell us how this feels.

A. Her peace is something that is hard to describe. The peace when I would see Our Holy Mother, even inwardly, is as if everything is totally stilled beyond description. I have never found this stillness anywhere in the world or at any other time in my life, only through the apparitions. Our Holy Mother's love is beyond description. It's as if you're the only person existing to her at that moment. You're so loved and you're so in love with Our Blessed Mother. That's about the only way I can describe it. You hear the word "love," but you really know in the depth of your heart what love is with Our Blessed Mother; it's not just a word. Your entire self is united to Our Lady in her love. It's such an experience that there are no words to describe it.

Q. During the apparitions of Our Lady are you able to touch her?

A. I have never found any reason why I couldn't touch Our Holy Mother. I have never so much touched Our Lady as she has touched me. Our Blessed Mother came on one occasion when I was having a very difficult time during the early stages of the apparitions. It was then I found people mocking me. This was difficult for me. Then, Our Lady appeared with a shawl. She came over to me and placed it around my shoulders. As soon as she did, all the suffering I was feeling at that time just disappeared. It was then that Our Holy Mother touched me. On another occasion, when I was upset by a newspaper story, I said to her, "Holy Mother, I can't ever face people again. I can't take any more of this. I'm not going to the prayer meeting because they'll probably tell me to get out and that I'm a bit crazy." On this occasion, I didn't see Our Blessed Mother, but I heard her voice clearly, like I would hear any human voice. I then felt the grip of Our Lady's hands so gently on my arms as Our Holy Mother pulled me forward and invited me to go and pray. She told me not to be afraid.

Q. Have you been kissed by the Blessed Mother?

A. No, I can't remember any particular time that Our Blessed Mother kissed me.

Q. Is the Blessed Mother like a real mother?

A. Yes, more real than my earthly mother, in every way. I love my earthly mother very much, but when Our Blessed Mother comes in this experience, you realize the difference between love and the pure love of God, and you feel you are the only child she has. Our Holy Mother comes as total trust, love, and peace. Our Holy Mother is the *complete* Mother.

Q. Tell us more about this complete Mother's love for all her children.

A. How do you describe the love of Our Blessed Mother? It's beyond anything in this entire world! You would give everything in this world to experience it continually. There is nothing that exists in the world that I have a deeper desire for.

The world is of no value; it's only a journey, and we're on that journey. But on the way, all the things of the world are a temptation to the flesh, and our flesh can be weak. We say we want this and we want that. When we want those things, it draws us away from God. It closes our heart to God. We're human and we want a certain amount of things. The flesh can lead us further and further down the wide road but not the narrow road.

The narrow road is the road of the cross. The flesh is only the house. When you deny the flesh you take care of the inner self to the point that you surrender to God. Then God fills your heart and inflames your soul. You can't serve two Gods or two masters—the world of the flesh and of God. You have to decide to serve one or the other. If God comes first, do you love Him above everything else? If yes, then you'll have to deny the flesh. The body is only the temporary house of the soul.

Q. Tell us about Our Lady's joy. Is Our Lady filled with joy?

A. Our Lady's joy is overwhelming. To the point, again, of being painful. It's so overwhelming that I get to the point where I just can't stop praising God. I'm singing and praising God in such a way that I nearly feel as if I want to just go to Heaven; just be with her and never be anywhere else. Sometimes it's like living in Heaven on earth. It's beyond description of normal joy, such as the joy of the birth of a child. There's joy in that, but not the real joy compared to the joy of Our Blessed Mother. Our Blessed Mother's joy is painfully beautiful. That's the only way to describe the feeling.

Q. What has Our Lady spoken of regarding love and charity for others?

A. Our Lady says if you do something, it's not of much use if you don't do it with love. If you give somebody something, it's not much good without love. If you happen to do works of charity and you say, "I'm giving it with love, but without wanting to do it, without the desire to do it for love of God," it's not much use. If something is done with love and charity, you want to do it for the love of God.

Q. Is the Virgin Mary always happy whenever she appears to you?

A. Not always. Sometimes Our Holy Mother is happy and sometimes she is sad. Sometimes Our Holy Mother is crying. Sometimes her tears turn to blood for her lost children, for her children who have gone astray or are going away from God. Our Holy Mother's desire, as a mother, is to lead her children to God for the salvation of their souls.

Q. Do you think about Our Lady and Our Lord all the time?

A. Practically. When I'm talking to others, I might be looking at the crucifix or I might be looking at a glass of water, but it won't matter what I'm looking at because I'm always thinking of them. I really get distracted at times, when something will crop up and I will have a particular worry or situation on my hands. I always come back to the fact that there's only one way to solve it; Jesus and Our Blessed Mother. I always hand it over to them with prayer.

Q. Has Our Lady cried often?

A. Yes, a number of times. But it is different with Our Blessed Mother. When the average person cries, the tears flow down from the corner of the eye. When Our Holy Mother cries, the tears flow from the very center of the eyes, very slowly, in one drop, till it reaches the end of her face, then it disappears. It then starts all over again. Sometimes the tears turn to blood. Again, the same thing occurs, the blood flows from the center of Our Holy Mother's eyes.

Q. Does Our Lady cry from both eyes or just one?

A. Both eyes, but when Our Holy Mother cries it breaks my heart. I would give my life to help stop the tears.

Q. Has the Blessed Mother told you why she is crying tears of blood during the apparition?

A. Yes, for her children. Our Holy Mother is crying for her children who have gone astray. She wants to bring them back to God.

Q. Has the Virgin Mary worn different dresses on special Holy Days?

A. On one Easter Sunday, Our Blessed Lady was the most beautiful I've ever seen her. Her "garment of light," as I call it, was a dress and a mantle of light. It was so beautiful, with three very tiny roses at the bottom. It was like a gown, such a beautiful dress. It was overflowing her feet. You could not see her feet at all. Three tiny roses were there and you could see Our Holy Mother's heart. It was very distinct and very clear.

Q. Could you see her real heart?

A. Yes, there are times I've seen Our Blessed Mother's real heart. I've also seen her heart exposed at other times; it looked gold, but like an artificial heart. There are times I've seen the Heart of Jesus. This was when Our Blessed Mother taught me the Rosary. The Heart of Jesus would pulsate. You could even see it beating. I could see the Heart become more alive. Now, I know what a heart looks like, though I've never seen a real human heart. On this occasion, there was a very, very fine gauze or something around the Heart of Jesus. I saw veins beginning to come into the Heart, protruding from it. Then, His Heart would pulsate. I was looking at the Heart of Jesus; I could feel it also beating in my heart as if my own heart was beating in union with the Heart of Jesus.

Q. Have you seen thorns around the Virgin Mary's heart or a sword piercing her heart?

A. No, but I did see Our Holy Mother's heart with an open wound in it and I could see blood dripping from her heart. I've also seen blood coming from the Heart of Jesus.

Q. Are you still having inner apparitions of Our Lady?

A. I see Our Lady inwardly. She comes through a white light. I can see Jesus or Our Blessed Mother in this way. I don't know how to explain it. I can see them with the eyes of my soul.

Q. Will you be having these inner apparitions of the Blessed Mother the rest of your life?

A. Yes, but it depends on my response to Our Lady. It's up to me. If I continue to respond to God, Our Holy Mother will continue to communicate with me. Our Lady told me that if I was to keep asking her questions, she would stop communicating with me. I wanted to know answers to questions for other people. If I were asking about somebody that was ill, there were times when Our Blessed Mother told me they would be healed and then they were healed. But then, I would get upset when these people thought that their healing was brought about by the power of mind over matter as, indeed, one person later expressed it. I was hurt for Jesus and for Our Blessed Mother. So after that, Our Holy Mother had forbidden me to ask questions. Our Lady advised me to pray and if it was important she would answer the questions.

I always feel love when Our Holy Mother comes and I feel at peace. Sometimes if a particular question pops into my mind I will still ask her. Sometimes Our Holy Mother may not reply. Sometimes she may reply. Three times I asked more questions and three times Our Lady told me not to ask any more questions. So on the third occasion, Our Holy Mother said she would stop communicating with me if I continued to ask her questions. Our Blessed Mother told me then to pray for any particular intention that I wanted to know, and if it was important she would reply.

Q. Do you mean Our Lady would reply without you even having to ask the question before she would know what it was?

A. Yes, because Our Holy Mother would know what was in my heart and what I felt before I asked.

Q. When you've had these experiences are you conscious of where you are?

A. On some occasions I know what's happening. On one occasion I felt this experience of the light coming over me. It felt like going under anesthesia. That's about the nearest thing I can compare it to. Sometimes my body reacts by itself and I have no control over it. When this happens I'm totally unaware of anyone or anything around me. Other times I can't move but I can hear people speaking and what they're saying. During these times, I'm aware of where I am but I can't move my body and I can't do anything about it. In one instance while I was in this state, I could hear the people saying, "Oh, my goodness, her face has changed." Another person said, "Oh, she looks like a corpse to me." I could hear everything they were saying, but I could still do nothing. It didn't matter to me at that time. The only thing I felt was an awareness of

> my hands being wet. When I came out of this state, the first thing I did was look at my hands and they were, indeed, wet. So when I looked at my hands, I didn't make any commotion or say anything about this experience. There were a number of people in the room at the time. Then all of a sudden, a lady at the end of the couch jumped up and said she saw a white cross in my hand, as did the others who were present.

Note: The remainder of the people could see it as well. On many occasions a crucifix would appear as if it was beneath the skin of the palm of Christina's hand and pushed upward. This was witnessed by a number of people. On other occasions, on the base of her thumb The Holy Face of Jesus, the Blessed Mother, or the face of Padre Pio appeared.

Different miraculous events witnessed by others included a bottle of holy oil that had already been used by Christina in prayer with others was empty one evening when people wanted her to use it and pray with them; Christina received an inner awareness that the bottle would now have oil and the people witnessed the oil coming into the bottle miraculously.

Christina continued:

> Sometimes when I come out of these experiences I'm very peaceful and tranquil. I could care less what people are saying, or who's saying what. I'm so peaceful that I cannot be bothered with listening to anyone talk. I prefer to be alone.

Q. Can you tell us about your own mother.

A. I have special memories in my life where my mother is concerned. Like all families in our area, we had moderate circumstances, but we were happy because we had love and peace.

Q. Did you pray as a child?

A. I used to pray quite a lot. I didn't know the Rosary yet, but I knew the "Hail Mary's" and "Our Father's."

Q. How have these experiences affected your relationship with your family?

A. I love my family, my husband, my parents, and all my relations very much. But my real mother now is my mother in Heaven,

Our Blessed Mother. The Eternal Father is my Father in Heaven. Jesus is my brother and Redeemer, the Holy Spirit, the Light of God, through which my Father and His Son unite to grant me the gifts of the inner life of God.

Q. Has any other member of your family experienced any revelations?

A. My daughter saw a cross coming out of my hand. Each beam ended in the shape of a shamrock. It was a three-dimensional cross. I saw it, too. After it was gone, the face of Jesus appeared to us in my hand. It looked like the first apparition I had of the head of Jesus, crowned with thorns. I didn't say what I was seeing in my hand to my daughter. I just said to her, "Do you see anything on my hand?" When she looked she said, "Yes, I see the face of Jesus." She had seen it, too.

Q. Christina, do you feel your experiences have allowed you to become holier?

A. I don't talk in terms of the word "holiness." I just know that God is working in my life, changing my life to peace, love, and recognition of the sufferings of others. This has allowed me to be able to say to God, "I am nothing." I constantly recognize my nothingness. I realize how tempted I can be and when the temptations come, I realize how quickly I can fall.

It's only through God's grace that I have come to love God in this way. I have finally come to the realization that all this is God's way and God's gift of freedom. All of this in my life is just to share with others, and to help them. All of this now gives me a deeper sense of love for all God's children. I mean it sincerely with all my heart. If I had the opportunities and the means to go where my heart would lead me, it would be to those who are alcoholics, drug addicts, and AIDS victims. I don't care what they are called, because they're all God's children who have just gone astray and feel as if they have let themselves down. They feel they've let their people down and been a failure to God and man. They may think God doesn't care about them and doesn't even exist.

I would like to help bring them to an awareness that God is very much in existence. God hasn't turned away from them.

It's through temptation and sin that they've turned away from God. But God will never stop loving them until they draw their last breath.

Q. Sometimes by the Power of God you can read souls. Is that correct?

A. I experience a light and I know things about people. I was scared of this at the beginning. It was so strange. But many people I met I suddenly knew as though they were like an open book to me. Some people would be smiling at me but I would know that they were insincere.

Priests would come to me and I would know what they were like, whether they were sincere or not. When priests come, they would sometimes be curious to know if my gift of knowledge was real.

I'll give you one example of a particular priest, Father John, a beautiful man. I felt very comfortable with him from the beginning. I told him of my experience and he was very quiet. He just listened to everything.

During this occasion, Father John began talking and I assumed praying in another language. I didn't pay close attention to what he was saying. Later, Father said he had been asking the Blessed Mother to guide him to know if this was the truth and if it was of God. During his prayer I experienced a light and Father John no longer existed to me. The light consumed me and I began to know things. I didn't hear him talking to me anymore nor was I aware of him or anything else. Later, he told me he had been talking to me, but I heard nothing. All I know is that he touched me. When he touched me it was like I was released halfway out of my human state or human condition. I wasn't unconscious, I wasn't out of it to the point that I was not aware of where I was. There was a sense of power going through me and I began talking. When it was over Father John was smiling and very joyful. I didn't know what to make of it or what had happened. While I was in the "light state," I saw Jesus and Our Blessed Mother. Jesus was on the Cross. When I saw Our Lady, she was smiling.

When it was all over, Father John told me that he had asked me ten questions in Spanish. He told me that he also asked the Blessed Mother to answer them through me in English to see if this was truly of God.

Q. What actually happened?

A. Obviously, what happened was the Blessed Mother had answered through me the ten questions Father wanted to know the answers to. Our Lady answered them in English through me, although he asked me in Spanish. Father told me what had happened and I had a somewhat vague memory of the answers that were given. Then this memory was totally taken from me. When this happened I said to him, "There's something strange happening to my mind, the knowledge given to me about you is taken from me." He said to me with a smile, "Christina, don't be troubled or wonder why, but I asked the Blessed Mother at the very start to make you unaware of the personal details regarding myself." He said that it was God's will that I wouldn't remember what was given to me. He was so full of joy.

This same priest came back days later. I saw the sins of priests that had made confessions to him and people he was dealing with in Argentina. A lot of different things he asked about were given to me. I can see the people committing their sins. I can see them and I didn't want this sight, but can't help what I'm given. Once I prayed so intensely that God would take this away. I prayed, "Don't give me this, give me something else, a cross or anything," I asked God. Lately, the intensity of this and the frequency of it is happening less to me. From time to time, instantly, it is given to me again. I'm not as burdened by it now as I was in the beginning. I would say that maybe the Lord is helping me to be able to accept it more easily, by giving it to me more gradually.

Q. Why has the Virgin Mary come to so many people in the world at this time of history, such as yourself?

A. Because as Our Lady herself said, "The world has never been so sinful." These are the end times of Satan and also the end times as we know them. Sinfulness is multiplying. Russia's errors, which she spoke of, are spreading. Sin seems to be multiplying at such a fast rate. The world just can't go on the way it is. So Our Blessed Mother is crying out as a mother to her children to repent. When Our Holy Mother talks about the sacraments, prayer, and loving one another, it's because she wants peace as God desires peace. This also must be to fulfill Scripture.

Q. Father McGinnity says that you have been given a great insight concerning Our Lady's role in salvation. Can you tell us what you were shown and told?

A. God the Father had always planned to use the Mother of His Son in a special way at the "end time" and this is going to come about now. It will lead to the Triumph of the Immaculate Heart. It is a resource to help rekindle faith in the world. Although she knew in the beginning only a shred of what was happening, the Holy Mother bore her heart being pierced all the time in silence. Later, especially at the Crucifixion, Our Lady understood it more. Her purity at all times kept her in total union with God. The Blessed Mother's Assumption took place only by means of the Holy Spirit of God and was the completion of the unifying of the Body and Blood of Jesus with her own. Our Holy Mother is being used in a greater way now than when she was on earth. Just as the two Hearts were inseparable, so their two offerings, their two acts of sacrifice were one. So much so that their blood being one is, in the Virgin Mary, now life-giving blood—her flesh and blood in union with Jesus. God is using her blood as a sacrifice, because united with Jesus the Redeemer, more so at this time, her sufferings are now in the Eternal Now of God, greater than ever. She is the vessel to bring Jesus to us. And the need is now greater than ever. In the one Sanctuary of Jesus' Heart, there are two altars: His own Heart and His Mother's Heart. Through that one sacrifice, He atones for the sins of the soul and accepts His Immaculate Mother's sufferings for sins of the flesh (which today are greater than ever in history), but it is

> Jesus' sacrifice which gives the single united offering infinite value.

Christina's spiritual director observes that this is a fascinating gift of understanding. In relation to this particular point of theology, Saint Paul, in Col. 1:24, makes us all "coredeemers" with Christ because we can "make up," he says, "what is still necessary to be undergone for the sake of Christ's Body, the Church." Christ's sacrifice was perfect as such and no one can add to its infinite worth. It is in the area of the application of Christ's sacrifice that we can help. It is interesting, therefore, that the understanding given Christina is that Our Lady suffers "for souls who say 'no' to God and who reject the life-giving Blood of Jesus." In addition, Father McGinnity stated that "Christina was also made aware that in the apparitions of Our Blessed Lady no one sees her as she is, but as a reflection of Our Holy Mother through the Holy Spirit. He portrays whatever aspect of Our Lady is appropriate for a given situation."

CHAPTER TEN

One with Christ

IN CHRIST, THE FULLNESS OF DEITY RESIDES IN BODILY FORM. YOURS IS A SHARE OF THIS FULLNESS, IN HIM WHO IS THE HEAD OF EVERY PRINCIPALITY AND POWER.

—COL. 2:9–10

To grasp the special relationship Christina Gallagher has with Jesus, it is important to understand a little of the Divine Savior's plan over the centuries to bring His merciful love into the world through *little souls*.

After the seventeenth-century revelations of the Sacred Heart to Sister Margaret Mary Alacoque, the Lord continued to reveal Himself more and more. Jesus explained to the nun that the love of His Heart must spread and manifest Itself to men and He would reveal great graces to her. This He did.

From these revelations, the Sacred Heart of Jesus became the focus of rich devotion. It was regarded as the "symbol of that boundless love which moved the Word to take Flesh, to institute the Holy Eucharist, to take sins upon Himself; and dying on the

Cross, to offer Himself as a victim and sacrifice to the Eternal Father."[1]

As the Lord's plan to bring special graces to souls who honored His Sacred Heart unfolded, Jesus promised to use many little souls. They were to transmit messages to the world, He said, and establish new devotions to His love and mercy. Once more He was true to His word.

Like Saint Margaret Mary, souls were chosen because of their weakness, their nothingness, such as Saint Thérèse of Lisieux, best known today as the Little Flower, and whom Christina admits is her favorite visitor. It was Saint Thérèse who promised someday God would work even greater marvels in still weaker souls than hers. Known for her "little way" of getting to Heaven by offering everything to God with love, the Virgin Mary even asked Christina to read Saint Thérèse autobiography.[2]

By the twentieth century, the Lord's plan for little souls continued to unfold, revealing to Sister Faustina that His work through her was intended to profit a great number of souls.

Other victim souls received numerous extraordinary communication with the supernatural world. All were chosen by Divine Will to come to intimately know their Jesus' love and mercy. All were chosen for their littleness.

Again, these were graces for the world. Many became victim souls. Yet there were slight differences in the purpose of their sacrifices.

Saint Thérèse of the Child Jesus offered herself as a victim of merciful love; Saint Margaret Mary, of both Justice and Mercy. Heavenly experiences, extensive revelations, abandonment, suffering, and charity characterized their lives in Christ; for these little souls truly became one with Him. Most saw the Lord with their eyes or "inner eyes" and embraced His divine beauty and nature. Most knew Him better than their neighbor.

Like all of them, the account of Christina Gallagher's revelations and victimhood in Christ is no less captivating and meaningful.

And here, Jesus has truly chosen another little soul to reveal His saving plan of love for souls. In just seven years they appear to have developed an intimate relationship and she knows Him well, both in her ability to describe His appearance as well as her understanding of His will.

Like the others, Christina has seen Jesus, with her eyes, and observed His actions. Physically, she compares Him to the reversed image reproduced from the "Shroud of Turin." This image, she says, looks like "the Jesus I know." Yet no picture she says has totally captured His appearance.

In order to be thorough, Christina explains she has seen Jesus in two forms: one that she refers to as His suffering body—His body from the Passion; and the other as His resurrected or glorified body. In either form His hair is shoulder length and His eyes are blue.

In the suffering body, Jesus appears thin and shattered. His cheeks are sunken and His eyes are bulging. His hair and beard are sparse and damaged and His near-death countenance accentuates the agony of His sacrifice.

In the resurrected body, Jesus appears younger-looking and joyous. He often smiles. His beard is full and His hair is very wavy and very shiny. The Savior in His resurrected body does not walk, but floats and usually is in a long white robe or with a red wrap that appears to be blowing in the wind.

But from both of these images, there seems to be special underlying reasons in her seeing the Lord at all.

Because there are no words to adequately describe the tortuous scenes of the Agony in the garden and the slow, grueling march to Calvary and Crucifixion, Christina's experiences of seeing Christ in His suffering body seem designed to convey a piercing impact upon our realization of Christ's sacrifice for mankind. No visual detail was spared. Her eyes witnessed the Savior's red blood flowing and His limbs penetrated by huge spike nails. From these revelations, it appears Jesus seeks to show us He truly lived and died for mankind. Yes, He was truly here on earth and His act of redemption was very real and very meaningful.

Indeed, mankind's present-day indifference to Christ's act of redemption is something that pains Christina to the marrow of her bones. Often feeling the futility of her words in describing these insights of God's gift of salvation, Christina seems to cling to their memory for her own strength and courage, something she finds she needs to do to continue her constant pleas for prayer, sacrifices, and atonement. It is an endless struggle.

As she confided to her spiritual director, "I am just at my breaking point. God has given me the strength to cope. Now, more than ever, I just live for God more and more."

These unforgettable sights of Christ scourged and crucified are constant, haunting reminders to Christina that she must continue on and get this message out to the people. She now understands it, along with her suffering. It is the primary purpose of her life. This urgent reality is never lost upon her, especially as she relays Our Lady's message for Ireland and the world.

But the powerfully real apparitions of Christ in His suffering body left the strongest and deepest impressions on her. These apparitions showed her the Lord is master and His justice is real.

In 1992, Jesus had His mother remind Christina of this urgency. It is an urgency the Virgin Mary tells her is greater than ever, and simply defies human comprehension. Yet it doesn't stop. It won't go away. Metaphorically, it is the thunder of God's approaching justice. All Christina can do is pray and offer more suffering.

Yes, more suffering. Herein lies the answer to understanding how Christina Gallagher has become one with Christ. It is through her suffering for souls—all souls—yet specifically the souls of priests, that she has come into the deepest union with Our Lord.

Like many victim souls, Christina is especially asked to suffer for the souls of priests. From this suffering, the Lord has taught her much. Christina sees now, in every priest, the Savior using His victim to pasture His flock. In this, she comprehends and understands the importance of their sublime dignity and calling, and subsequently how very special is her own mission.

Despite the weakness of the individual priest, the fruitfulness of his suffering united with that of Christ is of inestimable value for the pasturing of the flock. This greatness is generally unknown, not only to the laity, but even to the priests themselves.

In a powerful message given on the morning of Tuesday, April 23, 1991, the Lord explained to Christina His understanding and patience would have to give way, eventually, to His Justice; especially if His priest sons do not properly fulfill their callings.

My people, I am Jesus, your Lord God. Many of you stand on the edge of the Abyss of Death Eternal. I say to you, My people, wake up! My return to you is close at hand. My Holy Mother calls you to prepare you for My forthcoming. My Holy Mother's call has been unheard or scoffed at. My Mercy will be with you now for but a short time. My people, you are now living in the times of great darkness and distress. Wake up and be vigilant in prayer.

My priest sons, My Sacred Heart bleeds for your lack of love, and for your lack of courage to speak up for My true teachings. I tell you, My priest sons, if you do not fulfill My work on earth, and proclaim My Word in Truth to My people, you will force My hand to fall on you in Justice. I tell you this, because My Sacred Heart burns with love for you. I want My people to know My Word.

My people, pray! Pray for wisdom. I am Jesus, I am the Word; I am Wisdom and Truth; I am Life Eternal for you.

Christina knew this. After receiving this message, she understood with even more confidence the importance of her prayers and sacrifices for Our Savior's chosen priests. Her suffering took on a new and special meaning to her. "This," she proclaimed, "was her life's work."

Consequently, in her dual role as a visionary and a victim soul, Christina now understands her suffering may actually be of greater importance in God's plan than her role as His messenger. Here is perhaps the most intriguing realization about God's plan to now bring His victory into the world. Although many messages have been given to the world for its salvation, the Virgin Mary's report of a poor response seems to be irrelevant to her promise of the Triumph of her Immaculate Heart. This absolute guarantee of Our Holy Mother's victory reveals that at this time the Triumph will be more a result of the mysterious and powerful ways of God than of mankind's response to all the heavenly messages. What more mysterious way of God is there than the suffering on the cross? It is the ultimate mystery, the mystery of mysteries. Thus, it appears the prayers and sufferings of the little souls through Christ are truly the way of God's coming victory.

Even Pope John Paul II prophetically wrote that the offering of suffering to God is a practice that will bring unity among all mankind. The Holy Father said:

> And so there should come together in spirit beneath the cross on Calvary all suffering people who believe in Christ, and particularly those who suffer because of their faith in Him, Who is their Crucified and Risen One, so that the offering of their sufferings may hasten the fulfillment of the prayer of the Savior Himself that all may be one.
>
> (Salvifici Doloris,
> *On the Christian Meaning of Human Suffering*)

The suffering of many innocent people is so great that God will use it to raise His victims to the glory of eternal life. Suffering is the key to the Triumph and possibly the key to why God is able to do so much through Christina Gallagher. For without her suffering, without her victimhood in Christ, her other spiritual experiences—her apparitions and revelations—might not be possible.

Before we finish this book, after we've seen all there is to see and heard all there is to hear, let us come back to this mystery. Let us take a deeper look at what it's really like to be crucified in Christ, to be a little soul. For the key to the understanding of our salvation has always been found in the wounds of the Body of Our

Lord and now somewhat again in the wounds of the bodies of these brave little victim souls that somehow die to themselves in the wounds of Our Lord, and do not shrink from the call to suffer for love of their Lord to draw others to Him; souls like Christina Gallagher.

CHAPTER ELEVEN

"The Heart of Jesus Is Open to All"

NO ONE WHO COMES TO ME SHALL EVER BE HUNGRY, NO ONE WHO BELIEVES IN ME SHALL EVER THIRST.

—JOHN 6:35

Christina Gallagher's enigmatic existence does not make for an easy life. It's not a life that is humanly desired because it carries with it such great struggle, persecution, and doubt from others. Yet Christina must go forward. More than anything else it is a life of testimony in the Lord; testimony that must be given because it is an essential part of the Lord's plan to use this soul.

In Christina's own testimony, we explore the depth of her relationship with Jesus.

Q. Can you tell us about your first apparition?

A. I saw Jesus. It was my first experience of an apparition.

I went to pray at a grotto and the people would gather around a little cross that was placed there with a statue of Our Lady on the crossbeam. People were saying that they were seeing the little statue of Our Lady change to Our Lord and I was not seeing it at first. After a time I did see it change to a statue of Our Lord, but rather than believe, I disbelieved. I felt that if this was real I would have seen it before it was suggested; I had so much doubt that I felt like leaving the field. If we were going there to pray we should pray, not be looking for signs and wonders. But someone started to pray the Rosary and I couldn't be disrespectful of the Rosary, so I stayed. At some point during the Rosary a force moved my head to the right and upward and I found myself looking at the Head and Face of Jesus crowned with thorns. My entire body became as if paralyzed and I was deeply shaken by sorrow for my sins, but later realized it was not just my sin, but sin itself that had Jesus in this state. As it was revealed to me at a later stage in an inner knowledge, He redeemed our souls, leaving us free will, and all the souls of humanity make the Mystical Body of Christ; through our free will to sin we are tearing the Mystical Body of Christ apart and Jesus continues to suffer to redeem us and will continue to suffer to redeem us until the earth is purified from sin.

Q. Tell us about the experiences with Jesus you have mentioned.

A. It's not like a television screen vision. It is seeing with the eyes of my soul.

Q. So you are able to see Him?

A. I see Jesus, yes, but not always with my bodily eyes.

Q. When you see Jesus, what does the expression on His face look like? Is He smiling?

A. He briefly smiles. There's always a deep sense of love, but always a firmness. His lips barely move. When Our Blessed Mother speaks, it's much the same. It's as if her lips barely move. I don't know how her voice comes across as clearly and distinctly as it does.

Q. Does Jesus always stand still or does He walk toward you?

A. On one occasion when I saw Jesus in this way, with the eyes of my soul, He was looking toward the altar at my home. During this time, I felt a great sadness. I thought, Jesus won't look at me. At that moment, He turned right around. Normally, His expression is serious; very sincere, very loving, but serious. But when He turned around to look at me, I thought. How dare I think He should turn around to look at me. The moment He looked at me, enormous love came from Him. I wanted to fall at His feet, but I couldn't move.

Q. You've spoken of Jesus being angry and people have said that God does not get angry. It has been discussed that this was your way of expressing what you experienced when you were observing His unhappiness with mankind. Can you explain this anger you mentioned?

A. Exactly. This is when there is, as my spiritual director says, what's called the "just anger of God." It is hurting Jesus to see mankind's ways. His anger is expressed in different ways. Jesus portrays Himself as angry with sin and He hurts when He sees people sinning.

Q. Could you tell us how, in your opinion, Jesus' anger is different from a human being's anger?

A. It is like the time I saw Jesus in the sky. He looked down upon the world and obviously He was looking at the sin in the world. Then, I heard the echo of His voice which sounded so stern. He echoed the word "Woe." At that, He drew His hands over the world. I just felt myself tremble. Obviously, He was saying woe to the people and to sin, but it was mostly to the sin of the people.

Q. To be specific, the anger of Jesus is not expressed as a violent, ugly emotion, like human beings sometimes express it. Is it?

A. No, no. His anger is out of love for His people. If a father is hurt because of his son, he will have a sense of anger out of love for his son. Jesus would be looking at human weakness in accepting sin and rejecting Him. With people, there's no prayer, no sense or awareness of sin. People are getting deeper and deeper into sin. Jesus sees this in His people that He's redeemed with His Blood. Yet He thirsts and longs for the souls of His people to return to the light, graces, and the love He wishes to give them. Jesus invited me to give Him a drink. Three times He repeated the request. I was unsure as to how

I would give Him a drink. Jesus then said, "You are like a grape ripe to be crushed; when you are crushed, you give me a drink. I do not thirst for water or wine, I thirst for souls out of love." I've seen Jesus, at another time, in the sky when He again expressed this firmness in His justice. This time, He lashed out at the sky with this scourge. When He did, I saw the sky burst into millions of cracks of lightning. Jesus was obviously very hurt by the sin of the world; then everything turned into darkness. He repeated three times, He wanted peace.

During this experience, beside Jesus on His right-hand side was an angel whom I recognized as the Angel of Wrath in red. The Angel of Wrath held in his hand a cross of light with a circle around this entire cross. From behind came a white dove which perched on this cross of light. I could hear thunder as the lightning was cracking all over the sky. I was neither up where Jesus was nor was I on the earth. I was somewhere in between. I was very, very frightened. When the thunderbolts came, it sounded as if the earth was exploding. I looked down and I could see the road open up, as if the buildings themselves became sand and the people were falling into the cracks. I could see the horror and hear the screams. It was a really horrible scene.

Then I could see Our Blessed Mother before Jesus and she looked very small. I could only see Our Lady's mantle in the shape of her as if I was looking at a back view of Our Blessed Mother. Our Lady was crying and through the sobs of tears was saying, "Mercy, my Son—Mercy, my Son."

Q. Is there anything else in particular about Jesus' appearance that is very memorable to you?

A. No, only my love for Him. Only that I feel such great love for Him.

Q. Can you tell us about the love of Jesus?

A. The Love of Jesus is more than the love of the Blessed Mother. Although sometimes He may be very serious or stern. The love of Jesus for me is my life. He's my Redeemer; He's everything and all I ever want. How do you describe a love, again like Our Blessed Mother's, that fulfills you completely? It's like loving somebody you never want to lose, somebody you want to be always united with. I am on earth for whatever God desires. I want always to be able to say "Yes." Yes, but for whatever God wants to do with me. Through the messages, through the cross, through whatever He wants. All I desire is to do the will of God. This life has very little meaning for me. God is everything to me and my home is with God. Yes, even while I'm on earth.

Q. Can you tell us about the Mercy of Jesus?

A. I see both Jesus' mercy and His love. This is the Sacred Heart. Any time I think about His mercy, I think of His Sacred Heart. The Heart of Jesus is open to all. Jesus would never stop loving any soul. It is the person who turns away from God. While there is breath in that person, God will never stop reaching out to him because God knows only love. The Sacred Heart of Jesus is boundless mercy; it is the depth of His love for all His people, His redeemed. Jesus will always continue to reach out with love until a person finally takes his last breath. Then they have made their decision. They take their last breath and decide whether they want God or not.

Q. What has Jesus shown to you for us all to know?

A. Jesus has shown me very clearly that He's always with us and He never leaves us, and so is the Blessed Mother. It's in our sinfulness, weakness, and our humanness that we walk away from Him. He's always there for us.

Somebody once said that if Jesus came to earth at any particular place in the world, there would be millions of people there who would want to meet and touch Him. Yet there are so many churches throughout the entire world today where Jesus is already in the tabernacle, in the Holy Eucharist. His Body and His Blood are real and alive. It's not a dead Jesus we receive; it's a risen Jesus. It's a Jesus who feeds us with His flesh and blood; a Jesus that's full of love. Yet almost nobody cares.

Today, there's not the desire to rush to the Church to talk to Him, or to just simply keep Him company. I don't mean we should go to church and say, "Jesus, I want this, this, and this." We should say, "Jesus, I want to be here because I want to keep You company. In my nothingness, in my littleness, I want to be here to love You."

Q. How do you talk to Jesus?

A. Sometimes when I'm not in the church at night, I find in my little prayers that I'm saying, "Jesus, let my heart be united with You in every tabernacle throughout the entire world. I know that that's not possible as I'm here at this moment, but it is possible for You to do this in a sense while I'm sleeping, through my Guardian Angel or whatever way You choose." I just allow that every moment in my life be an act of love for Him. The Son of God humbled Himself in the stable at Bethlehem and on the cross of Calvary. His entire life was an act of love for us, right to the Cross. Can we not show Him even one bit of love in return? He's the giver of love. He gives total love to us. Can we not give Him something back without always giving in to human sins, again and again? When we give to another person, out of love for God, it is then that Jesus' love is shared with one another. This is allowing God to communicate in us. God's love is beyond anything I could ever express. It's so much beyond my mind and my heart that, through all I have experienced, I would want to die for Him. I would give my life in whatever way He wants. I pray that God would never put me to the test, but at the same time, I hope that I will always be able to say "Yes."

Q. Has Jesus spoken to you about Our Eternal Father—His Father?

A. Yes, He spoke about Him. He said to always do the will of the Father. When He showed me Hell, He said, "This is the abyss of sin, Hell for all those who do not love my Father." And that's when He said, "My daughter, unite your weakness with Me Who is all strength."

Q. Can we know Jesus the way you do? Can we come to know Jesus without having experienced everything you have experienced?

A. Yes. I do believe that anyone who wants to get to know Him can do so in the way that He has given to me. I do believe in Him. Those who were walking in faith must be able to believe because He is the Truth. Through our weakness and our human nature and flesh we will be tempted to think this is all craziness. Temptations will come into our mind, saying, "There's no need for this." It's like fasting—we say to ourselves, "You don't need it." Most people in the world today are living in such darkness that often they feel they don't need God. Anyone can come to God, but you have to first become childlike. They must humble themselves before God. One must truly learn to believe in God, through prayer, sacrifice, fasting, and especially through the sacraments. You have to come to God like a little child and He'll draw you inward to Himself.

Q. Jesus loves children. Has He spoken to you about children?

A. Only when He talked about the three sins that most greatly afflict His Heart. Those were abortion, the immoral abuse of the innocent, and the sacrificing of the innocent to Satan. These three sins all affect children, whom He loves because they are innocent and helpless.

Q. Has Jesus spoken to you about the personal judgment of individuals and the final judgment of the world?

A. He's talked about His hand coming over the world more swiftly than the wind and where everybody will have the opportunity to have conversion, to truly believe and know of His existence. On the other hand, because sin is so strong, they also can use their free will to return to sin.

Q. Has the Lord said to pray to Him or to His Father?

A. Jesus says, you can't come to the Father but through Me. Yes, we must recognize the Father and the Holy Spirit—the Three in One. As Jesus Himself said, "If you recognize the Father, you recognize Jesus." But I think I would have to go to Jesus each time. Only in the sense of using the name of Jesus to intercede with His Father for me.

Q. Should we go directly to Jesus or should we go to Jesus through the Virgin Mary?

A. When we go through the Virgin Mary, we are giving honor

to God in the sense that all of the Holy Trinity chose Our Blessed Mother. God the Father chose the Virgin Mary to bear Jesus, the Son of God, by the power of the Holy Spirit. The Virgin Mary is pureness before God. We would be foolish not to go to the Blessed Mother as our mother. As in the wedding feast at Cana, where Jesus changed the water into wine, when we go to Our Mother, Mary, we should ask her, "Holy Mother, please help us." With this, will Our Blessed Mother not go to Jesus and to God the Father to intercede for us? God will accept our prayers when we go to God the Most Holy Trinity. At the same time, He would love us to go to Him through the Virgin Mary, because she is our mother as well.

Q. Can you tell us about the love that Jesus has for Ireland?

A. Jesus and Our Blessed Mother have a great love for Ireland and they spoke to me about it. There were many people from Ireland who took the Word of God to the world. Many of them weren't recognized as saints by the Church on earth. But the martyrs of Ireland are crying out in Heaven to God for His mercy to be with Ireland. Our Blessed Mother said she desired Ireland to be "a light to go out to the world." So yes, God has a love for Ireland, but then again, God has a love for all the people of the world.

Q. Has Jesus spoken to you about the Pope?

A. Our Blessed Mother has spoken many times about the Pope. I've been shown the Pope a number of times on the ground with his stomach bleeding. I have wondered why I was shown the Pope a number of times in this way. So one day I asked the Blessed Mother why she was showing me the Pope so many times in this way. Our Holy Mother said that through prayer, God was removing the danger from the Pope that particular time; but it was being immediately replaced by another danger.

Q. I read that you did not know how to read and write and that Jesus answered your prayer and gave you these abilities. Can you tell us a little about this special prayer to God?

A. Yes, my mother was ill with tuberculosis for a number of years. She'd gone back and forth to the hospital. She didn't have the strength to teach us. I wasn't too bothered about not reading and writing and nobody would push me to learn. That was fine with me. Then I went past the stage of being able to catch up to others. After this, it was difficult to try to learn anything. Still I didn't care much, but it was a constant humiliation. Every day I went to school, I felt like I was invisible. My teacher's still alive and remembers this. When we'd come to the part where the classroom would read aloud, they would have to skip over me when my turn came. I was the invisible person in class because I couldn't read.

I used to wonder what I was doing even going to school, because it seemed I was just there for the sake of being there. All the time, I felt hurt being there. I felt I was just there to be humiliated. I suppose there was no point in the teacher asking me to read, because I didn't know how. So there's no point blaming the teacher, really, because I suppose he was sparing me the extra humiliation of trying to struggle with reading when it was never clear to me how to read. I left school before I was fourteen years old. There was nothing I could do, only housework. I was okay when I could wash the dishes, sweep or scrub the floor, or make the beds—that kind of thing.

One day the woman I worked for came up and said, "Christina, I haven't my glasses. Could you read the instructions on this page?" All I remember is I just stood there as if I was paralyzed. Humiliation overwhelmed me. I didn't know what to do. Then she said to me something like, "Can you not read?" I said, "No." I turned away and went upstairs. I thought I could never face her again. So I left that job. It was at that time I remembered hearing my father and my aunts talking about my mother. She was very ill. They said she was unconscious and she had a lobe of her lung removed and she was not going to survive. She had been unconscious for a time and they said there wasn't much chance of her survival. They had had a second operation to remove fluid from her lung and the medical staff felt she could not survive. They were all waiting for her death.

I loved my mother so much and I wanted to go see her, but I wasn't allowed. The memory of that time still affects me. I finally came to terms with the fact that the adults were permitted to see my sick mother and, because I was a child, I wasn't. So I said, well, even if I got to see her, I couldn't help her, but I know One who can help her. It was Jesus, because Jesus was a real person. So I went to Jesus and asked Him to help me. I went to Mass that Sunday as if the weight of the whole world was on my shoulders. I couldn't wait to get in the door. During the consecration at Mass, I started my talk with Jesus. But it wasn't until I received Him in the Holy Eucharist that I really got down to talking to Him.

I said, "Jesus, I'm asking You to do two things for me. I don't know how You're going to do them, but the one thing I do know is You can do them. One thing is to make my mother better, because I need her more than You do. And the second thing is to teach me to read and write enough to get by so I won't be humiliated like this again."

Q. When did Jesus answer your prayers?

A. Right after that time, my mother regained consciousness and her health went uphill. That was about twenty-six years ago. But I still ran away from newspapers and books because I didn't want anyone to ever find out again that I could not read or write. I'd forgotten about the second request I'd asked for from Jesus. Then one day—I don't actually know where I was —sometime later, all of a sudden I discovered I knew each symbol that was on the paper and I could read it. I couldn't figure this out, so I got a pen and paper and then I discovered I also could write. Still, I wasn't convinced that this was real. So I gave what I wrote to my sister. I remember giving it to her and asking her what was written on it. She answered the question I had written. It was true—it was real! I could read and write! So I told myself that maybe when a person grows up and develops something changes with their mind and that's how a person learned to read—your mind developed. But I quickly dismissed this idea. Then it happened. I realized that it was God who had answered my prayer in some unknown way. Now, I don't say I'm perfect at spelling. Today I write to people and some of my spelling is wrong, but I don't care about it anymore. Somehow, I can now read and write.

Q. On May 2, 1992, you received a ring from Jesus. The message that day also said that you had previously received another ring. Will you please tell us about these two rings?

A. Yes, I received a ring with a countersunk diamond. I later saw three diamonds on it. The first time Jesus didn't refer to it as a ring. He referred only to the stone. He said it was His gift to me. The gift of the virtue of His love.

The second ring indicated that it had something to do with the mystical marriage. Our Blessed Mother led me to Jesus, like a little child for Holy Communion, dressed in white, filled with expectancy and reverence. Then she put the ring onto my knuckle and Jesus moved it the rest of the way. Then Jesus looked to Heaven and said, "Nothing in Heaven or on earth will break this union."

Q. What do you think all of this means with the two rings?

A. I have no idea.

Q. Do you think it means a spiritual betrothal?

A. I don't exactly know what it means. All I understand is what is in my heart and soul and mind. All I want to do is live for God.

Q. Is Jesus' return, the Second Coming, close at hand?

A. Yes, all this is a preparation for the Second Coming of Christ.

Q. In late October 1993, you received a message that gave an indication of how much time is left before the purification. Can you tell us this message?

A. Jesus said to me, "Offer Me your will, your life, and your eternity." Then He told me, "My love is like a raging fire that consumes." Christ said that He longed " . . . with deep desire to give of Myself to all hearts." I then asked if the chastisement of the world is far away and I was told, "It is as My Father has appointed its hour. There is much work and little time."

Q. At the end of 1993, on December 25 and 27, you received

two important apparitions and a message from Jesus. Please tell us about them.

A. At the dawn Mass on Christmas Day, I saw Jesus approach in great light, very splendidly and slowly. I saw that as He approached a huge dark cloud was being crushed downward beneath Him (though never touching His feet).

I could hear three of the Beatitudes sounding:

"Blessed are the pure of Heart . . .

"Blessed are the Peacemakers . . .

"Blessed are they who hunger and thirst for what is right . . ."

Then Jesus spoke: "Woe to the man who chooses to ignore My words, for My coming will be faster than light. Soon."

I asked, "But how soon is Your 'soon,' Lord?"

Jesus looked straight at me and just said, "Soon."

After saying this, Jesus approached at an increasing speed. Then, two days later, on December 27, 1993, on the Feast of Saint John the Evangelist, during Mass, I saw a huge chalice with a silver stem and golden cup. After a while I could hear the sound of bubbling. Then I saw white bubbles of steam rising from the cup, and it overflowed in a white liquid. I had an awareness of blood, but did not see any. Then a dove appeared over the chalice, facing forward, with wings outstretched. It was crowned. It seemed restless to purify.

CHAPTER TWELVE

I, Your Father, Yahweh

"THIS WILL TAKE PLACE, SO THAT THEY MAY BELIEVE," . . . HE CONTINUED, "THAT THE LORD, THE GOD OF THEIR FATHERS, THE GOD OF ABRAHAM, THE GOD OF ISAAC, THE GOD OF JACOB, DID APPEAR TO YOU."

—EXOD. 4:5

With what sounded like a choir singing a name in the background, Christina was left bewildered as one of her heavenly friends departed. Who was she? The name did not sound familiar. This woman had come before, always dressed like a nun, always friendly, yet never identifying herself. One day when she appeared, Christina said, "In the name of God, who are you and what do you want?" And she heard an echo: "Catherine of Siena, Catherine of Siena, Catherine of Siena."

Indeed, it was the famous saint who came in love. Sent by God for many reasons, she generously shared with Christina the strength she was revered for in the fourteenth century. Not surprisingly, Saint Catherine's visitations soon became welcomed events. She became a good friend. Like the Virgin Mary, the holy nun also came with others, including Saint John the Evangelist.

Though silent during the first apparition. Saint Catherine later gave Christina plenty of advice regarding her prayer life and mission—advice based on wisdom and experience. On one visit the powerful saint tearfully implored Christina to pray for the religious. They were in danger, spiritual danger, she said, and needed help: "Pray for the Pope every day, and priests, bishops, and cardinals, and for my sister nuns," she told Christina. Like a secret envoy, the saint also disclosed that the time of the final battle was now upon the world. Yes, it was the final hour. She wanted her to know the Heavenly Army was with her for the duration.

From Saint Catherine's exhortation, we are again sadly reminded of the dangers threatening the Church today—great dangers, said to be multiplying. Although now more grave problems are nothing new for the Church, such perils were a big part of Saint Catherine's mission during her times.

Born on the Feast of the Annunciation in Siena in 1347, the renowned mystic is highly recognized in Church history for her efforts to defend the Holy See during the complex political and religious currents of her troubled times. She was a warrior. Someone God deliberately sent at the right time and place.[1]

Why Saint Catherine visited Christina is not exactly certain. Like her other heavenly friends, there appears to be a curious connection between the mission and life of this saint and Christina. During childhood both were first summoned by God. Both were illiterate. Saint Catherine's first apparition, like Christina's, was of Christ. Later in their lives, both received the stigmata. Most curiously, Saint Catherine first received the stigmata in her hands, feet, and heart while visiting a little church in Pisa—named Saint Christina. Both Christina and Saint Catherine received numerous celestial visitations of Our Lady and Our Lord, as well as of Satan. Saint Catherine was also terribly tormented by Satan and his demons during long intervals in which degrading temptations assaulted her.[2]

Like the Irish mystic, Saint Catherine received an invisible gold and pearl ring from Jesus, signifying her spiritual marriage in faith to Christ. A mystical marriage, like Christina's, which armed her with strength, courage, and reassurance of her special relationship with God.

But there's more. Probably as much as anything else, Saint Catherine was known for her four treatises written while in ecstasy, in the form of a conversation with the Eternal Father. After studying the book, *The Dialogue,* many scholars are convinced of the great spiritual union Saint Catherine had with the Eternal Father. It was a mystical union of love few understand. How many can say they know the Eternal Father? How many can say they have had a mystical experience with the First Person of the Most Holy Trinity?[3] Not many. Christina Gallagher just happens to be one. The Eternal Father has spoken and revealed Himself to her in a very special way.

Once when coming out of ecstasy, Saint Catherine espoused, "I have seen the secret things of God." These things the saint later admitted were not communicable by human words, because there were no words she could find. No words existed! Likewise, Christina Gallagher has also seen the secret things of God, yet more remarkably, even God Himself—God the Father. Yes, she has seen the Eternal Father. That sounds shocking. But on more than one occasion she received inner experiences of Him. These are mystical beyond words, beyond imagination, beyond our very comprehension. Like her other experiences, she struggles to describe these spiritual encounters. Yet they are a critical part of her revelations.

Over the last few years, Christina's relationship with God the Father has deepened. It has become closer. On October 5, 1992, He spoke to her of His Son:

"Little one, to you I will reveal the opening of the heavens and the closing of the Gate. To all who desire to come to Me—come through the Mercy of Jesus My Son and by means of His Mother. Those whose desire is to disown My

Son and His Mother will not find life. Only through Jesus My Son in His mercy will any soul find life. Those who desire to find life through Jesus must drink of Him. There are many false gods. Man has returned to adoring all that is of the world. Man is raising up the Antichrist through adoring false gods. Pray to her who is Wisdom. Only in her is Truth."

According to Father McGinnity, this message was of significance, because it may contain profound meaning for our times. It was a message deserving more than just a glance. After praying and studying it closely, the theologian ventured his opinion:

When the phrase "the heavens opened" occurs in Scripture (at the Baptism of Jesus), we are told "The Spirit came down" and Jesus undergoes Baptism for the sake of saving the world. Later, Jesus said, "I have a Baptism to be baptized with and how eager I am till it is completed." He meant His death, which would purify the world. The "opening of the heavens" which Christina is to see, would seem to be the cleansing of the world or purification. This is God's Spirit descending in an act much, like our Baptism, like Christ's death. It means dying to rise, letting go in order to gain, suffering to be renewed.

The "Closing of the Gate," when we return to Scripture, can have a clear and definite meaning in the context of the messages. Jesus in Saint John's Gospel remarks, "I am the gate of the sheepfold." He makes this remark in the lovely discourse about His tenderness and mercy as Good Shepherd. Now when the Father says to Christina that to her will be revealed "The Closing of the Gate," He may mean that she will see the end of this time of Mercy, when as Jesus said in the Gospels we have to enter through Him to find life. In other words, the time will come when, if we refuse His Mercy, we must face His Justice.

The phrase could mean the end of the time of Mercy, in which we now find ourselves. If people refuse this Mercy, then the cleansing of the world will follow. The Father will determine those who will be allowed in or kept out of the Gate; saved or lost at this important phase in the history of Salvation.

Further commentary on the October 5, 1992, message by Father McGinnity was offered:

To understand this message, it is necessary to apply the rules of Scriptural interpretation. In the interpretation of Scripture, one goes to other parts where a similar message or similar words are given. Earlier on the same day (October 5) Jesus used similar words and ideas. These throw light on the Heavenly Father's message, e.g., when the Father says ". . . must *drink of Him,"* He is speaking in a vein similar to Jesus earlier that day when He declared, "I am Peace, few come to *drink of Me."* That message was directed toward behavior within the Church—carelessness, desecration, and "the blind leading the blind," which is bad example and leadership. It seems then that "Who is who?" is a gentle way of saying "Be careful; people who lead may not be as trustworthy as you think they are." In other words, "Who is who?" raises doubt about the genuineness of those we automatically and unquestioningly follow.

In the earlier message about the "blind leading the blind" resulting in the "trampling of the blood of the Lamb" (the abuse of the Holy Sacrifice of the Mass), the question is asked rhetorically by Jesus, "How can My little ones give glory to their Lord God?" In other words, when the Sacrifice is dishonored through irreverence of malpractice, or more basically, when it is not preached for what it is, then people who depend on their spiritual leaders for the enlightenment of truth are deprived, go ignorant, and do not respond with reverence, adoration, and reparation. If they are not led to sorrow for sin, they will not cleanse themselves in Confession. So the Sacrifice will be profaned, because they are all given Holy Communion.

But the message implies that this is not primarily their fault. They are led by the blind. So accordingly as the true source of Life, the merciful Jesus is profaned and abandoned, the Church moves to false means of fulfillment, and is thus raising up the "false gods" that God the Father then mentions. The Church is led in a worldly way. A great amount of time is then spent on trivial, distracting programs and pursuits . . . all in the name of religion while less and less time is given to the Sacrifice of Jesus. The Father then directs attention to Our Lady whom He describes as "Wisdom." In other words, Our Holy Mother directs those who pray to her (as He desires) to the true source of Grace.

But the Eternal Father had even more to say to Christina. A few weeks later, in late October 1992, He again addressed her. This time it was with an important message for her own life, for her own cross.

To her surprise, He reminded her of a conversation she clearly remembers having with Him as a child. At that time, when she was five, the Eternal Father invited her to come into His Kingdom. Not surprisingly, she declined. It was a choice, she felt at the time, the Eternal Father accepted and blessed, especially since she never heard from Him again, and she was still in her bed the next morning. Now, over thirty years later, He talked to Christina of that conversation's significance:

My beloved daughter, I your Father reveal to you what is hidden from the learned. To the little, will My Kingdom belong. Jesus My Divine Son has blessed you and called you in the womb of your mother. To you I have spoken at the early age of five years—your time. It was you who made your choice. You chose the cross, for I your Father Yahweh longed to draw you from the cross, as I longed to draw My Divine Son. But Jesus My beloved, My Son—He too chose the cross for My people. You do not take the cross by yourself. For you could not—only through My Divine Son. Your share of it is little, yet it is great. Do you now understand what you asked Me or when I said, "So be it?"

"Yes, my Father, I understand, but only a little," responded Christina.

"Oh, My little one, *few have been chosen*. All have been called."

"But my Father," she replied, "I love You, though I am weak and nothing. How could You have chosen me?"

"Out of the love of the Heart of My Divine Son. Those of your generation, of your seed have surrendered to the cross. To them Jesus gave glory and rewarded them by calling forth one of their generation of seed to be blessed and chosen. That you are chosen is the fruit of their cross. I am your God, and so be it."

So be it. But since that night, Christina has disclosed other personal conversations with the Eternal Father—conversations she holds dearly in her heart, conversations that are not yet revealed, but that promise to be interesting. God the Father, she says, has promised to "reveal to her more of that which He has kept hidden from the learned and wise"—more of what He saves for the little, more of what He is saving for her.

From Christina's own words, we capture a little more of this unfathomable relationship:

Q. Christina, you had a mystical experience of the Eternal Father and the Blessed Trinity according to a published account. Can you describe that experience?

A. I was praying the Stations of the Cross with the meditations out of a prayer book.

While doing the Stations of the Cross, I became totally aware of seeing, with my eyes, a beam of light going up. Then I could see angels, and they were all like little babies. They were whiter than the light they were in. They ascended this beam of light, but they didn't fly up with their wings, although they had little wings. They seemed to move up the beam of light at will. At the top there was the most enormous area of white light. I've never seen anything like it.

Then I saw a man sitting in a big wooden chair. This chair was very broad and powerful-looking. It was a chair of authority. This man Who sat in it had white hair. Although He looked old, there wasn't a line or a blemish in His face. He was very beautiful. His face was identical to Jesus', only Jesus had brown hair and He had white hair, but Their faces were identical. When I saw them together, Jesus was on one side and the Blessed Mother was below Jesus on a step. I could see long steps, although they were nearly covered with light. And I remember saying, that is my Eternal Father, that is Jesus His Son, and that's Our Blessed Mother. I thought, where is the Holy Spirit? I then became aware, that very moment, that all of the light I could see was the Holy Spirit. Now during all of this there were clouds, white clouds of light. There were different clouds with angels on each of them. They floated over where the Eternal Father was sitting and Jesus and His Blessed Mother were standing. I could hear millions of little voices mingled together. They were singing, but their singing sounded like music. It was beautiful. It sounded as if children were singing from a distance. I could hear a lot of children singing and their voices were coming across as if on a breeze. It was like a beautiful sound from a distance, but it was softer, like music. I didn't know what they were singing, but it was so beautiful, all mingled together. It sounded so soft, like the wind itself, yet a beautiful sound came from it.

Q. On May 5, 1992, you were told the Holy Trinity dwells in you. Jesus said that you've found favor with God. Can you tell us about the meaning of this?

A. I was trying to find out what it meant because I had realized that Jesus would live in me, but I didn't realize that the Holy Trinity could live in anyone. Then Jesus said that He is One with His Father; that when a soul is chosen by God, they are one. He said, "When your heart is open to receive God (if I receive Him and He lives in me), then His Father also lives in me through the Holy Spirit." When I asked to understand this, He said, "When I sing in praise of Him, I sing in praise of the Father." He said, "It's all through the Holy Spirit, through His actions." This is the way of the Holy Spirit. However, that's not just for me. It is for many people who receive Jesus with an open heart. Jesus said, "Everyone is called, but few are chosen."

Q. What did the Eternal Father say to you about being among the Chosen?

A. When I asked about being chosen, He referred to the seed of my generation that Jesus had glorified. It was through their cross that Jesus gave them what they desired, which was a person of their generation to be chosen.

Q. Does this mean you? Are you this chosen person?

A. Yes, it just happened to be me.

Q. In October of 1992, the Eternal Father said to you that He spoke to you at the age of five. Do you remember this?

A. At that time, my mother was worried, because of the many illnesses I had. I had pneumonia and double pneumonia. On this particular occasion, I was so weak that my heart was not beating. I was not breathing. My mother was investigating and she put her ear down on my heart. Then my mother brought my father into the room. My mother believed the scream of crying from my father shocked my heart and it started beating again. It was at the same time that this experience with God happened to me. I was five years old when it happened.

I remember I had an experience with God. I heard a voice and I knew it to be God, saying He was coming to take me to Heaven. I said I didn't want to go to Heaven yet, that I wanted to remain on earth. I wanted to live and I wanted to grow up and be like Mommy and Daddy. I wanted to get married and have one or two children. As it turned out, I did get married. I have two beautiful children, but because of complications I can't have any more children. But now, going back over everything in my life, this conversation I had as a child with God and hearing His voice is a realization more strongly, now.

Q. Why do you think the Eternal Father spoke to you? What were the circumstances?

A. As a child, I was often very sick. My parents didn't know for a number of nights whether I was going to live or die. I didn't realize that I was so ill. I wondered if God was going to take me to Heaven or not. I would pull the blanket over me and say, "If You're going to take me, it'd be just like going on a holiday." I knew it was a holiday that would never end and that I wouldn't come back. Then this voice came again. The same words again were said to me about going to Heaven and I ended up saying the same thing to God. I told Him I wanted to live. At the end of this conversation with God, the second time around, I heard the words, "So be it." Then I knew that meant, "I can live! Now everything will be all right," I thought. I took it as meaning that I could live.

Q. Christina, on October 5, 1992, you received a message from Jesus. He spoke to you about being a victim soul with Him. Then the Eternal Father spoke to you. Can you tell us about Our Heavenly Father speaking to you?

A. It's strange during these experiences because you instantly know the difference in the voice, although the voice may be the same. The Eternal Father to me has a stronger, more powerful something in His voice. He has a more firm tone, yet there is something very beautiful and gentle about His voice. It's more overpowering. I know when He's speaking to me; I know instantly it's Our Eternal Father. He has spoken to me on a number of occasions—a number of occasions recently. He has given me other messages. He would say things like, "My daughter, I am your Father." One night, He repeated this a number of times. Then He invited me to arise. I just said, "Precious Blood of Jesus cover me. In the name of God, if this is not of You, be gone in Jesus' Name." This voice kept repeating, "My daughter, I am your Father. Arise and pray."

Q. Your spiritual director reports that you were given knowledge concerning the Seven Degrees of the Spirit and how a soul moves toward holiness. Can you explain some of this?

A. In January 1994, I was given an awareness of the means whereby a soul advances in holiness. It concerned ascending the *seven steps to perfection,* which I had been shown sometime back, but did not really then understand. I was given that God desires the Seven Degrees of His Spirit to permeate the person who is being perfected in the seven faculties of *heart, soul, mind, body, will, intellect,* and *memory.*

The Seven Steps to Perfection

Christina has been given the gift of knowledge from Almighty God to understand how there are seven steps, stages, or degrees on the path to perfection, or the path of purification.

I saw seven steps, and the more we respond, surrendering to the Cross for the love of Christ, the more we are drawn into the degrees of His Spirit with God raising the soul to a higher degree.

The heart of the Holy Trinity is the Godhead and from the heart of the Godhead comes the beacon of light which is the Holy Spirit. Through this beacon God desires to radiate His Spirit and draw the soul to a higher level of union with Himself.

From the unity and love of the heart of the Godhead, the desire of God is to draw each soul in a deeper way into Himself.

Every soul is redeemed by Jesus and, in that way, is part of the Mystical Body of Jesus. By the person decreasing in self and allowing God to increase in his or her soul, God desires to draw each one to a level of mystical union or marriage with Christ. Many, however, do not achieve this union because they will not decrease in self to allow God to increase within them.

What Our Lady Asks

When Our Blessed Mother asks, through her message, for prayer, sacrifice, and fasting, these teach us to decrease in self in childlike humility before God by depriving the flesh and opening the heart to permit the Spirit to freely flow in the seven areas of our being, that is, heart (the main channel or entrance leading to the will), will, mind, intellect, memory, body, and, lastly, the soul.

These first six areas, depending on their response, can lead the soul into light or darkness. Everything is first of all desired in the heart and the heart then requires the will, the mind, the intellect, the memory, and the body to respond in an open channel to permit the seven degrees of the Spirit to purify and strengthen the six areas of our being, whose response will leave the soul in either light or darkness.

The *heart,* because it is the main channel leading to the other faculties, and is itself the source of desire which leaves the other channels open or closed in willing, choosing, or action, needs to be purified of its weakness, because the heart can be open or closed to God.

The *will* can become so unyielding to God's will that it stubbornly resists the prompting of God and becomes shaped in a pattern of self-interest and self-concern and can become too weak to decide for God.

The *mind* can be molded more and more by the thinking

of the world, the expectations of people, and the standards of earthly judgment.

The *intellect* can lose its realization of God's Wisdom being supreme, a greater treasure than all human expertise and greatness. It can even rationalize what suits itself and begin even to justify as right what is objectively wrong. A loss of humility before God leads us to trust in ourselves and less in Him: more in our personal potential and less in Him Who is indeed the source and giver of every talent we possess. God may then need to prevent pride from building up and taking us over for then we would lose the greatest gift, God Himself. But as he removes our securities we are made to feel vulnerable and helpless of ourselves.

The *memory* can be clouded from consciousness of the merciful deeds of God in our past and need a purifying and strengthening from the clutter of personal concerns that accumulate and block our loving dependence on the God Who loves us with an everlasting love. To make us realize this, He will have to bring us down to a realization that we are nothing and that we draw all from Him Who is the giver of life itself.

Our *body,* through its weaknesses as a result of original sin and because of constant temptations from the other deadly spirits—apart from pride—that can gain many influences over the bodily appetites and temperament of a person through their attacks of greed, lust, anger, gluttony, envy, and sloth, will need strengthening for the mastery over self that is imparted by the Spirit's gift of self-control. This spiritual reinforcement of our higher faculties over our lower appetites will shatter our composure the more dependent on the flesh we have permitted ourselves to become.

The *soul,* through failure of the other faculties to respond to God, can experience only light or darkness. Although this work of purifying is not the release of the Holy Spirit as in the Sacrament of Confirmation, it will inevitably result in a freedom of movement for the Spirit already received through the Sacrament, for He is hindered and hampered by our imperfections and impurities and the residue of past sins already forgiven.

Purification Can Be Painful

The seven degrees of the Spirit of God can be at work at any given moment, or there can be three, four, or any number of degrees of the Spirit at work at any time. For instance, if the heart is open and the mind is weak and Jesus wants to purify the mind, sometimes the darkness experienced feels like abandonment. The mind is not able to understand, and thinks God has abandoned it until God can, in His degree, penetrate sufficiently to purify that particular area of the mind; then one can receive the Light and gain the understanding of the Spirit of God.

If somebody is living with bad thoughts, and God is purifying and strengthening the mind, it has the ability then to overcome the bad thoughts, but when God withdraws that degree of the Spirit from the mind, the mind is in shock, as it were. It feels like a depression, a feeling of distress while the purifying is taking place.

As the Spirit of God progresses and works through each area, it is a painful procedure, and the key to everything is surrender: surrender everything for the love of God.

Until God purifies a particular area, it is like being in a darkness, depending on how open or how blocked the particular area is, and depending on which degree of the Spirit of God is at work. The higher degree of the Spirit, the more powerful it will be and the greater will be the shock caused.

God might bring a person to a particular level and that level can be purified and doing well, but that person can, of their own free will, fall to the temptation of Satan in sin and darkness. The memory, for instance, can forget the mercy of

God and the truth. Then God may have to repeat, in His mercy and goodness, His purification of that person's memory again and reawaken its faculty.

If the will is weak, God will have to work on the will. It is the temptation of the flesh in our free will to decide against the desire God has given in the heart. And if God is working on the will in any degree of His Spirit, the will can get shaky, feel fragile, and even seem about to collapse.

Surrender Is the Key

The key is surrender. Everything has to be surrendered. As we get to know ourselves we get to realize our own nothingness, that without God we are nothing, and the will more than any other faculty is instructed and taught by this. We realize that we depend on God for absolutely everything, for His gifts of Light, Wisdom, and Mercy and the degrees of the Holy Spirit in every area of our lives.

The Holy Spirit wants to strengthen all the areas of our being, and since all these areas work together, if there is something blocking any one area the other areas suffer. The quicker we surrender everything to God, for love of Him, the better. Understand ourselves and our nothingness in the sight of God, and come with hearts totally open and bent on receiving everything from God in humility."

When Things Go Wrong

"It is easy to surrender when everything is going right," Christina says, "but when things go wrong for us, when a person may say, 'Where is God in all this?,' we find excuses and have negative thoughts and feel as if we've had enough, then we can fall back to where we were previously. But, if we can surrender out of love of

God, and not even be interested in questioning, then it is as if the heart is allowed to open up to a greater extent, and the Spirit can flow freely, through this channel, into the soul."

Priests

Christina understood that

Whereas consolations of soul follow the process of purification for those God is drawing to perfection through the seven steps, with priests it is generally different. The meaning of the priesthood is to be a victim in union with Jesus: priests share in a special way in the victimhood of Christ, the Great High Priest Who is sacrificed for the sins of the world. The priests who are enduring the purification process will, therefore, experience emptiness during and following it, because the benefits will be applied by God to the souls whom they pasture in their shepherding of God's flock. Jesus pastures His sheep by means of the priest's ministry. So priests will be benefiting the flock in their charge in a deeply spiritual way as they themselves are led closer to perfection by means of the seven steps.

It would be nothing strange for a priest to go through his entire priestly life feeling no spiritual consolation, a prey to many temptations, emotional loneliness, inner emptiness, and as if abandoned by God. In addition, priests suffer the lack of knowledge to understand the spiritual fruitfulness God draws from their victimhood—the wealth of spiritual riches to lavish on His little lambs.

But God also expects the people (His little lambs) to respond to the greatness of spiritual wealth in the sacraments which He provides for them through the victimhood of His priests, by their response in prayer and sacrifice to keep holy the anointed ones of God.

As in the Scriptures, Jesus questioned Peter three times,

"Do you love Me?" and each time Peter replied, "I do." Jesus desired that he feed the sheep. He was to fulfill this in the suffering and death Jesus immediately prophesied for him. So Jesus' intention in saying "feed My sheep" is "suffer for My sheep." The cross is the pasture!

The Grace of God and How We Receive It

"The highest degree of grace is received through receiving the Holy Eucharist at the Sacrifice of the Mass for the person who is in the state of grace. This requirement of being in the state of grace shows the importance of the Sacrament of Penance," Christina says. "Through the Sacrament of Penance comes the second highest degree of grace we can receive." "The third highest degree of grace comes through prayer and our good deeds for fellow members of the Mystical Body. This grace comes as an outpouring from the enormous beacon of Light, the Spirit of God, in unity with every soul, through its higher degrees."

Holiness

"Holiness," she says, "is not, therefore, to be equated merely with health of mind or well-being of body. To be holy means to be wholly in union with the Spirit of God. In this union we draw upon the living source of the everlasting spring of the Spirit of God."

What Happens at Death

"When released from the body each soul is destined for immortal life, and its future in eternity is determined by its state when death takes place and the soul is released from the body. When the body dies and the soul is released, it suddenly finds itself in the full light of awareness, able to see itself as it stands in the sight of God. It then realizes the darkness to which the body's actions condemned it. The sensitivity of the soul to the enormity of the Light of God is like the naked eye before the brilliance of a thousand suns, and the soul in darkness quivers in pain. It plunges itself into the sea of Hell to avoid the pain of the enormity of the Light."

Purgatory

"The soul destined for Purgatory seeks shade at the level in Purgatory appropriate to its own imperfection. It will automatically plunge itself into Purgatory to be cleansed and purified, aware of all the sins for which it failed to atone sufficiently; it will gladly go to whatever level of Purgatory is necessary, and it will be eternally grateful to God, in the knowledge that it will one day gain His Presence in Heaven."

The Reality of Hell

Asked about a soul which dies in mortal sin, Christina said that:

> During life, if a soul gets deeper and deeper into sin and darkness and blindness, God will call and call that soul, time after time, urging it to respond to the Light. But if a person does not want to hear, does not want to see, and refuses to respond, the body will make of that soul a living hell, in all the faculties of that person, and it will respond only to the temptation of the Devil.
>
> If the person dies in that state, his soul, on being released from its mortality, realizes that it cannot come before the greatness and Light of God in that state, because it just could not bear it. The pain would be too great, because if that soul had been prepared for Hell by the life lived by the body on earth, and it came before the greatness of God—total Love

and Goodness—in the enormity of that Light and Goodness, the soul would suffer enormous agony.

So it is not so much God condemning it or casting it into Hell, as the soul itself, unable to bear the pain of the enormity of the Light of God, casting itself into Hell, she said.

The reality of Hell shows us the importance of Confession, and of true repentance for our sins.

Heaven

"The soul, when it dies and is purified for Heaven according to the degree of its response to the Spirit and grace of God, will be drawn to an outer level of that Light of God in Heaven. It will be totally fulfilled according to the completion of its own capacity for God. To the extent of the decrease of self on earth, thereby permitting the increase of the Spirit of God, this capacity is increased in the souls who receive a high degree of God's calling in life. They will be drawn into the deeper areas of the Godhead. Such a soul could be described as a shining crystal allowing the Light of God to radiate or reflect through it, bringing greater glory to God."

Saints

"Hence, to pray through Our Lady does not distract from the glory of God, but actually enhances God's glory for she is what she is in the Blessed Trinity, being the only person at freedom in the Spirit of God to go to the Godhead of the Holy Trinity.

"To pray through the saints glorifies God because they are all united in the Spirit of God at whatever level to which they have been drawn. Because they have been drawn into Heaven through the action of their response to His Spirit during their earthly life,

God would joyfully permit His Spirit to respond to the earthly soul seeking help through them."

The Call to Life in the Holy Trinity

Christina explains that:

> In the Holy Trinity, we have the Father and Jesus, and uniting Jesus and the Father, the Holy Spirit; tremendous Light and Wisdom, with all His Gifts; together with the awe, greatness, love, and union between the Father and the Son, God's infinite Mercy and Justice. The Father created the World, the Son redeemed it, and the Holy Spirit purifies and draws it to Himself. God desires to draw to Himself those who have been redeemed and are loved, but through sin they experience darkness and are unable to respond to the Light and the Truth.
>
> God created us to love and adore Him, but being in the world and responding to the darkness of sin, we start to love and serve self. That is the temptation of the world and the flesh that will lead us into a darkness that will blind us from perceiving the Light of God. Although the world is the creation of God, it is the Devil's kingdom that tempts the flesh. Because it is redeemed, the soul can choose, through free will, the desires of the flesh and the world or the eternal home God has prepared by following Jesus. Jesus is the Way, the Truth, and the Life.

God Desires to Save All

Christina says that "God wants all souls to be saved and Jesus died for all of mankind, but God has given each created person free will, and Our Lady has emphasized over and over again that all a person has to do is stop sinning and turn back. She is pleading all over the world with her children to come back to her Son before it is too late while they still have time. And this is why Our Blessed Mother even weeps tears of blood, because so many souls are being lost."

Free Will

Explaining how she understands free will, and how it is left to each one of us to accept or reject God's grace, Christina says the image that was given to her about how God has given us free will and is always offering us His grace was in the form of two trees, a Black Tree of Darkness and a White Tree of Light.

I saw from the Tree of Light many white roots going in every direction and there were larger black roots on the Tree of Darkness, and all these roots were intertwined with the narrower roots of the Tree of Light.

Then it was as if there were little ants running along on the roots, representing people, and each of those on the white roots of the Tree of Light had a little white dot of light on them. They would be going grand until they met a place where the roots intertwined, then they would halt at the crossroads and not know which way to go. They might then drift off on the other black root of the Tree of Darkness and their light would go out. Then they might come again to another meeting place of the two sets of roots, and some would go back on to the white roots of the Tree of Light and their light would be seen again.

As they came nearer to the trunks of the two trees, those who reached the Tree of Light just disappeared into the Light while those on the black roots coming nearer to the Tree of Darkness seemed to go at great speed, as if rushing into

Hell. That is how it was given to me, and I was shown no in-between.

As I understood it, this was a representation of how free will and the grace of God work, how we receive it and then reject it, and how God always forgives us through Confession throughout our lifetime, but He has given us free will and He does not force us to accept it.

The Role of a Victim Soul in the Mystical Body of Christ to Circulate God's Grace of Conversion

"The more a person surrenders to God, the more the Lord will invite that person to surrender, and the more the person will be enabled by God to receive and respond to His Spirit, Love, and Grace, surrendering in total abandonment and trust.

"What this means is that God wills the sins of others to be purified, through the victim or suffering soul who surrenders and offers his or her sacrifice to God to be purified in its uniting with the sacrifice of Jesus, thus permitting God to draw many other souls to Himself." As Christina says,

Look at the crucifix and see the outstretched arms of Jesus. He went on the cross to redeem us. He was born in a stable to show us He wanted nothing of the world. He had no roof over His Head, showing us the unimportance of everything of the world. Yet He was the Son of God, teaching us as He said, what He had been taught by His Father through the Spirit. So everything that Jesus knew was through the Spirit and He was teaching us the way, the way home—how to gain Eternal Life. He was teaching us that to be nothing in the eyes of the world is the way home through Him.

That is why if we see self as important or see our progress in the world's eyes, see anything of the flesh as important, then we have gained nothing. It is only if we gain it through God's Love and Spirit that we gain anything and that we permit God to develop in us, to grow in us. Our souls, then, will be more and more transformed into the likeness and Image of Christ. The more we permit our souls to be transformed, the more will the radiance of God's Spirit and Light reach out and touch others, by the decrease of self and the increase of the Spirit of God.

❖

"This is," as Christina understands it, "how the accepted sufferings and sacrifices of one person who trusts and surrenders are used by God to help others in the Mystical Body who are in darkness and sorely in need of His grace. This is how, through the purifying action of God's Spirit in a victim soul, others, too, can be drawn back to God. This work of purification, then, in individuals is not intended to benefit themselves only. God in His love is drawing good out of it for the conversion of lost souls."

The Paralyzed Hand and the Working Hand

Christina was given the example of the two hands, the paralyzed hand and the working hand. "If a person has a paralyzed hand and cannot use it, then that person must compensate by using the other hand much more.

"The paralyzed hand represents the person who cannot be bothered with God and is without God's enlightenment; the other hand is the other person in the Mystical Body who is prepared to suffer and cooperate with the Spirit of God in order to convert the other. What Jesus wants to do is to flow His grace of conversion from the working hand to the paralyzed hand and renew His life in that soul."

Christina explains further what she has been given:

❖

When we hear about a conversion, the grace for the renewal of life in that soul comes from the suffering of someone else. With the Mystical Body, God will use the victim soul to help those who are in the darkness of sin. He will take the victim soul to Himself and give it His gifts and graces in a greater way, and will nourish it and give the victim soul the strength and ability to surrender in all things to Him, to be crushed like a grape.

The victim soul is the working hand, and the soul in darkness that does not want to know about the Light is the paralyzed hand. . . . It hasn't got the ability, because of darkness and sin, to draw on the Light and ask for the forgiveness of God. When someone is far away from God, in deep sin, that person does not recognize the truth or the reality of the true presence of God; so Jesus will use the victim soul and crush it, and the grace and the Light of His Spirit can then flow freely to the person in darkness, giving the soul his life anew—renewing God's life in that person.

So when we hear about a person being converted, that conversion has come about through the surrender of a victim soul. God does not interfere with the person's free will, but He will use the victim soul's efforts united with His Divine Life and Mercy to help the soul in need.

MESSAGE

The dialogue in a personal message dated September 24, 1988 (see *Please Come Back to Me and My Son*), sheds more light on this teaching:

Our Lady: My dear child, if only you were to know what good my dear Son has permitted, with your acceptance of pain. I cry tears of joy.

Christina: My dear Mother, my pain is but nothing. I long so much for God to save souls, including my own.

Our Lady: If you accept all God permits you in suffering, many will be saved. [Our Blessed Lady then promised Christina that she would later understand the mystery of God—"What was hidden from the learned and given to the little ones."] "I know you do not understand what is becoming of your body. When you accept the cross my Son Jesus permits you to carry, you are purified in soul and body and save many others. My child, your cross will be heavy and your pain greater at times. Be at peace. Accept, with all the love in your heart. . . . My tears of joy and sorrow will fall on you to comfort and console you. You are surrendering your body and soul to God. I ask you to try to pray more. Keep your heart with Jesus my Son, asking Him to save souls. My Son will grant you what you ask in prayer. . . . Tell my Son it is because you love Him that you accept it with love. . . ."

In the following questions and answers, Christina explains even more of the mysteries revealed to her.

Q. Did Jesus or the Virgin Mary tell you anything else about the Holy Spirit?

A. I was told by Our Holy Mother, "The Word of God is alive, it is Spirit; the Light of God is Wisdom; the Light and Word of God is life, for those who receive it."

Q. Have you seen the Eternal Father when He speaks to you?

A. Yes, I've seen Him on a number of occasions, like when I saw Him the time that I saw Heaven. And I saw Him on other occasions. It's hard to describe Him. He can take many forms in His own right. I've become aware and I can inwardly see, on some occasions, where He's like immense light. I am conscious of the enormity of Him and the tininess of me. I see myself like a grain of sand in relation to Him. Yet all the Eternal Father's greatness and enormity are impossible to describe. It's like being in an open space with the sky surrounding me. His pureness is beyond expression. Now these experiences, when they happen, are given to me in a manner I cannot fully comprehend.

Q. Have you seen how the people are dressed in Heaven?

A. The only ones I saw in Heaven were the Eternal Father, Jesus, and Our Blessed Mother. They were all in white and a radiant light was everywhere.

Q. So you haven't seen any people in Heaven?

A. No, no people in Heaven.

Q. Tell us about the Eternal Father's love.

A. It is an enormous love, yet there is—even though He's so great—no limit to the depth of His love, which will reach down to a tiny grain of sand, like myself, to raise me up to be united with Him in Jesus.

(In 1994, Christina said, "My understanding of souls in Heaven [those who die in the state of grace] is that they are released into the Light and Spirit of God to the degree to which God has drawn them in their openness of heart and response to His will in that Light and Spirit of God. The degree of their reward depends on their response to God while on earth. Some souls are drawn into the inner or higher degrees of the Light and Spirit of God depending on the reward God has given them for their sacrifices. The Light in the Spirit of God is like a million suns. The soul that is drawn into the inner or higher degrees must be as clear as a crystal that the light will reflect through the soul, and they will radiate and bring greater joy to the Glory of God. Souls in Heaven are aware of other souls in Heaven and on earth through the knowledge of God. In that knowledge they can only love as God loves.")

Q. You have been told the meaning of the twenty-fifth day of each month is special for the Eternal Father. Can you tell us why?

A. Our Blessed Mother told me: The two means the two hearts of Jesus and Mary, the united heart of Jesus and Mary. The five represents the five major wounds of Jesus, and the two and five added together represent the seven sorrows of Our Blessed Mother. So on the twenty-fifth of any month, it means that the sacrifices of Jesus and the Blessed Mother are offered in union with the prayers of Our Blessed Mother's children, or the children of God, to Our Eternal Father in union with their hearts and their sacrifices.

Q. So this means the twenty-fifth of any month of the year is a special day to be offered up to the Eternal Father?

A. Yes. That's what I understand from what Our Lady has given me on the meaning of the twenty-fifth. That's why it's so powerful because it's an offering of the major wounds of Jesus and an offering of their two hearts suffering together. With the sacrifice of that, they're offering the Seven Sorrows of Our Blessed Mother.

Q. We know that Jesus was born on the twenty-fifth of December. Is this why?

A. Yes, but again, it all represents the sorrow, the sacrifice, and the triumph.

CHAPTER THIRTEEN

Where Angels Tread

THEN I SAW A MIGHTY ANGEL COME DOWN FROM HEAVEN WRAPPED IN A CLOUD, WITH A RAINBOW ABOUT HIS HEAD; HIS FACE SHONE LIKE THE SUN AND HIS LEGS WERE PILLARS OF FIRE.

—REV. 10:1

No one could argue there could be a greater experience than to gaze upon the Face of the Eternal Father. This special grace defies comprehension, though Christina has tried to present a good account. Yet the delights of the world of the spirit are many, for God has made it that way for Himself as well as for us.

Long before God made man, He created angels. Although they have names and faces and can speak to us, they are still remarkably different and unique. One thing is for sure, their full nature is still somewhat a mystery.

"The angel," wrote Saint Thomas, "is the most excellent of all creatures because among all creatures he bears the greatest resemblance to the Creator."[1]

"The angels are spirits," wrote Saint Augustine, "but it is not because they are spirits that they are angels. They become angels when they are sent, for the name 'angel' refers to their office not to their nature."[2]

As pure spirits, angels are created intelligences, altogether above matter and free from any relation to it, both in their existence and their operation. They are close friends of God, endowed with free will, like human beings. They are constantly able to see God, constantly in communication with Him. Likewise, Scripture is rich with stories of their interactions with humans. Like the Virgin Mary's apparitions, God has permitted many people to see angels and receive their messages.

Again, Christina Gallagher is one such soul. Yes, Christina has seen angels many times. She has seen them on earth and in Heaven. With her eyes, she has observed them joyfully singing praises to the Most Holy Trinity.

The extraordinary angelic experiences kept repeating themselves. Over and over the angels came, often singing "Ave Maria" and "Glory to God on High," often singing in perfect harmony, like a choir. Their voices were like music that came across like a whispering wind unlike anything heard on earth.

"There have been big angels and small angels, transparent and differently colored angels," says Christina. "I have seen angels that are like people. I have seen the Angel of Wrath and the Angel of Peace."

In another mystical experience, Christina gazed upon a beautiful fountain with see-through birds as little angels playfully hovered above. On still other occasions she has witnessed tiny angels without wings moving—as if through will—up and down the heavens.

Just as, by God's permission, angels assume human forms when appearing to men, so, too, are they permitted to produce a human voice and speak our human language. As messengers, they must speak, especially our Guardian Angels.

Once Christina's own Guardian Angel, who she thought was Saint Jude, appeared to her. His name is Carmello. Catching her off guard, he assured her she should not be troubled and that he would, "take her trouble away and give her peace," which somehow he immediately did.

Yet most of the angels who have appeared to Christina have been silent, as their presence was all God wished her to know. Christina has been visited by the Angel of Ireland, the Angel of Wrath, the Angel of Peace, and even the Archangel, Blessed Michael.

The Angel of Ireland was an impressive sight. While beautiful, this angel emitted an overwhelming sense of power and protection. In one apparition, she watched him "as he moved over Ireland." Dublin and Cork were identifiable to Christina while other areas were not. Christina said, "The Angel of Ireland was in pure white light. There was also a mist of light coming from him. He released it and then it scattered like a mist." This light, says Christina, was symbolic of the graces people were receiving in response to their suffering and sacrifice.

The angel of God's Justice, the Angel of Wrath, was a magnificent angel in red apparel who left her "feeling the enormity of his power and authority as the Angel of God's Justice." As with Sister Faustina, he was shown to Christina to be the angel God calls upon to strike out against evil.

Like the Angel of Ireland, the Angel of Wrath emitted such a forceful presence that at first she was so overwhelmed that she said, "Lord take this angel away." Finally, she realized it was not evil, but his extraordinary perfection that overwhelmed her.

The Angel of Peace, the apparent counterpart to the Angel of Wrath, immediately appeared. Dressed in white with gold around his neck, this magnificent angel literally radiated peacefulness. It was a peace she could immediately feel, like when the Queen of Peace appeared to her. "Peace poured out of him," she says.

Finally, Blessed Michael the Archangel has also visited. He appeared to her as very powerful with a great sword, drawing it to reassure her of his protection. According to Christina, "He was enormous. He looked like a huge man, with wings, in radiant white light. I've seen him in different forms. He was handsome. He had a strong face. His power caused a feeling of faintness, almost fear within me.

"Repeatedly, he made gestures with his sword. Blessed Michael seemed so much more powerful than the Devil. He has a greater power than anyone other than God and Our Blessed Mother. I felt the tremendous sense of his protection. It's a spiritual power of peace and security. It filled me with awe."

Blessed Michael first appeared to Christina during a time Satan was relentlessly attacking her. Since the Virgin Mary's assurance of his protection, Christina says she has intuitively sensed the Prince of the Heavenly Host's constant presence—a presence she again can literally feel.

Christina's description of Blessed Michael's awesome power has been recounted before. In the year 590, in Rome, the powerful Archangel appeared in response to the prayers of Pope Gregory the Great for the end of a plague. Standing atop the Castle of San Angelo, Blessed Michael again drew his sword to show the people their prayers were answered. Indeed, they were. The plague suddenly ended. Throughout history, Blessed Michael had defended the just, aiding Constantine the Great during his woes and Saint Joan of Arc when she saved France.

Since Blessed Michael's appearances to Christina, things have radically changed for her. "He's always there," says Christina. "I feel a whole lot happier now. Even with Blessed Michael near me, I still say his prayer quite often."

After a particularly difficult experience with the Devil in which he physically left claw marks on Christina's arm, God gave her a gift of not having a paralyzing fear anymore. This gift was given by God in response to Christina's great fear that Satan would touch her during one of his appearances. This attack was only permitted to give Christina the greater gift of taking away the fear. It shows a greater depth of the love and the mercy of God.

Yet even with the constant awareness of Blessed Michael's presence, the Queen of Peace reminds Christina that she must continually implore his assistance. "My child, use Holy Water more often. Implore Blessed Michael the Archangel more often. Ask him to protect you."

We are to do the same. There is no need to be afraid. No need to worry. Christina says that we just need to call on Blessed Michael, our friend, our protector, too. It is extremely important that we unhesitatingly request his empirical protection; these are the times of the great heavenly battle written of in the Book of Revelation. Blessed Michael is to be the chief defender of the faithful in this battle.

Indeed, this is a battle that centers around many of these special angels. From the strong angel who proclaims, "who is worthy to open the book, and to loose the seals," to the seven angels who "come forth and pour out the seven vials of the wrath of God upon the earth," the Book of Revelation makes it clear these angels will play the key role in God's final victory. Following the Lord's commands, they will serve as the celestial front line, going toe to toe with the enemy, right up until the end.

It appears the end is drawing nearer. Among all these incredible angels, the knowledge of another mysterious angel has recently become known to Christina. He is an angel God sent to earth once before at a decisive moment in history. Now, Jesus told Christina, this angel must come again.

He is the Angel of the Passover, written of in the Book of Exodus. His coming, his imminent arrival is perhaps one of the most important revelations God has given Christina.

On Sunday, September 5, 1993, the Queen of Peace relayed God's order for his impending visit. It was the second time this angel was spoken of to Christina.

> My children, I come with a message of love and peace. I weep for your safety in body and soul. I offer you the armor of protection in the Light of God.
>
> You think you are wise and learned. You are not, but foolish and blind. Read the Word of your Lord God. With His Blood you were redeemed.
>
> My children, I plead with you, wake up before it is too late. The Angel of the Passover is close at hand. I desire you to be wise and learned in the Light of God.
>
> Take up your armor. Put it on without fear.

I am your Mother and I lead this battle. As God chose me to bring forth your Redeemer through the fruit of my womb, I once again bring Him to you in Glory, as King, because I am the Handmaid of God, and share in His Glory and Victory for the redemption of the human race. In that Glory, my Immaculate Heart will Triumph.

My children, do not hesitate to respond; live my message of love and peace. Through it, you will have hope and life. My blessings I impart to you, in the name of the Father, and of the Son, and of the Holy Spirit.

In the book of Exodus, the Angel of the Passover, described as the Angel of Death, or Destroyer, played a decisive role in the departure of the Israelites from Egypt. When God told Moses and Aaron that on the night of the Passover, all the firstborn of Egypt would die, it was this angel who came to fulfill the mission. When he came, only the firstborn of those who had obeyed God's commands and had marked their doors with the Blood of the Passover sacrifice were spared. The next day, those Israelites were released from their captivity.

What will happen this time? The answer is somewhere in the Book of Revelation.

We do know that when the time comes to separate the wheat from the chaff, the just from the unjust, this awesome angel is probably one of the ones who will come to fulfill God's command.

CHAPTER FOURTEEN

The Church Triumphant

. . . For the Lord God shall give them light, and they shall reign forever.

—Rev. 22:5

The Catholic Church has declared hundreds of saints. Many of whom the faithful have never heard of and never will. Yet there will still never be too many saints. The reason—the saints are in union with God. They tell us of God and they draw us closer to God.[1]

Even outside the Catholic Church, one cannot but sense an irresistible attraction toward them. While this attraction may stem from curiosity, it is apt gradually to engender admiration, if not imitation.[2] For this reason, the saints are the best promoters and champions of the Church, and it is not surprising then that God would send them to Christina Gallagher so they may be better known for their incredible assistance in our salvation.

Like so many of her experiences, Christina's accounts of the apparitions of the saints are captivating. They are especially important because they allow us to better understand how they are constantly at work, constantly helping us by their intercession, that's what they do best. They intercede. They speak up for us. If we're hurting, they plead with God for spiritual medicine and if we're in danger, they call Heaven to our aid. The saints can seek anything for us. They are our intercessors before God. All we have to do is ask.

There is a significance in the particular saints God has sent to be with Christina to accomplish the work assigned to her. Saint Patrick; Saint Joseph; Padre Pio; Saint Brigid; Saint Thérèse of Lisieux; Sister Faustina; Saint John the Evangelist; Saint Anthony, who is Christina's proclaimed patron; and Saint Philomena, who is the patroness of Our Lady Queen of Peace House of Prayer, are just some. She has also seen Saints Peter and Paul. In late 1993, she received visitations from Teresa Higginson, a nineteenth-century English mystic who was known for the devotion to the Sacred Head as the seat of Divine Wisdom.

Saint Patrick, the patron saint of Ireland, came to Christina on December 8, 1992, the Feast of the Immaculate Conception:

> Saint Patrick came and I ran to him. He took me up in one hand. I could see and feel his hair and his beard. He held a lamb in his other hand. The hand I was in had his staff in it and he told me to hold it. It was wooden and curved like a snake. Then it turned to gold and looked ornate and fancy. I asked him why he asked me to hold the staff. He said that it contained the power of God. He smiled and said people once thought the staff was magic, but it contained the power of God. I touched the lamb and asked what he was doing with the lamb. He said it was the Lamb of God. Through sacrifice, he said, all the little victims were in union with the Lamb of God.
>
> Then Saint Patrick was looking at the sky and raised up the staff as a black cloud was whirling toward us. I asked him what it was. He said it was the darkness of death to blind God's people. Whatever he was saying to the dark cloud I

did not hear. Then I was looking at the sky spin as if the sun was coming out. But it got so bright as the sky was still spinning and I could see the face of God Our Father, Who looked with pleasure at Saint Patrick.

Then I was asking him questions about the victim souls and I said was he one, and he smiled and looked at his feet and said, "Why do you think I walked barefoot?" I told him about how I felt and asked had he felt abandoned by God. He again smiled and said, "Yes, but that was my glory," that God's love and zeal were in his heart.

Then Blessed Michael came. It was to let me know he was with me. "Saint Patrick, why are you always by the sea or water?" I then asked. He replied, "Because that is where God first spoke to me. I love the sea." (On the occasions when he has appeared to Christina, it has always been near water.) I asked Saint Patrick was he Irish, because his accent sounded Irish. He did not answer that, but said on the 17th of March, the Irish celebrate Saint Patrick's Day wherever they are. He was joyous as he said this. "Others say I did not ever exist," he went on. As he was walking along the shore of the sea on the little pebbles on the ground, how safe I felt. I could smell beautiful perfume.

❖

Father McGinnity describes this special experience, though different from bilocation and more than an apparition as such, as one in which the visionary is transposed from the here and now to a level of mystical reality in which sensory perception remains. The soul receives the Truth of God conveyed in an apparently natural way.

The significance of this special apparition of Saint Patrick, his intercession before God the Father on behalf of Ireland, and his encouragement of Christina, the victim soul, became clearly evident when political events in Ireland quickly unfolded and showed sinister attempts to introduce abortion, legalized practice of homosexuality, divorce, and euthanasia, in direct confrontation with the law of God.

Christina has had many apparitions such as this, but rather than describing them all, the best way to grasp these encounters is in her own words.

Q. Tell us about the angels and saints you've seen.

A. The angels and saints whom I've seen are God's communicators to intercede for us to the hearts of the Blessed Mother and Jesus Christ. Our Blessed Mother and God want all people to be aware of them. They're our helpers, not our enemies or beings to be afraid of. To me they are now very real. They're real friends, more than anyone on earth. We can trust them, whereas our friends around us can't always be trusted.

Q. What did Padre Pio look like? Does his face look like it does in his picture?

A. He had a brown gown, the same as in his picture. He was radiantly glowing with joy. I've never seen that radiance in any picture of him.

Q. Did Padre Pio speak to you?

A. Yes, Padre Pio spoke to me privately regarding somebody else. He tried to explain to me something because I really didn't understand what this particular person was going through. When Padre Pio came to me and spoke, he talked a lot about this person and about this person's life. After he explained all of this to me, I could understand the person's situation.

Q. Tell us about your apparitions of Saint Joseph?

A. Saint Joseph is always very kind and gentle. There's a gentleness about him like Our Blessed Mother. I see Saint Joseph, sometimes holding a lily. One night when I saw Saint Joseph bent over me in bed, I felt this deep love and peace from him. He transmitted to me an awareness of his protection and help.

Q. What did he look like?

A. He was a tall, thin, almost elderly man with white hair. He wore these garments that wrap around the body; one simple piece of cloth. They were the kind of clothes you wouldn't see today.

Q. Did Saint Joseph speak to you?

A. He said I was to be at peace and that I wasn't to be afraid.

Q. Can you describe what Saint Bernadette looked like? Did she speak?

A. When I saw her, Saint Bernadette was looking at Our Blessed Mother. I can't exactly say her age, maybe ten or twelve. She had very little hands. She had on a brown dress and a gray headpiece. She had a sallow complexion and black hair. She was so childlike and beautiful.

Q. How did you know who she was?

A. I didn't know who she was. I gave the description to somebody else and they said she was Saint Bernadette. I had heard of Lourdes, but I didn't know enough about Saint Bernadette. A priest once described her to me. He said to me one day, when I was talking about my experience, "you're another Bernadette." He said this because he was referring to my lack of formal schooling. He thought that might be why Saint Bernadette appeared with Our Blessed Mother to me. I don't know.

Q. Tell us what Saint Thérèse, the Little Flower, looks like and what she has said to you.

A. Oh, she's very gentle, very kind, very loving, and the most beautiful of them all. She's the one I feel is really my closest friend. I think of them all as my friends. When I need help or even if I'm making a decision, my little friend, Saint Thérèse, the Little Flower, always seems to come to my aid.

Q. Have you any memorable or special apparitions of her that you can share?

A. I saw during Mass Saint Thérèse come first from behind the altar and then Saint Bernadette. Saint Bernadette was small. Saint Thérèse had one rose, huge; lemon-colored with a rim of red—extremely beautiful. They seemed to be sharing among themselves. Saint Thérèse bowed toward the priest.

The Holy Eucharist in enormous light then appeared. I saw them, the Holy Souls, in a gray cloud, all raising their hands to the Holy Eucharist. Then little drops of blood began to stream down the center of the Holy Eucharist.

The clouds began to turn from gray to white and the hands

of the souls reaching from the clouds grew calm. From this I understood these souls were raised to a higher level of Purgatory, but not fully released on this occasion.

Q. You mentioned that you saw Saint Teresa of Avila. Can you tell us about your experience with Saint Teresa of Avila?

A. When I visited my friends in the north, who had great devotion to Saint Teresa of Avila, I certainly had no intentions of praying to her in any way. I didn't want to hear anything about her. I just wanted my Little Flower, Saint Thérèse of Lisieux, my close friend. Then it was at a Mass in this particular family's home that I saw Saint Teresa of Avila. She was looking at my spiritual director and observing every move he made. Then she looked at me, very firmly. I left with an uncomfortable feeling about her until the second time, when I had an encounter with her. This time, she went to the lady who had devotion to her. She looked at her, smiled, and came forward to me. This time, in a matter of seconds, I became aware of Saint Teresa's personality. She was so strong-minded. When she made up her mind about something, if there was a brick wall there, with her faith in God she could walk through it. I found she was such a strong person inwardly with her faith in union with God that nothing could stand in her way in the accomplishment of her work for God. What was also given to me about her was that she could be this strong and yet so gentle. I was inwardly aware of all of this. After that, there came such a bond between us. She took my hand and placed three little roses in it. After that, to me Saint Teresa was fine. I had no problem with her. I now really love her. I feel I know her. Although I don't regard myself as being anything like her. I can now feel in myself a sense of her strength in God and love for God, drawing me to also be stronger. I can now recognize a little of her personality in myself.

Q. Are you saying that the sternness you originally perceived in Saint Teresa of Avila was because of her personality?

A. Yes. She had to be strong in faith and in union with God because of the work she had to do. She let nothing stand in the way of her accomplishing the work given by God.

Q. Can you tell us about Saint Patrick and the revelation you had from him with regard to the House of Prayer?

A. Yes. It was beautiful. I could see Blessed Michael over the church. It had no roof. Then he would go down into the church and he would come back up. As he did, I would hear the screaming of demons. I was totally aware of the religious, both inside and outside of the church. I was aware that some were spiritually dead. Then Blessed Michael would come up with a tabernacle. He would open the tabernacle, take out the Holy Eucharist and bring it in his hand. He would then hand the tabernacle to an angel. There were a number of different angels present. They would then take different tabernacles and they would disappear. This action of Blessed Michael was repeated over and over. Each time he would go down, I would hear the screaming of devils. Then I was wondering what this could all mean—no roof on the church. They were trapped. I told my spiritual director, but neither one of us knew what all this meant. So then Saint Patrick came to me again. I was praying at home, I asked Saint Patrick about Blessed Michael protecting me and about what I had seen with the church. What did that all mean? He said the church with the roof off represented the state of the Church today; that the authorities within the church were throwing away the treasures of God. Then he spoke about Blessed Michael protecting the Holy Eucharist. He said the House of Prayer was symbolic of the Church.

At that time, the roof of the real House of Prayer, we were told, didn't have to come off for repair. But two days later, I was told the roof did have to come off. Saint Patrick referred to the roof coming off the House of Prayer as being symbolic of the Church at large today and it also had to be stripped down. He then reminded me of the message I got about the Church being shaken to its very foundation. This was represented by what was actually happening to the House of Prayer. Everything had to be pulled down in it. It then had to be rewiring new plumbing, and a new roof. When he told me this, it was easier for me to accept the enormous suffering to be endured during the radical overhaul of the House of Prayer. Saint Patrick said man works from the bottom up. But God doesn't. God works from the top down. This is like the suffering that will happen, both in and out of the Church. The chastisement that will come will purify. I asked Saint Patrick, from the way he was talking, if the Church was going to disappear, the Catholic Church. He reassured me "no," but it will be purified and made stronger than ever and the gates of Hell will not prevail against it.

Q. You said you have seen Bishop Fulton Sheen?

A. I didn't know who he was till I went to New York and I saw a picture. I said to my spiritual director, "This is the man I saw with the group that was helping Our Blessed Mother."

Q. I read that Sister Faustina and Saint John the Evangelist also appeared to you. Can you tell us about this?

A. I've seen Sister Faustina a number of times and I've seen John the Evangelist twice. On one occasion, I saw them both together during a vigil, yet there were no words spoken. So I asked my spiritual director why would I be seeing Sister Faustina and John the Evangelist?

Q. How did you know it was Sister Faustina?

A. I knew from a picture that I had of Sister Faustina. Somebody sent me a picture and told me about her.

Q. How did you know it was John the Evangelist?

A. On one occasion when I saw John the Evangelist, he was called out of a crowd of different saints who accompanied Our Blessed Mother to the earth at this time by Catherine of Siena and called by his name. He emerged from the crowd in this apparition and I could see him.

Q. Why did Sister Faustina and Saint John the Evangelist appear to you?

A. I later described this apparition to my spiritual director and talked to him about Sister Faustina and Saint John the Evangelist. I was trying to understand why I received an apparition of those two people without any apparent connection. It didn't seem to mean anything to me at first. So my spiritual director said to me he would think about it. He went away and a week later he got back to me and said, "Christina, did you get any enlightenment with regards to Sister Faustina and Saint John the Evangelist?" I said, "No." Then he said, "It makes sense to me." I said, "In what way?" He said, "Saint John the Evangelist has to do with The Apocalypse, or the end times as it's called in the Book of Revelation." Father McGinnity explained that the apparition means that it's the end times, and Saint John the Evangelist was the one who wrote about these times in The Apocalypse. That was the first time I knew he did that. He was shown with Sister Faustina as an indication that we are living in the time of Mercy which precedes the Justice of God.

On December 27, 1993, Saint John the Evangelist appeared, during a Mass, in light. He went on his knees in reverence, then stood up and took up a book. I wondered what book is this? Then it was given to me; it was the Book of Life. (This is also the book Christina saw Jesus hold over Los Angeles, California, in a 1992 apparition.)

CHAPTER FIFTEEN

The Abyss of Sin

DEPART FROM ME, YE CURSED, INTO EVERLASTING FIRE, WHICH WAS PREPARED FOR THE DEVIL AND HIS ANGELS.

—MATT. 25:41

Reinforced by towering apparitions of God's coming Justice, the urgent messages to Christina Gallagher calling for conversion are no different than those given at Fatima.

It's the same message. While stressing urgency, the messages bring the lessons of the Gospel—love, peace, faith, and hope—all while reminding people of the dangers and consequences of sin, consequences not only for this life, but especially the next. The ultimate consequence is no secret. It's a place called Hell, and it's been widely proclaimed. As the prophet Isaiah wrote:

> Behold, the wrath of the Lord burneth and is heavy to bear, His lips are filled with indignation and His tongue as a devouring fire.

The dogma of Hell is the most terrible truth of the Christian faith. We are as sure of its existence as we are of the existence of

God and this world. Nothing, in fact, is more clearly revealed by God than the dogma of Hell. References are numerous throughout Scripture. Jesus Christ proclaims it as many as fifteen times in the New Testament.[1]

Theologians tell us that without Hell, there would be no ultimate evil to avoid, no inevitable price to pay. Without Hell, each individual would have a mixture of good and evil in their life which they could find acceptable to their pleasures. Take away Hell and the balance, meaning, and value of a person's actions in this life are totally gone. They disintegrate. Behavior becomes situational with no eternal consequences.[2]

Without Hell, mankind becomes humanistic, misguided by ethical relativism and rationalism. Consequently, justice and injustice become blurred and the moral foundation of all civilization vulnerable. As far back as 1884, Pope Leo XIII wrote specifically of this in *Humanun Genus (The Human Race),* prophetically warning of the fallacies of human nature, especially human reason.[3]

Over the centuries, many saints and privileged souls have seen Hell. All have stated pretty much the same. Hell, they say, is hell. The greatest suffering for a soul in Hell is the knowledge of the loss of God forever. On this the saints have firmly agreed. Those who have seen Hell also confirmed Hell's darkness, stench, pain, and fire. It is truly, they say, a world of immense fire. Saint Bridget, in her accounts, even ventured that the heat of Hell fire is "so great that if the world were wrapped in flames, the heat of the conflagration would be nothing in comparison with Hell."

This reality of a world of fire and darkness, with no love or peace, was shown to Christina. Like the children of Fatima, she's never forgotten it. Indeed, her account of Hell closely mirrors those given at Fatima and by numerous saints. None of which makes one feel very peaceful or secure.

At Fatima, in 1917, the Blessed Virgin showed Jacinta, Francisco, and Lucia this underworld of fire and implored, "You have seen Hell, where the souls of poor sinners go. In order to save them, God wishes to establish in the world devotion to my Immaculate Heart."

Years later Sister Lucia still couldn't forget a detail. "We could see a vast sea of fire. Plunged into the flames were demons and lost souls as if they were red hot coals, transparent and black or bronze-colored in human form, which floated about the conflagration, burned by the flames that issued from them." Lucia recalled they were without equilibrium and shrieked with sorrow and despair. She remembers the devils were distinguished by other horrible and loathsome forms of animals which were frightful and unknown. "If the vision hadn't vanished," insists Lucia, "I think we would have died of fright and horror."[4]

Christina Gallagher reveals the same recurring nightmare. On March 29, 1989, Jesus showed Christina Hell. It was gripping. "Terrifying," she says. A miserable sight. She says she gazed at a sea of fire spread across a vast area. "Hell," she said, "was so enormous."

This huge area, filled with bursting flames, held many helpless people. They were immersed in the flames and their bodies appeared in "different shapes and black in color." Christina watched these bodies go in and out of the flames, suffering to the extent it was "unbearable to watch." The flames, she concluded, seemed to be "going through them."

After seeing Hell, Our Lord told her, "This is the abyss of sin, Hell for all those who do not love My Father. My daughter, unite your weakness with Me Who is all strength."

For Christina, like Lucia, Hell was unforgettable.

❖

Hell was just total fire. Jesus was with me through the whole experience. It was a terrifying experience beyond words; I never want to experience it again. It was a great darkness and very frightening. All I could see was an endless sea of fire, and somehow I could look down through it, with enormous flames going into flames. And there were the shapes of bodies in it, as if in a sea, swimming in this fire. The bodies were black and the intense flames were going through them. I could look down through the flames. There was an enormous amount of bodies. I felt an awful sense of terror. I could do nothing but quiver. I pray nobody will ever have to go to Hell.

Her intercession to save thousands of souls from Hell has already been sought. Once, after five weeks of suffering, she was invited to surrender to crucifixion.

Christina complied, telling the Lord, "If necessary, crucify me."

After this, she witnessed the appearance of many angry demons. The next day, Jesus informed her that through her suffering, five thousand souls were saved from the brink of Hell; those souls were still alive, Jesus explained to her. When Christina inquired, "What if they go back to their sinful ways?" Jesus replied, "I have touched them in such a way that they will be spiritually saved and healed in the eternal life."

Like many of the saints, Christina says those who go to Hell choose this fate—reasoning that offends against all logic, but true.

As I understand it, it has to do with free will and sin. You know, some people are not aware they're committing sin. That's where the pastors of any Church must come in. They are to make people aware of the reality of sin. So many people don't recognize sin. But God is Mercy and God is so full of love that people who are not aware of sin may go through a great suffering to make themselves aware. It's like a purification. God desires salvation for everyone but it's entirely up to man to come and seek God's helping hand. If they do, that's fine.

There are those who decide they know they are doing wrong and still have no intentions of changing their ways. These people may want everything of the world in preference to God—power and luxury—and they know it's wrong. Consciously, they are aware of it and know they are serving the Devil. He's the prince or the king of this world.

This is his kingdom—this world. I now realize how the flesh tempts us. The flesh is weak. We must turn to God and beg God for His grace through prayer and the sacraments. We must decrease in self and permit the Spirit of God to increase.

Prayer, fasting, and all that we can offer up is what God is asking us to do. God is giving us strength through His grace, through prayer, and through the sacraments. When man intentionally turns away from God and doesn't want to know Him, then he must clearly understand the road he's on is the road to Hell. Yes, man therefore chooses Hell himself by his actions.

After the shocking scene of Hell, the Blessed Mother again offered Christina encouragement. Our Lady reminded her of the sad state of affairs the world was in. It is a world, said the Virgin Mary, where many more souls are going to go to Hell if the messages continue to be unlived. "My daughter, do not be afraid of those of the world. Put all in the world beneath your feet and work only for Salvation. The Purification is close at hand. Many will be lost for the sins of the world and the sins of the flesh. You, my daughter, must make reparation for those who talk in blasphemy about my Son in the See of Peter. My Son is surrounded by many whose hearts are full of hate and jealousy."

In late October 1992, with the experience of Hell still stamped in Christina's memory, the Queen of Peace again pleaded:

There are many calamities to come to the world. The soul of humanity will be cleansed. God desires that I come to many parts of the world to warn my children. Some respond for a time, others do not want to know me. There are many who will go to Hell. The majority go to Purgatory, and those who go to Heaven are those from Purgatory. Pray, pray, pray.

My Heart is pierced and full of sorrow. I desire to give my

children many graces and peace. They desire to remain in darkness and sin and run after all the desires of the flesh and the world. The world does not hold peace, only death.

Then Jesus spoke, "There will be tribulation after tribulation. You who are sealed with My Blood are cohorts in My Sacred Heart and the Heart of My Mother."

A despondent Christina beseeched Our Lady, "Holy Mother, what can I do?" But there was no reply. The answer had already been given.

CHAPTER SIXTEEN

"Satan Is Trying to Destroy My Plan"

. . . THE DRAGON WENT OFF TO MAKE WAR ON THE REST OF HER OFFSPRING.

—REV. 12:17

With these words from the Virgin Mary, a dark and frightful chapter of Christina's experiences are brought to light. It's a remarkable reality most people would find hard to believe. Some would laugh. Yet there's nothing funny about it.

Since 1988, Christina says she has encountered Lucifer at least a dozen times and other demons at least another dozen times. This was pure evil incarnate, as if Hell itself was stalking her. Christina wrote to Father McGinnity, "The Devil is causing such destruction all around me, and he plagues me every way I turn."

These horrifying experiences began out of nowhere. At 3:00 A.M., just six weeks after her apparition of Christ at a grotto in County Sligo, Christina's heart and mind awoke to a living nightmare. A strange noise startled her. When she looked up, it was the Evil One—Satan—standing in her bedroom. Panicked, she thought her life was over. If not for an invisible defender, she says the demon would have mauled her to pieces.

"I felt there was a battle going on beside my bed. I could see the Devil, crystal clear, and I had no idea who else was there. He was trying to reach me, but an invisible defender held him back. It was the most horrible terror. I knew it was evil. It was part animal and part human. The face was human with strange reactions. The eyes were pure fiery red. While I could not see it, I felt an invisible hand cover my entire body with what felt like a liquid substance."

Desperately, she grabbed a leaflet with a prayer, "Oh, Jesus, in our present dangers wash us with your most Precious Blood." But the demon wouldn't budge.

Gradually, somehow overcoming the deathly fear, she moved to escape. She carefully advanced forward with Satan directly in front of her, slowly backpedaling with her step for step. Finally, after what seemed an eternity, she made it to her kitchen. After reaching for a prayer book her children had received at confirmation, she again begged God for help. Still the Devil wouldn't budge.

"There were times all my energy drained out of me. Times I didn't know again if I would live or die. Yet he still wouldn't leave."

Finally, after more than two hours of cold sweat and terror, it was over. Satan was gone, vanishing instantly.

As her fear subsided and a tranquil peace filled her, she realized that if ever she understood why we should pray from the heart, it was then. At that time, she didn't know why Lucifer was permitted a visit, or why he wanted to attack her. A local priest gave her no answers and she pleaded with God, "Please, Lord, that I may never see anything again, either good or evil!"

But that was not to be. The more the Virgin Mary came, the more the demon came. One day, returning home in her car, she felt a great presence of evil. Immediately, she knew what it was. He was back again.

Suddenly, out of nowhere, an invisible force grabbed and turned the wheel of her car, nearly sending it off the road. Stunned, she fought with all her strength to hold on as the car swerved more and more out of control. At that same moment, she saw him, Satan, "like a black puppet jeering at me and laughing at me."

As a feeling of terror overcame her, she wasn't sure what would happen next. An accident was imminent. Finally, in a desperate prayer to the Most Holy Trinity, imploring the intercession of the angels, the saints, and anyone else in Heaven who could help, the demon was cast off.

Since then, the Devil has been relentless in his assaults on her. Each time, he comes differently, always changing approaches, always trying to secure an advantage. But deception camouflages his intrusions only so much as the pure evil that comes with him cannot be concealed. "It's an experience that rocks the soul, rocks every cell in your body," says Christina. "He is terrifying."

Satan's disguises are many, too. He has taken on the form of a human being, a half-human, and even an animal. For Christina, it was a brutal learning process. Dark shadows, mysterious smells, sudden unnatural sounds are now instantly recognized for what they are, her nemesis from Hell.

❖

> It's strange. I've had many encounters where maybe in the kitchen I would hear a bang—an unnatural bang. At different times, smells may come or a noise may happen. But it's like the minute anything happens, or I see a shadow or a shape of an animal or human form, I become aware instantly of what it is. Immediately, I turn it over to God. I start to praise Jesus and God Our Father and the Holy Spirit. I start praising God in my own ways, whatever comes to my heart. Often, I'm offering the very attack, that moment in time of what Satan's trying to do; I'm offering it to God. Then Satan seems to disappear. In some ways I feel myself being drawn into prayer at a deeper level with a greater sincerity and love. Then it's all over.

After so many evil experiences, so many demonic attacks, so many nightmares, even when Christina can't see or hear him, she now recognizes his presence. His dark presence, a "great cold and hate," permeates the air and fills her with a terrorizing shudder, a shudder so deep, so strong it often induces paralysis. Christina recounted,

> After I saw the Blessed Mother there were more apparitions of the Devil. On one occasion in Dublin, I saw him in a vile form, but it talked like a human. He was accompanied by other demons in a different form. At one point he promised me anything in his kingdom, which he referred to as earth. I kept praying to Jesus. Then he would get furious and say he would destroy me, he would spit a gray-white slimy froth and blow it toward where I was and it would burst into flames just short of striking me. I was left shattered to pieces. I thought I was going to be burned to death. I didn't know if I was going to live or die in that situation.

This level of demonic terror, says Christina, is indescribable if not experienced. Who would want to? For Christina, her encounters with him have been paralyzing and chilling. "I was going through experiences of the Evil One frightening me almost to death," she recalled.

On numerous occasions, Satan has shouted and cursed at her and told her she was crazy. In fits of rage, he has mocked and unmercifully taunted her with degrading language, as if she were a child.

Once, the demon asked, "Where is your God now?" Then unhesitatingly answered himself, "He doesn't want you and neither do I."

Threats of "destroying" her and the House of Prayer were

endless. Christina said of her schizophrenic antagonist, "He's like two people. One minute he would be talking calmly and coaxing me. The next minute, if he was making no headway, he would get furious as if he were another person. The fury was terrible. He told me that he would make all the people believe I was a blasphemist and a liar and that he would destroy the Matrix Medal and the House of Prayer."

All of this is like living in a war zone, a spiritual war zone. Satan never sleeps, never rests, never retreats. He is always on the offensive. From her many demonic attacks Christina now understands that fear is Satan's main advantage. It's his game. Like a little spider, he creates big fears. Even the Blessed Mother told her, "Fear is holding you back. Fear is not of God, but of the Prince of Darkness. He holds you still in darkness. Do everything for the love of my Son, Jesus."

From her experiences, Christina now counsels others on Satan's presence.

❖

> We must always remember that God is the Light and Satan is the darkness, and while a darkened room may frighten, light can instantly disperse all darkness. By opening our hearts to God, Who is the Light, we vanquish the Devil's dark power and need have no fear. The only power he has is that permitted by God. Man can also give Satan scope through his free will, failure to pray, and refusal to live within the Commandments of God.
>
> There's no peace. There's no love, only distractions. We are drawn into everything. In portions of the world, there is no consideration or love for others. We need God, and with God and through God's grace and help, we obtain peace. The Blessed Mother wants us to recognize others' needs. We should love them as God desires us to love one another as He loved us. When the Devil tries to distract us and annoy us, we lose our peace. When we have no peace and feel distracted, we cannot really pray properly.

There's a difference if somebody's trying to pray, and finds their mind drifts to something that happened that day. They may be worried about what's on their mind. That's different than when the Devil constantly tries to draw us away from prayer. If we're praying the Rosary, we may find many difficulties. Anger and annoyance can blow up in our family between those who want to pray the Rosary and those who do not.

All this is the Devil trying to stop us. But people come to realize that when they've switched over to God, they can overcome Satan's attacks by the grace and love of God through Our Blessed Mother's intercession. They will then be able to do God's will and be released from temptations. How do we overcome Satan's temptations? By sacraments, prayer from the heart, fasting and sacrifice, love—all these things Satan cannot stand. The thing Satan hates most is for a human to love and trust God.

Evil never quits during our times. The Blessed Virgin told Christina that Satan's power and anger have exploded throughout the world, that demons now rage upon the earth, loosed from their pit. It's war. The demons can't win yet they won't surrender. Like Our Lady, they have come for souls, and no soul is off limits.

According to her spiritual director, Christina was shown through infused knowledge how Satan sometimes gains a foothold on a soul through the most unassuming means. Father McGinnity relates:

Christina was made aware that people must be careful about whom they permit to "lay hands" on them and pray over them: that some tap into sources of power and energy which are not of God. These can even bring odd cases of apparent healing.

Through prayer we tap into grace through the Spirit of

> God and crush the desires of the world—desires which can otherwise reawaken the serpent within. Occult practices and eventually possession can result from the seeking of evil powers. These powers and energies are from the serpent—the Evil One.

❖

Once again, all of this is a battle for people's will. People, when they want power, choose evil, choose Satan, choose Hell, when they choose sin. Christina tells us, "Because of our free will, God calls us to remember to use it properly by discernment through prayer. We are called to make the right choices. Yet Satan calls, too. Through prayer and the sacraments, our willpower to do God's will is strengthened. But Satan, through temptations and deception, is also ever present. He is constantly trying to influence our free will to reject God."

In Ireland, the Virgin Mary has proclaimed to Christina her coming Triumph. Although Our Lady told Christina on December 28, 1992, this victory was close, Our Lady reminded her to pray. To pray like never before:

❖

> My children, pray like never before. Satan is trying to destroy my plan. You, my children of light, love your enemies. Only through prayer and sacrifice will you be able to obtain the graces to open your hearts and love. Do not dwell on the past, only on the present. Pray for those who are blind and refuse to respond to the truth of my message. Pray and love all around you. I offer you my love to inflame the hearts that are cold. Through the light of my love it will disperse darkness.
>
> My dear child, the world is in grave danger. God desires its purification to be in stages. But the man of destruction desires to let the children of the world rule my children of light and turn all into darkness. My Immaculate Heart will triumph with you, little ones, but you must continue to

receive my love, to surrender all your trials and sufferings to Jesus. I am your Mother of Love and I desire to offer you, little ones, to Jesus with the Triumph of My Immaculate Heart.

❖

Satan at the moment is trying to destroy so many in every way he can. Seemingly, the last message the Virgin Mary gave was for the youth. Satan wants to use them as instruments of destruction. Our Lady has desired us to pray like never before. In other words, the Devil and his coworkers are stronger than ever, because all the devils in Hell are now loosed upon the earth.

Christina says, "But we have no need to fear the darkness if we are in the light, if we permit and allow Jesus to live in our lives. That is what Our Blessed Mother has taught me. The less I feared Satan, and the more I trusted God, the more I was able to accept God's Will."

We must not deny Satan's existence. Christina says Our Lady told her that if we deny Satan's existence, we deny sin. When we deny sin, we deny Christ and His Sacrifice of Redemption on Calvary—a sacrifice made, the Blessed Mother stresses, to "redeem us of our sin."

This denial of Satan, like the denial of Hell, says Christina, causes us to "let our guard down and place our souls in danger, which is exactly what Satan has always sought to do."

Indeed, as Saint Peter admonished, "Be sober and vigilant, your opponent, the Devil, is prowling around like a roaring lion looking for someone to devour." (1 Peter 5:8)

CHAPTER SEVENTEEN

The Chamber of Suffering

. . . THE WORK OF EACH WILL BE MADE CLEAR. THE DAY WILL DISCLOSE IT. THAT DAY WILL MAKE ITS APPEARANCE WITH FIRE, AND FIRE WILL TEST THE QUALITY OF EACH MAN'S WORK. IF THE BUILDING A MAN HAS RAISED ON THIS FOUNDATION STILL STANDS, HE WILL RECEIVE HIS RECOMPENSE; IF A MAN'S BUILDING BURNS, HE WILL SUFFER LOSS. HE HIMSELF WILL BE SAVED, BUT ONLY AS ONE FLEEING THROUGH FIRE.

—1 COR. 3:13–15

Around the same time Christina was shown Hell, she was also shown Purgatory and its suffering inhabitants. It was another dire sight. Some of these poor souls were also experiencing the effects of fire, only this fire was the fire of purification, not damnation.

The reality of Purgatory shocked Christina. Like most people, it was not something she contemplated. Today there is little mention of Purgatory, even among Catholics. It is, however, a teaching handed down from the apostles and found in Sacred Scripture.

Purgatory is said to be a necessary part of the Justice of God, which responds to all sin. The Church teaches that even the least sin displeases God. Thus, His Mercy, which pardons, contains His Justice, which cleanses.[1]

Purgatory, therefore, is a place of justice. Many saints have witnessed and written about this transitory state. It is a frightening place, yet unlike Hell, it contains peace and hope.

In Purgatory as in Hell there is a double pain—the pain of loss and the pain of the senses. The pain of loss consists of being temporarily deprived of the sight of God, Who is the Supreme Good, the beatific end for which our souls are made. This is a moral thirst that torments the soul's love for God. The pain of senses is similar to what we experience in our flesh.[2]

Although its nature is not defined by the (Catholic) faith, the doctors of the Church believe this world of suffering is in a foggy, misty place of darkness, a vast area said to be ash gray and cloudy with different levels, some fiery.

From what Christina witnessed, Purgatory was just that. The Irish mystic saw three levels of Purgatory. In each of them, she witnessed souls imprisoned. She especially shuddered at seeing a lower level of Purgatory, a place she was told was not the lowest. The lowest was called the Chamber of Suffering. It is a place written of in the pages of old Catholic history books detailing private revelation. It is described as a frightful sight.

Saint Lydwine of Schiedam, who died in 1433, wrote of such a chamber from her own experiences in ecstasy. Upon seeing this lowest level of Purgatory, Saint Lydwine saw what appeared to be walled pits in an immense prison of fire. She inquired of her guide, an angel, "Is this then Hell, my brother?"

"No, sister," replied the angel, "but this part of Purgatory is bordering on Hell."[3]

Another of Christina's experiences of Purgatory was being taken through a dismal passageway with a series of doorways on either side leading at the end to a wider door space from which Christina's soul recoiled, but toward which she was relentlessly impelled. Christina had to stop at each doorway where she experienced the inner agonies being endured by the various souls in these different caverns. The final one was the most horrific. Yet as soon as she surrendered to go there she was instantly consumed in a ball of light.

Like other witnesses to Purgatory, Christina remembers it as a dismal place of "gray ashes and little light," with all types of people, even priests, in great distress. Those she saw were in constant torment and hungered to see God. Purgatory even emitted a horrid smell. Christina said, "It was horrible; really, really horrible."

Like earthly prisoners, the souls in Purgatory longed to be released from their sadness, captivity, and suffering. They wanted to get out. When these souls saw Christina they immediately begged her for help.

From his notes, Christina's spiritual director reports the Irish seer has been visited by many souls from Purgatory—priests, laity, even bishops—all asking for her prayers, all wanting to be released.

On November 2, 1992, Christina received an experience that described the plight of those in Purgatory. "The souls in Purgatory—I can see them in a sea of gray cloud, reaching up to me and calling me by name saying, 'Christina, pray for me, pray for me,' and reaching up for my Rosary beads." On December 4, 1993, she again saw them pleading for help with hands stretched out. Christina said it reminded her of the way people in Saint Peter's Square in Rome reach out to touch the Holy Father.

On another occasion she was taken by Jesus through a narrow path, down some steps into a dark tunnel that led to Purgatory. She came to some gates that opened as if by remote control. Here, she saw many people dressed in brown-colored garments with hoods on their heads, two of whom she immediately recognized. These poor souls had their heads flexed downward as if in agony. Says Christina,

> The ground was mucky looking, sort of muddy and smelly. I could feel a particular agony and sadness for those souls. I didn't know these people in the sense of having a

relationship with them or of knowing them personally, but I knew them to see: a priest and a layperson. They didn't get very near us. But at the moment when I was there, it seemed they were almost as close to me as my own mother or father. I loved them so much. All of a sudden, Jesus left me. I was then trapped against what looked like a wall. It's hard to describe. I couldn't move, but I didn't mind. I just kept crying out, "Jesus please release those two souls, and if it's your will, let me stay here, but release those two souls." During this experience, I had resigned myself to wait there, to go through whatever I had to go through in suffering. I saw demons playing with fire which they took in their paws and which they threw toward me in my helpless state. It was more painful than when earthly fire burns the flesh. Yet my longing for those two souls to be released was beyond anything I could understand. Then after this, an enormous ball of white light came and I was taken into it. Then it was all over.

Afterward, the Lord confirmed to her the two souls—the priest and the layperson—were, indeed, released. In late October 1993, at the House of Prayer, many souls from different levels of Purgatory again appeared and pleaded with Christina for her prayers and sufferings. One of them, a soul of English descent, spoke to Christina about the "faith of England, and said it would be raised up through Jesus and in union with His Holy Mother, 'Mediatrix of All Graces.' "

From all of this, Christina has learned the great value of our intercession for the release of souls from Purgatory and of the role the House of Prayer is to have in God's plan for the souls in Purgatory. Poor souls will do anything, says Christina, to be freed from their captivity, their suffering.

Indeed, Saint Catherine of Siena, in order to spare her father the pains of Purgatory, even offered herself to Divine Justice to suffer in his place. Not surprisingly, God accepted her offer. It is said that from this Saint Catherine suffered excruciating torments the rest of her life till death, but her father was set free.

Like Saint Catherine, we are also in a position to help release souls, especially by prayers, lots of prayers. "Our prayers," says Christina, "are the keys to their freedom."

CHAPTER EIGHTEEN

The Sign of the Power of the Antichrist

THE COMING OF THE LAWLESS ONE BY THE ACTIVITY OF SATAN WILL BE WITH ALL POWER AND WITH PRETENDED SIGNS AND WONDERS, AND WITH ALL WICKED DECEPTION FOR THOSE WHO ARE TO PERISH, BECAUSE THEY REFUSED TO LOVE THE TRUTH AND SO BE SAVED.

—2 THESS. 2:9–10

Before we can speak of Christina Gallagher's experiences with a man referred to as the *Antichrist,* we need to examine the history of this baffling prophecy. It's a long and strange history. Yet of all the events that are foretold to come, this may be the most mysterious, the most complex, and one of the most important.

From Scripture, the word "Antichrist" is comprised of two Greek words: "anti," meaning against, and "Xpistos," meaning Christ, which signifies "against Christ." Since the times of the apostles, it has been said that the Antichrist shall be supremely inimical to Jesus Christ. The Good Book also calls him, "the man of sin, the son of perdition, the beast that ascended out of the abyss, the lawless one, the abomination of desolation."[1]

Throughout history, the fathers and theologians of the Catholic

Church have regarded this coming tyrant as the most impious of men, literally the incarnation of Satan. As for Antichrist's family name, it is not known. Still, it is known that the number obtained from the addition of the Greek letters with which it is written will be *666.*[2]

In the Book of Revelation, Saint John writes, "Behold wherein wisdom cometh, let him that understands count the number of the beast, for it is the number of the man. It is the number 666." Saint John calls this number "The number of the man," because the number six, which designates the day on which man was created, enters into its composition in three different ways: namely in its concrete form, six, as a multiple of ten; and as a multiple of one hundred, which in total equals 666.[3]

Today there is one question to which everyone seeks an answer. When will this monster, the very personification of the Antichrist, come?

The debate is still hot and heavy. From their writings, theologians appear to conclude that he will come when certain primary conditions foretold in Scripture are met.

According to these scholars, when the whole world shall renounce Christ and reject the authority of His Church and say, "We will not have this man reign over us." (Luke 19:14) "We have no king but Caesar." (John 19:15) It is then that God will deliver the world to the man of sin. He will then consign it to the darkness of vice and error because it rejected light and truth. But there's more to these conditions.[4]

According to Church scholars, the Holy Catholic Church is destined to pass through a great persecution. This persecution will make all the previous ones seem insignificant. As far back as the fourth century, Saint Augustine wrote that this persecution will be violent, like the one against the early Christians. It will also include deception by false brethren. Then a combination of these two persecutions will consequently prove more redoubtable than either of them alone.

This scenario is not easy to discern because prefigures of the lawless one have appeared in almost every century. When heresy, apostasy, schism, incredulity, and impiousness are displayed in full regalia; when many will give in to their passions and drink from the pool of iniquity, then will the Antichrist appear.[5]

But there are still greater complexities that surround the fulfillment of this ancient prophecy. Over the centuries, theologians have also insisted that a political preparation, along with a religious preparation, must come before this demonic being will appear. This means that all intellectual and moral reasoning must be subjected to the prevailing trends of thought, contradicting all that is good.[6]

This, theologians say, will then create a vacuum. A vacuum that will be filled by a world hungry to have a philosophy and an authority to believe in and subscribe to. Then this new authority will replace Christianity. It will be a babel of extravagant and absurd ideas. Finally, it will lead to a state of perversion that will find the world in the hands of the "Man of Perdition."[7]

Has the time now arrived? Many Protestant and Catholic leaders think so. The signs of the times concur to the affirmative. The world is a mess. All social and moral restraints have collapsed. From abortion to euthanasia; from occult practices to New Age religions; from the total rejection of the Ten Commandments to the denial of the law of love that Christ gave—the world is ripe for the appearance of the "man of sin."

Other foretold conditions also appear to be falling into place. A world filled with tribulation as defined by Scripture must occur first. This is certainly happening now as nature and civilization erupt, causing untold suffering. The Jews must return to their homeland, which again, has occurred. A false peace must be proclaimed throughout the world. With the fall of communism, and Israel's peace initiative with its neighbors, never has world peace been more heralded. Peace, peace, peace, everyone is talking peace. From Cambodia to South Africa, there's been an explosion of peace initiatives everywhere.

According to her spiritual director, Christina Gallagher does say she has seen the Antichrist. The Irish mystic has been shown a man in his fifties, "who looks like a bishop," and exudes a "feeling of horror." Christina tells us, "His face had a sallow complexion.

His hair was cut short and was very black. He had a roundish, bold-looking face with very dark eyes. He was broad shouldered. His looks were piercing and penetrating. They were unusual. He did not smile. He seemed to be a priest or a bishop. I'm not saying he was. I've seen him twenty, twenty-five times; always the same. I would know him instantly if I saw him on television or in reality. I would know him instantly." She says she was shown this man "a number of times," and during each apparition, she heard Our Blessed Mother's voice repeat the word "Antichrist."

Why has she seen this man so often? Was this the face of the Antichrist? According to Father McGinnity, Christina is positively sure. But the Virgin Mary also told her other information concerning specific events which she says are related to the coming of Antichrist.

Back in late 1991, Christina was given three dates and told to observe what would occur on these dates. In retrospect, world affairs of rather insignificant prominence and noteworthiness that occurred on these dates had a significant effect on world conditions necessary for the rising to power of the Antichrist. Her spiritual director gives us this account:

> In November of 1991, Our Lady said to Christina Gallagher. "Observe what will happen in the world on these three dates." Our Holy Mother gave Mrs. Gallagher three dates. (At the time, the message was written down by Christina and given to her spiritual director. Mrs. Gallagher did not know what it meant, but her spiritual director thought the first date, December 9, might refer to the important Maastricht meeting in Holland or perhaps to a Gorbachev/Yeltsin encounter due to take place on the same day.) On December 10, when Our Blessed Mother came to Christina, she asked Our Lady: "What was yesterday about?" and added, "Was it the meeting in Europe?" Our Lady paused and then said, "Yes. That meeting was a sign of the power of the Antichrist. Few realize how soon he will raise himself up."

On December 9, at Maastricht in Holland, a treaty was signed bearing the same name. Its aim is to unite Europe economically, but it is also the formulation of security policy that would inevitably affect the legislation of would-be member states. One immediate consequence of membership in this body would be the surrender of national autonomy and the impossibility of maintaining social policies not in line with its lax and liberal legislation. Abortion, for example, would be considered "a service" and the practice of homosexuality a "personal right," and so on.

The second date was January 3, 1992. On that date it was announced that a major meeting in Washington would suspend regulations in order to invite the Eastern European countries to join the International Monetary Union.

The third date Our Lady mentioned was not the polling day for Ireland's vote on Maastricht. Instead, June 15 was the date that the panicky and manipulative Irish government hurriedly bribed the nation with a promise to farmers of a 30 percent grant increase if they would ratify the Maastricht Treaty. The actual polling day of June 18 fell paradoxically on the Feast of Corpus Christi. As the Body and Blood of Christ was traded for thirty pieces of silver, the Irish people, misled and misinformed, were enticed by a promise of 30 percent grant increases to vote Ireland into Maastricht!

The three dates are all linked with the power of the Antichrist to get control of the governments of the world, and so the money of the world, and to render it almost impossible for people to exercise their own rights and freedom.

Christina adds, "I know it is linked up to the Maastricht Treaty and the uniting of the currencies. This is through the Maastricht Referendum."

Still, to bring all of this into a proper perspective, Father McGinnity reminds us that while an individual can be used as an Antichrist, any force or power at work against the Kingdom of God can also be described as an Antichrist. As in the past, we still do not know for sure the exact identity of the Son of Perdition or the time of his reign. Yet the feeling is that he will make his presence known very soon.

It is important that Christina's own words be presented for examination concerning this fascinating prophecy.

Q. You have had experiences concerning the Antichrist. Describe them for us.

A. I was seeing this man time and time again. I had no idea who he was at first. I just saw his face and his head. I saw him a number of times and I didn't think there was anything wrong with him, but I used to feel from him a sort of horror. There was something different about his eyes. His eyes were so piercing. I could feel his eyes penetrate me and I didn't like it. I didn't know what to make of this, so I asked God one day, talking in prayer. I said, "Dear God, who is this?" much like the way I asked Catherine of Siena. The next thing I knew I heard an echo of the Virgin Mary's voice saying, "Antichrist." I got the shock of my life. I've seen this man a number of times since then, but I just ask the Precious Blood of Jesus to cover me.

Q. Is the Antichrist figure you saw a young-looking man or an old-looking man?

A. He's a man in his fifties. He has a round face and he's bald on top with very short black hair, in a fine haircut. He would remind me of somebody like a bishop. There's something very strange and very peculiar about his eyes. They were dark brown or black. I guess he was not a bad-looking man. In a sense you would never think that there was any evil concerning him. From what I can understand of what Our Blessed Mother has said about Antichrist, there will be a number of them; a number in the world right now who are "Anti-Christs" or "anti" of Christ.

Q. It is prophesied that one specific man will be the Antichrist. Do you think this one man that you are seeing is going to be the ultimate one? Do you think he is the one the Bible tells us is the Antichrist?

A. If I were to tell you I knew for certain that this was the man, I would be lying. I can only assume it is possible that he is what's called in the Bible the Antichrist. But that's my own opinion, because other than that, I wouldn't know why this apparition was given to me.

Q. So you're saying that the Antichrist figure you have been shown, in your opinion, is quite possibly The Antichrist.

A. If he's not the Antichrist, I wonder why the Lord permitted me to see him and hear the word "Antichrist," because I didn't know anything about the Antichrist at that particular stage in my life. I don't think it would be given to me otherwise. The Virgin Mary said to me, "Few realize how soon the Antichrist will raise himself up." There are many Antichrists now, but one, as time goes on, will be elected at the top.

Q. Have you seen this man on the scene of political leaders that exist today?

A. No, but I don't watch television and I don't get newspapers, so possibly he exists. He may exist, but I haven't seen him yet.

Q. From the apparition of the Antichrist that you witnessed is this a person who is alive today?

A. If I was to say he's alive today, I would be going on assumption. Because we are in the "end times," and from all that the Blessed Mother has been saying to me I can only assume that he must be in the world today.

PART III

Messages from Above

CHAPTER NINETEEN

Searching for Meaning in the Revelations

I BEGAN TO SEE HOW TRUE IT IS THAT GOD SHOWS NO PARTIALITY. RATHER, THE MAN OF ANY NATION WHO FEARS GOD AND ACTS UPRIGHTLY IS ACCEPTABLE TO HIM. THIS IS THE MESSAGE HE HAS SENT THE SONS OF ISRAEL, THE GOOD NEWS OF PEACE PROCLAIMED THROUGH JESUS CHRIST, WHO IS LORD OF ALL.

—ACTS 10:34–36

Throughout the centuries, from every corner of the globe, the Virgin Mary has brought a message of evangelical appeal, and prophetic warning from Heaven to her children. It is a serious message; a message the world has repeatedly neglected and forgotten, or worse, totally ignored.

Why do we need these appeals? Where has our world gone wrong? What has happened to our faith? How did we get in this mess?

Christina's revelations specifically cite God's recognition of man's errant ways, and consequently man's need to come back to God, come back before it's too late.

Upon examination, it appears the apparitions and messages

given by God to Christina serve a dual function. The primary function is to reawaken faith and bring a return to God, much like the Gospel and the preaching of Saint John the Baptist. Ever so boldly, Saint John called for conversion and the Baptism of repentance. The Virgin Mary's messages likewise call for conversion. The secondary function of her experiences is one of prophetic impact. These prophetic messages carry the reminders of Scripture. The message remains the same—God is the answer to our problems, not man. We need only turn to Him. But now, unlike before, there is an immediate urgency. It is an urgency the messages repeat, over and over. Our Lady says that: "Now is the time for the fulfillment of one era and the beginning of another." Time for the fulfillment of prophecies, even old prophecies which take root in Scripture. Some of them are even from the Book of Genesis.

Christina's messages are the message of the Gospel. Our Lady's words call for "peace, prayer, conversion, penance, sacrifice, and atonement." They urge Catholics to receive the Sacrament of Penance and to attend the Holy Sacrifice of the Mass. Most important, Our Lady implores us to love Jesus in the Holy Eucharist. These messages are always the most important because they invite us to respond in faith to God's invitation to return to His love. We need to hear this because when we respond to God's love, we are assured of the outcome of the prophetic ingredients of the messages in our own lives. Whenever God calls us we have nothing to fear when we are in His Light.

"What Our Blessed Mother is asking us to do," says Christina, "is to pray constantly, pray from the heart, especially the Rosary; turn back to God while there is time, sincerely repent of our sins and go to Confession; love God in the Mass and in the Holy Eucharist; be united and love one another, and stop finding fault, bickering, and fighting with one another. The messages tell us, through the power of the Resurrection, God has brought us all into the Mystical Body of Christ."

Indeed, Christina's insightful reflection of the primary function of Heaven's messages to us during these times is perfect, bringing to mind the words of Saint Paul, "You then, are the Body of Christ, every one of you is a member of It." (1 Cor. 12:27)

Still, regardless of how many messages God sends, it is up to us to respond. We have to take action. As the Blessed Mother told Christina, "I want to help, but you must decide."

Over the past seven years, the revelations to Christina have shown us a Savior who suffered much for our salvation and continues to be hurt by our sinfulness and indifference. Christina tells us this suffering of His is real and deep. Yet repeatedly, her experiences of Jesus while they overwhelmingly emphasize His endless love and constant call to salvation also stress His pain and suffering from rejection, through sin. Christ repeatedly shows Christina, by word and encounter, His immense longing for all souls. It is a hunger and a thirst for souls that is infinite.

In her own surrender, we have discussed how Christina Gallagher as a victim soul has abandoned herself to the will of God. Again, it is this total surrender to God that is the key message Heaven wants to get through to us.

As we look at Christina's life in Christ, we need to remind ourselves of the significant importance of her response to God's call for complete surrender. As with all stigmatists, we are often confused or overawed by the phenomena of their wounds, and lose sight of the deep implications of the soul's trusting relationship with God. It is this trusting relationship that is the real message all of us are called to live. Indeed, we are clearly reminded of this in Our Lord's image of Divine Mercy, where the words, "Jesus I Trust In You," boldly invite all who gaze upon the Risen Savior to embrace His complete love, trust, and mercy.[1]

God is trying unceasingly to get our attention. Whether it be through a living sign of suffering like Christina or through the messages that God not only desires people to read, but to live, all of this is to call us back to Him. For God is trying to make us aware of the threatening dangers that now besiege our planet.

War, disease, family disintegration, poverty, apostasy—a catastrophic crisis surrounds us. Heaven says that mankind is living in a cesspool of sin and atheism. From the messages of the Queen of Peace, it is reported that these dangers are now especially grave for the survival of the world. As Our Lady told Christina on May 6, 1993:

My child, the world of sin is causing and bringing about its own destruction. Time is short before the Second Coming of my Son Jesus. There will be wars spreading from country to country. There will be more diseases than there will be names for. Hunger cries will reach Heaven.

The inhabitants of the earth will wish they had not been born and so many will curse God. They will not beg God's Mercy.

My child, let this message be known. Fear not, my children. Know you only suffer what God so desires for poor sinners.

This secondary function to Christina's messages, the prophetic cries of alarm, flow constantly throughout her revelations and apparitions.

Over the past several years, her mystical experiences have ranged from seeing Pope John Paul II under great duress to an entire world about to be let go by the supporting hands of Jesus Christ. Symbolically these vividly descriptive scenes synthesize for us many of the warnings the Virgin Mary has given us. Heaven apparently is preparing earth for the promised events involving purification: events that draw ever so near; events, the chosen souls tell us, that have no reprieve, only potential mitigation and promised fulfillment.

On August 20, 1991, Christina viewed the frightening scene of Jesus holding a globe of the world with His hands and then suddenly vanishing. He was replaced by a pillar and it was crumbling. It could no longer support the world. After that troubling sight, the Virgin Mary confirmed the approaching times of tribulation.

My child, I, your Immaculate Mother, desire you to open your heart and offer all distraction to my Heart.

The world is held up by pillars. The Pillar is Jesus Christ. The pillars are about to fall. My Divine Son Jesus is soon releasing His hand, the Pillar of God. The world will be plunged into the depths of its sin, and drink of its bitterness. My child, do not let my words trouble you. I desire to give you messages. Be attentive and keep your heart open to receive what I give you. I hold you under my Mantle, my child."

It was also after this that Our Blessed Mother urged Christina's spiritual director to read "The Seven Seals" of the Apocalypse, "especially the seventh seal," she said. From this apparition, Christina thought the entire world would be hurled into Hell. "Plunged," as the Virgin Mary explained, "into the depths of its sin." Although Our Blessed Mother has delivered these harsh words before, this revelation echoed those messages with a new degree of reality. For God knows pictures speak louder than words. And through this revelation, He sought to send His children His strongest message yet—to Christina Gallagher through Our Holy Mother.

The Blessed Mother added, "Pray in meditation on the Passion of Jesus." A moment later, Our Lady added, "The clock, its alarm is set. The hour is close. Pray, pray, pray!"

Describing how much the scene had affected her, Christina said she was so shattered and frightened that she phoned up a friend, and eventually spoke to her spiritual director, despite the late hour. She was crying and it took her more than a day to recover from it.

"I have been through other experiences, and have been shown frightening apparitions and encountered the Evil One, but in relation to God, this was the most frightening I have gone through," she said. She wondered how the message ought to be printed, as she did not want it to cause any alarm. "That is not what Our Lady would desire," she said.

While several prophetic messages to Christina clearly detail that the purification of the world is near, the Virgin Mary always reminds Christina that she has come to the world to present all souls to God. In this disclosure we find the heart of Our Blessed Mother's prophetic call. This repeated reminder of Our Lady's mission appears to tell us that the Blessed Mother can save us from Hell if we respond, but not necessarily from all the tragic events that are on the horizon.

Indeed, Christina implies that hard times are ahead, no matter who we are or what we do, the Blessed Mother said this is because, "Mankind has never indulged in Satan's work like now," and because people "desire to remain in darkness and sin."

Yet Christina's messages tell us the greatest period of Mercy the world has ever known is now upon us, but is already merging with a period of His Justice.

To help incite response to the Lord's Mercy, the Virgin Mary's prophetic messages to Christina stress the reality of evil, sin, Satan, and Hell in today's world. These messages bring about a deeper awareness of the love and mercy of God and also of His forthcoming justice.

In many of the prophetic messages given to Christina, the sins of the world are mentioned. The sin of abortion, we are specifically advised, is one of the three sins that grieve Our Lord's heart the most; along with "the immoral abuse of the innocents and the sacrificing of the innocents to Satan." As the Queen of Peace confirmed to Christina: "Abortion is the greatest sin against God. It permits the Devil to work like never before." On more than one occasion, Our Lady revealed that through abortion, people are sinning against the Holy Spirit, because "Life comes through the Holy Spirit." Yet immediately Christina reminds us that so does forgiveness. His forgiveness is what God's Mercy is all about, regardless of any sin we commit, even abortion. It is why Jesus told Sister Faustina, "I desire the whole world know My infinite Mercy."[2]

Reaching out for God's forgiveness must come through the Church for Catholics. This is the heart of the messages given to Christina Gallagher. The work and survival of the true teaching of Christ is truly why Our Mother has now come, and, according to Christina, to call her children back to the free-flowing fountain of the mercy and love of the Heart of her Son Jesus. In retrospect, her many apparitions are like a rudder that corrects the course of the ship. In the messages to Christina, we repeatedly see Heaven's special call to the Church and its priests, bishops, and religious. This call is also a mission special to Christina. Through the Virgin Mary's words to the religious, the Church is revealed to be in great danger of betrayal. These deceptive actions, like the betrayal by Judas, are in the process of occurring and will bring about a great crisis within the Church. Our Lady's messages foretell that this crisis will be the Church's calvary and crucifixion. But it will be followed by its glorious resurrection in the Triumph of the Immaculate Heart.

In the coming chapters, as you read Christina's messages and examine Our Lord and Our Lady's words, you will see this call to faith, hope, and love. Her revelations show us that God wants to forgive, forget, and invite His children to be part of His plan for the salvation of the world. All we need to do is say "Yes," and His love will take over. Much the way Christina did when she was called, or rather when she was chosen.

Indeed, Christina was chosen.

She was chosen to be a special soul in which the Most Holy Trinity wished to come and dwell. On May 5, 1992, Jesus desired Christina to have a better understanding of this calling. Once again, He gently shared with her a secret of their intimacy.

"My little one, do you understand that I live in you?"

"Yes, Jesus," replied Christina.

"Not only I live in you, but also does the Most Holy Trinity. All who love Me, love My Father and the Holy Spirit. Your heart is the dwelling place of the Most Holy Trinity."

Christina confessed to Jesus, "I know you live in me, but how can you say the Most Holy Trinity is living in my heart?"

He assured her, "My little one, all who love Me, love My Father and the Holy Spirit. In that way their hearts are open to the Most Holy Trinity."

Yes, the Most Holy Trinity dwells in Christina Gallagher, who was born and raised in an area of Ireland historically called to suffering and to God. It all makes sense. There are no mistakes here. No coincidences or accidents. History holds that Ireland opened its homeland to receive the Most Holy Trinity many centuries before. As far back as the fifth century, Saint Patrick, Christina's fatherly friend and visitor from Heaven, had defied and openly opposed the idol-worshipping Druids in Ireland by a simple illustration of the reality of the Most Holy Trinity.

Responding to the Druids' proclamation that the Trinity was absurd as three could not exist in one, Saint Patrick stooped down and pulled up a shamrock, which has three leaves on one stem. Confidently, he enlightened his antagonists, "To prove the reality and possibility of the existence of the Father, Son, and Holy Ghost, I have only to pluck up this humble plant, on which we have trodden, and convince you that truth can be attested by the simplest symbol of illustration." The Most Holy Trinity was therefore boldly proclaimed in Ireland long ago. Today it remains firmly rooted in the hearts of the faithful.

As anxious as Christina is to have the messages shared with all who will listen, she is equally adamant for people to recognize that she is no better than anyone else. Every heart, she insists, is called to be a dwelling place for the Most Holy Trinity. "But, people must not delay their response anymore," she painfully sighs. "Time is short and will soon run out!"

To better understand the Virgin Mary's call, key topics in the messages given to Christina are reviewed in the upcoming chapters. These revelations span the role of the Mass and the sacraments in our life to Our Lord and Our Lady's special messages concerning the Holy Father, apostasy, and the tribulation.

The messages again seek a response. They call, even beg, for all souls to return to God. Like the Gospel, these messages are Good News, to be proclaimed for all to hear and especially to live and spread.

Like Christina Gallagher, we are all now called to invite the Most Holy Trinity into our hearts and to share in God's coming Triumph. Like never before in history, this coming victory of God will be a triumph of truth that the world, like the pagan Druids, will not be able to deny.

CHAPTER TWENTY

Heart to Heart Prayer

I CALL UPON YOU, O LORD; COME QUICKLY TO ME; GIVE EAR TO MY VOICE WHEN I CALL TO YOU. LET MY PRAYER BE AS INCENSE BEFORE YOU, AND THE LIFTING UP OF MY HANDS AS AN EVENING SACRIFICE.

—Ps. 141:1–2

God is an infinite God!

To possess His grace is to possess God Himself. To persevere in the possession of this grace until death is so great a favor, that according to the teachings of the Fathers of the Church, no one can merit it, even were he to perform all the good works of all the saints in Heaven. God bestows this gift gratuitously and the Lord grants it, as Saint Augustine teaches, to all those who pray daily for it.[1] Saint Augustine wrote, "We must pray for it every day, because even the just are every day in danger of losing it." Saint Paul the apostle wrote, "He that striveth for the mastery is not crowned except he strive lawfully." This lawful striving must come through prayer.[2]

Indeed, in order to do God's Will there must be prayer. As the saints have stressed, the Virgin Mary tells Christina this prayer must come from the heart.

From the first of Christina's apparitions on January 21, 1988, Our Lady requested she make every effort to have her prayer joined to the depth of her soul. "I want you to pray more as much as you can. I know you have your family to think about, but my Son and I are giving you the graces you need through your prayers. So I say to you, 'Rid yourself of fear.' I know you do not understand all, but you will. You have accepted in your heart how to pray, but you must know I want you to pray more and more. Do not waste time, my child, I love you."

This was not easy for Christina, she admits ashamedly: "I used to get around the Rosary speedily. I wasn't thinking of what I was saying." On August 22, 1991, Our Lady once again encouraged her to continue to learn the value of prayer from the heart: "Yes, I desire many works and much prayer. My child, pray, pray, pray! The Devil wants to destroy my plan for Ireland and the world. By your prayer, sacrifice, and suffering offered to Jesus, my Son, will disarm all his snares. Be patient. Be vigilant in prayer and good works. Love all those you meet, my child, my heart is your heart. I will give you my graces that you are in need of, through prayer. Pray my beautiful Rosary often. My Son Jesus desires a great work from you. Respond to His Love."

Not surprisingly, the majority of Our Lady's messages to Christina Gallagher are meant for everyone. There is a reason for this. The Virgin Mary's messages call people back to faith—all people. Regardless of religion, her messages invite believers back to God, but people must make the effort to respond, a true effort from their hearts. This can only come through prayer.

During painful trials, the faithful must persevere and persist in prayer. As Our Lady promised her, God wishes to heal His broken people, but this must come through trust in Him and faith, strengthened by prayer:

"My Son Jesus wants you to triumph over all evil. Please pray more, and fast for three days. Ask my Son Jesus to strengthen your faith when you are weakest. My Son has made known to you words of healing but without strong faith, it cannot be. Be strong, my dear child. Do not go to Holy Mass out of habit. Love my Son when you are at Holy Mass."

As the apparitions to Christina continued, the Blessed Mother's invitations to prayer were constant. On February 24, 1988, Our Lady urged her to follow the path that the Queen of Peace invites everyone to take to get to God. It is the path of the saints, who were often no more than reformed sinners. It is the holy path of prayer.

Christina adds, "To pray from the heart." Our Lady said, "When you speak to a person you know what you are saying—when you speak to me know what you say." We should meditate on the mysteries of the Rosary and know what we are saying and to whom we are speaking. Because at that time we are living the mysteries of Our Blessed Mother with Jesus, from Our Blessed Mother's "yes" to God to the sufferings of Jesus in our redemption to the Resurrection of Christ, and how we in our "yes" can be raised and united in the Resurrection of Christ.

CHAPTER TWENTY-ONE

The Cornerstone of Life

SET YOUR HEART ON THE GREATER GIFTS.

—1 COR. 12:31

Saint Teresa of Avila was so overwhelmed with God's goodness the saint once asked the Risen Savior, "How can I thank you?" Our Lord replied, "Attend one Mass!"

Over the centuries private revelation is filled with testimonies to the value of the Mass—a value, not only for souls, but for the Church and the world.

"What can be greater than being at Mass where during the Consecration we are taken to the foot of the cross with our Blessed Mother? It is the same sacrifice," says Christina.

Without question, Christina Gallagher tells us, the Holy Sacrifice of the Mass is the ultimate prayer. Nothing is greater. Nothing is more powerful. Indeed, the saints steadfastly proclaimed it. We are told the Mass is of infinite value to the very survival of the planet. Padre Pio, the stigmatist and mystic, reportedly said the world could exist more easily without the sun than without the Mass. People say he meant this literally.

Others have concurred. Saint Gertrude was told that for each Mass we attend with devotion, Our Lord sends a saint to comfort us at death. In fact, many saints have said that having a Mass for the intention of a living person is of even greater value than for the deceased. The great doctor of the Church, Saint Anselm, declared that a single Mass offered for oneself during life may be worth more than a thousand after death. Pope Benedict XV echoed this view.

To Christina Gallagher, the Blessed Mother continues to repeat this request. Christina says: "Our Lady is constantly urging her children to go to Mass, daily if they can. The Blessed Mother wants the Mass to become the cornerstone of her children's life, upon which all else is built."

In Ireland, the Queen of Peace calls for a childlike abandonment to God's will in our lives. This will automatically lead us to Jesus at His table in the Mass. From many messages to Christina, we are assured that through the Mass and the sacraments our lives can be changed. Every day, the graces received in the sacraments help us become like children in our faith again. Our Holy Mother tells us this change in our lives cannot come about by our own will. We are not strong enough. We're too weak, too easily distracted. The Blessed Mother insists that we need this spiritual help.

In October 1992, Our Lady enlightened Christina more about the Mass and its value. "My child, if you could see the world through my eyes and realize the value of the Holy Sacrifice of the Mass and the value of praying the Rosary from your heart, you would go to the Mass many times each day and you would pray the Rosary from your heart constantly."

As if to emphasize the love and peace which come into one's life through God's sacramental gifts, the Irish stigmatist unexpectedly experienced Eucharistic miracles on two occasions.

Once while attending Mass at a church in Northern Ireland, the Holy Eucharist miraculously changed to flesh in her mouth. On another occasion, when offered the chalice by Our Lady, Christina saw and tasted the Precious Blood in the form of actual blood. Both times, she was shocked. Christina says,

❋

Everything slowed down. It was as if I were outside the world. I went back to my seat after I received the Holy Eucharist. Then I became unaware of the people. I became very peaceful. There, I could feel the Holy Eucharist growing in my mouth. It became like jelly, or flesh. I was thinking, "Dear Lord, how am I going to swallow this. Am I going to choke?" But automatically, it went down. I could feel it go down. I swallowed the Holy Eucharist without any trouble. On another occasion, I received the Precious Blood from the chalice handed to me by Our Lady. I was handed the chalice, but I could feel a different liquid in my mouth. Instantly I knew what it was. It was the Precious Blood. It tasted different, but like the pains in my hands, I did not look.

❋

Over the past five years, Christina has repeatedly received messages from Our Lord and Our Lady encouraging frequent use of the sacraments. On February 28, 1988, Our Lady instructed, "My child, tell all my children to *come back to me and my Son.* We are waiting and we love all our children. Repent, go to Confession. Unburden yourselves of all sin and receive my Son's Body and Blood worthily. Pray and make sacrifice. In return, I will give you peace in your hearts."

Ever available, peace through the sacraments is rejected by many, and this brings pain and sorrow to the Blessed Mother. From a message on July 1, 1988, the Blessed Mother informed Christina even some consecrated souls did not believe, that "Jesus' Body and Blood are present in the Consecration of the Mass. They do not believe that the bread and wine are changed into His Body and Blood. . . . We must love Jesus in the Mass and Holy Communion. . . ."

Just two weeks later on July 14, 1988, Our Lady admonished her children: ". . . Do not go to Holy Mass out of habit. Love my Son when you are at Holy Mass. . . ." Our Holy Mother wanted to make sure we didn't misunderstand her. On August 11, 1988, she implored Christina to understand that, more than anything else, Our Lord wishes to meet us at His table: ". . . My children, go to Holy Mass. Offer it to the Father, to console the Heart of my Son Jesus."

While the Mass and the sacraments bring with them gifts of joy, they also bring protection. The Blessed Mother, true to her role as our Mother, says the faithful must avail of this protection. On August 15, 1988, the Virgin Mary reminded Christina of the necessity of frequent Reconciliation and how the sacraments provide additional protection, but sadly so few accept it: "My children have abandoned the Sacrament of Penance. Do they not know they cannot be set free of Satan's influence and work without asking forgiveness? That is why it is so important, my children, to offer all the hurt of your heart to my Son with love. It can do a great good for many. . . ."

In her own words, Christina explains what she has learned about our need to frequently come to the Lord in the sacraments and the Mass.

Q. How do we, in our lives, stay focused on Jesus?

A. I know I can be drawn away through every distraction but for the grace of God. We should constantly be petitioning God through prayer, sacrifice, fasting. The Holy Eucharist—above all things—will help us. In receiving the Holy Eucharist, we must receive It worthily. Our Blessed Mother said all these things contribute to the Grace of God that you receive. All of this helps to draw you closer to God and to bring you constantly into an awareness of God.

Q. What has Our Lady taught you about Our Lord's presence in the Holy Eucharist?

A. On the second apparition, when Our Blessed Mother came from a distance, there was a Light over Her heart. Then, when Our Holy Mother came close up, I could see it was the Holy Eucharist and the Light was radiating from it. Our Lady was joyous and drew my attention to look down as she was looking down.

After that, I was wondering why the Holy Eucharist was over Our Blessed Mother's heart. It's only been these last couple of months that I thought about it. So I prayed and said, "Holy Mother, if you want me to know the meaning of what that was all about, then you'll reveal it." She didn't reveal it in words; it was revealed inwardly. I was aware that she held Jesus over her heart, meaning that she loved Jesus in the Holy Eucharist. Our Lady would give reverence to Him by carrying Him over her heart, meaning that we should carry Him over our hearts and in our hearts. The Light around it, for me, signified the graces we can receive by receiving the Holy Eucharist, worthily—in a proper way. Our Holy Mother said we can receive the Holy Eucharist only when we have made a proper Confession. Our Blessed Mother desires her children to unburden themselves of all sin and receive her Son's Body and Blood worthily.

Q. Has Our Lady spoken to you about the Mass and the Holy Eucharist? What has she said about the Mass and the Holy Eucharist?

A. When Our Blessed Mother spoke about the Holy Eucharist and the sacraments, she was talking about the Mass itself. Mass, with the celebration of the Holy Eucharist, is the Reality of Jesus. It is to love Jesus in prayer and adoration. Our Holy Mother said to come to Jesus and love Him. Our Lady has said this so many times. I didn't write down many things because it was as if she was talking directly just to me on some occasions. But when Our Holy Mother would refer to all of this, it was always to love Jesus more and to love Jesus in the Holy Eucharist.

Q. Has Our Lord spoken of Confession, the sacraments, and of repentance?

A. Yes. Jesus requested that we make an act of reparation for the abuse of the Holy Eucharist by receiving on tongue only. This was not a command. It was a desire. Someone I shared it with later said that I was going against the Church's teaching, but a week later Jesus repeated the same request. When I told Jesus of my plight regarding this person, Jesus then replied, "My little one, I am The Church." Our Blessed Mother has also spoken about it. Our Lady has asked that we be absolved of all sin and receive her Son's Body worthily, in the Holy Eucharist. This is what Our Blessed Mother had said to me in an apparition. We must desire the Holy Eucharist in our heart.

Q. What would you say to someone who has committed an abortion, concerning God's forgiveness?

A. I'd say to them to go to Confession and ask for God's forgiveness and mercy. Then make much repentance and sacrifice with sincerity to God and use the Baptism of desire. God is forgiving to anyone who turns to Him, because that's what His love and mercy are. God is crying out to everybody with total love.

CHAPTER TWENTY-TWO

"Arm Yourselves with My Rosary"

GOD HAS GIVEN US THE WISDOM TO UNDERSTAND FULLY THE MYSTERY, THE PLAN HE WAS TO DECREE IN CHRIST, TO BE CARRIED OUT IN THE FULLNESS OF TIME. . . .

—EPH. 1:9–10

Wherever the Virgin Mary appears, her call to the Rosary is always there. It's the Blessed Mother's universal message. It's Our Lady's open call to arms. Over the last several centuries, almost every chosen soul has repeated this invitation to pray the Rosary, for the Rosary is a powerful prayer with a great history.

This has been especially true in Ireland, where Father Patrick Peyton's worldwide Family Rosary Crusade became known for the expression, "The family that prays together stays together." Over the years, this County Mayo priest's endless work for the Rosary touched the lives of millions, as the Rosary remains recognized by the Church as invaluable to the spiritual health of its people.

In *Familiaris Consortio,* Pope John Paul II wrote of the Rosary's infinite value:

> We now desire, as a continuation of the thought of our predecessors, to recommend strongly the recitation of the Family Rosary. . . . There is no doubt that . . . the Rosary should be considered as one of the best and most efficacious prayers in common that the Christian family is invited to recite.

For centuries the Irish were known for their faithfulness to praying the Rosary causing, it is suspected, the Blessed Mother to wear a rose on her forehead at Knock in 1879. Throughout all of the Virgin Mary's apparitions today, the Queen of Peace explicitly reminds her children of her Rosary, over and over again.

Christina says Our Holy Mother calls us to use it as the spiritual weapon it was designed to be. To her Our Lady even prescribed it as a tool for discernment: "Do the Rosary Novena. If you do it, you will understand." To Christina, the Blessed Mother revealed that Satan hates the Rosary and its power over him. "It can defeat him when prayed from the heart."

Specifically, Christina says the Queen of Peace asks us to use this powerful weapon every day in our homes and once a week in church, especially now as both the Church and the family have come under such serious demonic attack.

Of this unfolding spiritual war, the Virgin Mary told Christina what must be done: "My child, the calamity has started. The influence of the Prince of Darkness is all around you. Arm yourselves with my Rosary. My Church will be shaken, even to its very foundation. My children who want to be saved must repent. Repent, I say, to all my children. Arm yourselves with my Rosary. Let it never be out of your hearts. My chosen children, you are now like lambs among wolves. Stand firm, have no fear, for the Hand of the Mighty One is with you. . . ."

On different occasions, the Queen of Peace confirmed to Christina Her desires concerning the Rosary:

I want it offered for peace and for the conversion of sinners.
I desire you to pray the Rosary more often.
It will protect them during the times of trial and suffering.

I plead with you, arm yourselves with my Rosary.
I love it when my children pray the Rosary.

The Creed is a holy summary of all Christian Truths and the Our Father and Glory Be give direct tribute to the Most Holy Trinity. But a Hail Mary gives praise to God and brings the Virgin Mary great joy, because it is a salutation given to the Mother of God by the Most Holy Trinity. According to many great mystics this anthem is often repeated in Heaven by the angels.

One day, Our Lady explained to Saint Mechtilde exactly what the words of the Hail Mary signified:

By the word *Hail* (Ave), I learned that in His infinite power, God had preserved me from all sin and its attendant misery, which the first woman had been subjected to.

The name *Mary,* which means "lady of light," shows that God has filled me with wisdom and light, like a shining star, to light up Heaven and earth.

The words *full of grace* remind me that the Holy Spirit has showered so many graces upon me that I am able to give these graces in abundance to those who ask for them. I am able to give them through me as Mediatrix.

When people say *The Lord is with thee* they renew the indescribable joy that was mine when the Eternal Word became incarnate in my womb.

When you say *Blessed art thou among women,* I praise almighty God's divine Mercy, which lifted me to this exalted plane of happiness.

And at the words, *Blessed is the Fruit of Thy Womb, Jesus,* the whole of Heaven rejoices with me to see my Son Jesus Christ adored and glorified for having saved mankind.[1]

On May 22, 1988, just three months after Christina's apparitions began, Our Lady personally instructed her about this special prayer, so she would be able to encourage more people to pray it, especially at the new House of Prayer. "I would like you to pray the Rosary to me from your heart. Offer each Hail Mary as a beautiful white rose or precious jewel, and the Lord's Prayer as a very fine red rose or special jewel, to clothe me in. But you must know that you cannot have precious jewels that will not sparkle, or beautiful roses that are only ready to be thrown away. My child, if you do not pray the Rosary from your heart, with love and joy, the roses or jewels you offer to clothe me in will be lost forever. Pray the Rosary with love and joy and it will last for all eternity. Please, my child, do not disappoint me. Let it be a garment that will sparkle . . . pray my beautiful Rosary."

Since that day, Christina's understanding of the Rosary has grown immensely. As she now does at the House of Prayer, Christina invites her listeners to embrace the Rosary's mysteries in order to pray it well:

> In the Joyful Mysteries we see the reality of our Blessed Mother's surrender to God, her yes to God and her yes for our redemption. It is her surrender.
>
> In the Sorrowful Mysteries, we see the ugliness of sin and what we did to Christ through sin, yet God in His Love and Mercy redeems us in our disobedience.
>
> The Glorious Mysteries bring us to a great awareness that if we say "Yes" to God, we can also be raised up to share in the glory of the Risen Christ in the home prepared by our Father. Most assuredly, the value of meditation on the mysteries is the key to the power contained in the Rosary.

In Ireland, the Blessed Mother has called upon her "little flock" to especially pray the Rosary for unbelievers, those lost souls who cause her so much sorrow and anguish. To this very end, she implored me to pray the Rosary more and use it also for my own needed strength: "Pray the Rosary for some of my lost souls. . . . Remember I am with you. There are some troubles ahead of you, but your cross will not get too heavy for you. You will be able to carry it. Pray, pray for strength to overcome darkness. Pray to my heart. Console my many wounds there. You are close to my wounded heart. Always stay close to my heart and the Heart of my Divine Son. Be not afraid. . . ."

Adding infinite merit to this call to use the power of the Rosary, Our Lord has even spoken to her of its significance, especially for souls who are far from God. In a message on September 24, 1988, Jesus specifically requested Christina to pray the Rosary to Him: "Pray the Rosary to My Heart for souls who are in great darkness. Offer all your pain to My Merciful Heart. You have experienced the greatest pain of the Crown of Thorns. Do not fear when you suffer pain, I am close to you. . . ."

Through her own words, Christina gives us more insight into the power of prayer, especially the Rosary, and how prayer can help our conversion to be pure and lasting.

Q. What advice has the Blessed Mother given you concerning your prayer life and praying the Rosary?

A. Our Lady has advised me to pray and receive the sacraments. This is what Our Holy Mother wants for everybody, not just for me. Our Blessed Mother desires all people to become aware of God and God's existence and to love God. Our Lady says you receive that awareness through the sacraments and prayer. Our Holy Mother talks about the Rosary. Once Our Lady referred to the Rosary and said, "When you speak to a person, you know what you say." I said, "Yes." Then Our Lady said, "When you speak to me, know what you say. In the Rosary, you can live the mysteries of my life with Jesus." The Rosary is a very powerful prayer because Jesus said to me at another time: "The Rosary acts as a shield—to protect you." If you have this awareness and you pray the Rosary from your heart and in conversation with God or Our Holy Mother, you should meditate on the mysteries of the Rosary. Then, in your heart, you're bringing about the Reality of Jesus as truly as if you're living in the time of Jesus and Our Blessed Mother. This is because you're allowing God's grace to enter your heart and increase your awareness. You also receive that protection Jesus spoke of. There is a great protection, from Heaven, through the Rosary.

Q. In your personal life has Our Lady given you any specific advice?

A. Yes, Our Holy Mother asked me to pray the Rosary more. Pray, pray, pray.

Q. How much does the Virgin Mary wish us to pray the Rosary each day?

A. There is not a time limit. Our Lady means that I should say the Rosary and pray it properly. Sometimes I would sit down or kneel down to do it. Then Our Holy Mother would appear and say, "My child, pray, pray, pray . . ." inviting me to pray the Rosary from the heart. Often I thought, "Holy Mother, you know I can't be constantly praying the Rosary because I have to do my work if I'm to keep my life in any way normal. My life wouldn't work any other way." Then I started to offer my work as a prayer as well as the Rosary. When I would wash the dishes, I would invite Our Blessed Mother to receive the act of washing the dishes as a prayer, or when I was sweeping or washing the floor or whatever work I was doing, I would ask Our Lady to receive it as a prayer and I would offer it to Jesus. Our Holy Mother never contradicted me in that. This meant to me that Our Lady was obviously satisfied with what I had done. It's not the amount of prayer that is important, but the constant awareness of offering it to Jesus or Our Blessed Mother. Make your life a prayer and offer everything to Our Holy Mother and, in return, she will offer everything to God.

Q. Has Our Lady spoken to you about praying in front of blessed objects and statues?

A. People say you shouldn't idolize a statue, that it is only a statue. That bothered me for a while when I first heard this. I asked Our Blessed Mother and she said, "Yes, keep blessed objects."

Our Lady didn't say statues. Our Lady didn't say anything except to keep blessed objects around you and use holy water often. So I was praying that Our Holy Mother would enlighten me or help me regarding statues. After awhile I had this realization. I don't know the Bible in depth. Even when I read it, I might not always understand what it's actually saying at times, but I do know that there is a part in it somewhere where Jesus says even the stones will cry out. I realized then what better stones than the mortar in the statues of His mother, to remind people of His words in the Bible. Our Holy Mother is crying out through the mortar to her children because they've gone far astray. Statues are known to have wept tears or tears of blood or change in appearance. This shows the depth of the cry from the heart of Jesus through the image of His mother for lost souls.

Q. There are Protestant groups who say that Catholics worship idols when they pray to statues. What would you say to that?

A. The statues are reminders to us. If you walk into a house and see a lot of statues, a person is never particularly looking at the statues, so much as being reminded by them of Our Blessed Mother or Jesus. When I pray, no matter how many statues are around me, I find myself closing my eyes to concentrate as I'm talking to Our Blessed Mother. I'm not looking at the blessed objects. You see, Our Blessed Mother says to put blessed objects around us because the Devil hates anything that's blessed. He hates holy water and our blessed medals.

Q. What have you learned that can help us to know when we are doing God's will?

A. Through the Holy Spirit and prayer, we must ask God to take our will away. Then our conscience in union with the Holy Spirit of God will begin to automatically tell us and guide us in God's will. We must understand the difference between right and wrong and ask help from our Guardian Angel. I see our Guardian Angel as important. This is how God communicates to us. Our Guardian Angel always wants to intercede for our every spiritual need. Our Guardian Angel is used by God to inspire us to do good, and the Holy Spirit guides us to respond to the will of God.

Q. You've spoken in a book about the "pure conversion." What does pure conversion mean?

A. Pure conversion is from the pure grace of God; when somebody is open in heart to receive God's grace with a complete conversion. There's also a conversion in which somebody comes halfway along the road to conversion and then turns back to their old self. A pure conversion is when somebody's completely spiritually healed. That doesn't mean they can't still drift back to their old self, but at least they will get a taste of God through a pure conversion. With a pure conversion, there's less chance of turning back to one's old self because one thirsts more and more for God through a depth of longing from within oneself for God.

Q. How should we pray to Jesus?

A. We should pray the Rosary as I described. When we can't pray a Rosary and we have to get on with our work, we then need to bring Jesus and Our Blessed Mother into our hearts and our minds with us at work. We need to offer everything we do as a prayer.

Some people feel they can only pray five decades of the Rosary each day, but if you had a beautiful treasure in your house, and the house had fifteen windows, you would not say that you only had time to close five of the fifteen windows; surely you would make sure to close all fifteen windows. In the same way we have within us the beautiful treasure of our immortal soul redeemed by the Precious Blood of Jesus. Satan desires to attack and plunder this treasure. Our Blessed Lady can shield us through the weapon of the Most Holy Rosary when we share these mysteries with her. She can ward off the attacks of Satan in the various approaches he makes to our souls. The body represents the house and the fifteen decades represent the fifteen windows. As we pray each decade, we close a window.

Q. What else has Our Lady said about the graces available to us?

A. In early January 1994, Our Lady said to me during Mass that Our Holy Mother desired to give many gifts to her children but their hearts remain closed. That is why the world has so much suffering. As Our Blessed Mother said this, she lowered her hands and white rays came from her hands and heart as she uttered the words, "I desire to give many graces to my children."

CHAPTER TWENTY-THREE

Calling All to Suffering and Sacrifice

CHRIST SUFFERED IN THE FLESH, THEREFORE ARM YOURSELVES IN HIS SAME MENTALITY. HE WHO HAS SUFFERED IN THE FLESH HAS BROKEN WITH SIN.

—1 PET. 4:1

The apparition was clear to Christina. Countless people all wearing the same Middle-Eastern headdress, their veils tied around their heads; it looked as if they were under concrete slabs. Telephoning her spiritual director to discuss this scene brought only the conclusion that it was a call to prayer, intense prayer and sacrifice.

Four weeks later, the news on television carried the exact scene. It was the aftermath of an earthquake in Iran; five thousand dead and fifty thousand people affected. On their way to worship at Mecca, thousands were trapped in an underground tunnel dressed exactly as she had described in the apparition. Pinned under concrete walls, it was a scene of massive death. Just then, the Virgin Mary spoke: "You were shown this not to prevent the catastrophe but to prepare their souls for God." So the decision to pray was correct. Her prayers were the preparation and hopefully her prayers were answered.

On another occasion, Christina was taken to the bedside of a man. This man had been very badly injured. His leg was bound and he was going to die. While there, she was given a prayer very similar to the Divine Mercy Chaplet. She began to recite it.

As she was praying, she miraculously witnessed a younger version of the afflicted man rise from his injured body and move upward. Jesus rose up to accompany his soul while the man's Guardian Angel ascended on the other side. Finally, she saw Heaven open up and receive them all. It was a beautiful sight. Later that same night Christina was shown many souls unprepared for death and was asked once more to pray and sacrifice for them.

Offering her own life as a testimony, these types of experiences and messages to Christina Gallagher are explicit in bringing to the forefront the necessity of redemptive suffering in this world today. It is a call that is imperative. Our Blessed Mother tells us that prayers and sacrifices must atone for sin or the world will sink into deeper misery.

This call for atonement and sacrifice is ever present in her message to Christina and often repeated. The Virgin Mary reminded her, "The more you suffer, the greater the sacrifice." It is also echoed in Scripture, "For it is your special privilege to take Christ's part—not only to believe in Him but also to suffer for Him." (1 Pet. 4:13, 16)

Christina Gallagher as a victim soul suffers in Christ. We must also understand that this call for sacrifice is also meant for us. Our Holy Mother tells us that all who are aware of this call must offer up their sufferings and sacrifices in atonement for the ocean of sin that exists in the world today.

Sacrifice, the Virgin Mary tells us, is essential. Our Lady also says no sacrifice is too small. This is not surprising, because it is again a message from Scripture. Saint Paul taught that to all who make up the Body of Christ we must be "Always bearing about in our body the mortification of Jesus, that the life also of Jesus may be made manifest in our bodies. . . . For that which is at present momentary and light of our tribulation, worketh for us above measure exceedingly an eternal weight of glory." (2 Cor. 4:10–17)

The messages to Christina Gallagher are much more than just a call to sacrifice. Through the messages given to her and in the example of her life, we learn to accept and offer our personal suffering for the atonement of sins in union with Christ's suffering. This brings us to a more personal awareness of the value of sacrifice. It is an awareness almost totally unknown in today's world of sensual consumption.

As Our Lady instructed her: "Always know when you suffer pain that my dear Son is close by. And I, your Mother, the Mother of your Lord, am with you. My tears of joy and sorrow will fall on you to comfort and console you. You are surrendering your body and soul to God. I ask you to pray more. Keep your heart with Jesus, my Son, always asking Him to save souls. My Son will grant you what you ask in prayer. Show Him how you love by acceptance."

Indeed, Our Lady's words once again remind us of the words of an apostle, this time Saint Peter:

> But if you partake of the sufferings of Christ, rejoice that when His glory can be revealed, you may also be glad with exceeding joy.
>
> (1 Pet. 4:13)

On occasion, Our Lady and Our Lord have also spoken to Christina specifically of fasting as a way to sacrifice. Through their messages to her, we are especially reminded to fast for the conversion of sinners. Our Blessed Mother reminds her children that every little denial can be used as a sacrifice to receive graces for sinners. Christina also stresses we must especially do this with joy, much like the Lord spoke in Scripture of our need to make no public display of our fast.

From her own fasting, Christina was led to understand its benefit for our souls. She explains: "When we fast, we take luxury out of eating and deprive the flesh; by doing this, we allow God, through the Sacrifice of the Cross, to work in our souls. Fasting teaches us to surrender and not to look for worldly things, like more power, more money, and all the other things that attract us." Christina also reminds us that by depriving ourselves, God guides us more and more away from the things of this world that are unimportant.

Our Lady desires fasting. First, Our Holy Mother mentioned sacrifice; sacrifice and praying the Rosary. Then Our Lady mentioned fasting. Our Blessed Mother hasn't mentioned any particular way to fast to me. Then, I thought, why is there so much need for fasting? Why do people need to fast? I questioned to myself. Then the reality of the need for fasting was given to me. Fasting is to deprive the flesh. In the beginning, I found it so difficult to fast. On the day I was supposed to fast, that's the day I would end up eating twice as much. This used to really bother me, because it upset me after I had eaten and not fasted. So I prayed and I said, "Please, please give me whatever I need in God's grace so that I will be able to fast." I pleaded with the Blessed Mother.

Then something happened so that when I got up in the morning, I wouldn't have a sense of hunger. I suppose it's no effort to fast when it's like that, because I would go for two days, three days, and even up to nine or ten days and I'd not feel one single urge of hunger. I was certainly a bit tired and weak in the flesh, but strong spiritually. God taught me in His own way the value of fasting, because I now understand that to deprive the flesh is to open my heart to allow Him to work more openly in my heart and soul. All Our Lady wants us to do is surrender, hand ourselves over to her, and let her do what is best.

To sacrifice, says Christina, whether it be fasting or some other form of self-denial, we must realize our need to call upon God's strength to help us. We cannot do it alone. We also cannot let our pride limit our effort. This call to sacrifice, besides being beneficial to our soul, is also for the benefit of the souls of others, souls who may be headed for Hell were it not for our sacrifices.

CHAPTER TWENTY-FOUR

One Fold, One Shepherd

I FOR MY PART DECLARE TO YOU, YOU ARE "ROCK," AND ON THIS ROCK I WILL BUILD MY CHURCH, AND THE JAWS OF DEATH SHALL NOT PREVAIL AGAINST IT.

—MATT. 16:18

There is no substitute for the Church and its role in our spiritual lives. This is unequivocal. The Queen of Peace centers almost all of her messages to Christina in some way around this fact. This is not hard to understand. Our relationship with the Church is inseparable from our ability to respond to the Virgin Mary's requests. The Word of God and the sacraments are the food, Our Blessed Mother reminds us, we must eat to have life. The Church is where we find this spiritual nourishment. While the messages, signs, and miracles are designed to bring us closer to God, it is only through the Church this can properly occur.

Likewise, the revelations given to Christina highlight the responsibilities of the Church's priests and bishops to meet our spiritual needs. The Virgin Mary reminds them they are our anointed shepherds. To be effective and provide the total truth, their leadership and instruction must come from the heart. Our Lady says we are dependent upon them, and they must realize the importance of their work. Indeed, this marriage of faith and trust between the flock and its shepherds is one of the Blessed Mother's main objectives. As Mother of the Church, she strives for it. Our Lady wants the Church to be strong and whole.

Throughout her messages to Christina as the Queen of Peace calls her children back to God, the Virgin Mary constantly reminds the priests, her beloved sons, to have nothing else on their minds but our spiritual survival. From world politics to Church politics, everything is secondary to the nurturing of souls. That is their call, nothing else is of equal importance. They are to stay focused. Likewise, the Blessed Mother reminds her children to pray for their shepherds, especially as the Church enters the greatest battle between good and evil the world has ever known.

The Virgin Mary's messages to Christina also touch on many aspects of the Lord's desire to help His people through His Church. From the value of Mass and the Holy Eucharist to the power of prayer, the heavenly messages are direct concerning our need to be part of the Church. Over and over they invite the faithful to return to the Church and the sacraments. Also encouraged are the special devotions such as the Scapular, the Rosary, and the novenas to the saints.

In an enlightenment on December 21, 1992, God allowed Christina to understand more of the mysteries of His Mystical Body:

> This morning I received an enlightenment or knowledge about Jesus and the Virgin Mary. I was conscious of Our Blessed Mother being the Virgin Mary, and Jesus blood of her blood, flesh of her flesh, because it was not through man, but God she conceived Jesus. The veil of the temple was being split. It was split in three states representing the Holy Trinity:
>
> First, at the birth of Jesus; through the Holy Mother being

a virgin, her virginity was split, but to return, as a first sign of Jesus Son of God, the Redeemer coming to bring light and life to a world in the darkness and bondage of sin.

Stage two; the perfect split of the veil of the temple takes place as Jesus on the Cross is redeeming the world.

Stage three; this is complete through the purification which will split the sinful from the good as we are the Mystical Body of Christ. When Jesus returns in glory, sin is destroyed forever.

Our Holy Mother, it was given to me, was Coredeemer, but not Redeemer. Our Holy Mother's part in the redemption was as Coredeemer for the flesh of man. Jesus was the Redeemer for the soul, uniting them as His Mystical Body. Jesus suffers for the souls of mankind through each soul being a member of the Mystical Body.

In this Mystical Body is where we belong. Like the saints have taught, the revelations to Christina call us to decide for God and come back to the teachings of the Church. It's that simple. We must act. During our crucial times, the Lord is calling each of us to His imitation. We must live what the Church teaches and boldly stand behind the Holy Father, His chosen Vicar.

But what about the crisis in the Church and the smoke of Satan of which Pope Paul VI spoke? From her many revelations concerning the Church, Christina now especially prays for the intentions of bishops, cardinals, and the Pope. Indeed, the Queen of Peace calls us to do the same, because the Church is in dire times. Christina has received messages concerning the Lord's dismay over His shepherds. These unpublished messages are said to reflect His anguish over their shortcomings.

Without a doubt, this turmoil is said to have weakened the Church and placed the Holy Father in constant danger. From all indications, it is the further unfolding of Pope Paul VI's prophecy.

Through Christina's messages, there appears to be a coming moment of confusion for the Church. It will be a decisive moment. Apparently, this confusion will also center around the Papacy. Many specific messages allude to this future crisis:

The power of darkness overshadows my Church and the world. (1988)

So many of my sons, priests, and bishops have broken their apostolic seal. (1988)

My Church will be shaken even to its very foundation. (1988)

Pray and sacrifice for those who talk in blasphemy about My Son in the See of Peter. My Son is surrounded by many whose hearts are full of hate and jealousy. (1989)

My child, pray the Lord's Prayer seven times for the protection of Pope John Paul II. He is in many ways of danger. Many of those he leads in the light of My Son do not follow his commands. The Church will be shaken! (1989)

Pray for the Pope every day, for priests and cardinals. (1990)

Each day pray for the Vicar of My Son, Jesus. He begins Calvary with me. (1992)

Pray for Christ's Vicar on earth. He is my chosen one. Never have you received one who like him has given all and lives in grace to fulfill Christ's work on earth. (1992)

He (the Pope) ascends Calvary with me, the Father awaits His sacrifice. (1993)

In late 1992, Christina received two troublesome revelations concerning the Pope and the Church. In one of these she saw the Holy Father as a large figure with a red cape. The Pope had a frightened look on his face as an invisible force tried to tear his cloak from him. Then she saw a pack of dogs behind the Pope in pursuit. Again the Holy Father appeared frightened.

❖

On another occasion, I saw Jesus lash streaks of lightning out through the sky. The thunderbolts sounded like the earth was exploding. People were falling to the ground and screaming with horror. Then Our Blessed Mother appeared before Jesus, and pleaded for her Son to have Mercy on us. I found myself looking at the Vatican in Rome. I was looking at Pope John Paul II sitting in a chair of dark wood with red velvet. He seemed very worried and was staring straight ahead. I saw the Holy Father get up off the chair and walk toward me as if he was looking directly at me, but then he just bypassed me. After that I was drawn to look back at the chair. I was looking at the red velvet and the carved wood of the chair and it looked so beautiful. I didn't have much time to look at it, because the next thing I knew, it was smashed to the ground.

I got such a shock seeing the chair hit the ground and crash. It now looked like an old battered chair. I just thought, how could that have happened? When I looked up, I could see four devils or evil spirits there and I felt very troubled. I felt a great sense of sadness. Then I found myself outside the Vatican. Next I saw long steps outside. I was standing on one of those steps, crying and earnestly inquiring, "Where is the Pope? Where is the Pope?" Then I could see Pope John Paul II; he was looking at his hands. It was as if he had the wounds of Jesus in his hands. There was blood coming from the center of his hands and dripping on the ground. He stood looking at it as if in shock.

Then I was drawn away from the Pope and I saw this round dome, which was the dome of Saint Peter's Basilica. There was black smoke or a black cloud coming from behind the Vatican and it covered the dome quickly. It happened so quickly. I was so distraught about it, and then it was over. Then it seemed as if I was back in Ireland again, but in some place I didn't recognize. I was in a field without grass. Suddenly, I could see the Evil One in a huge form. He was half human and half animal. He had claws and paws and he was clapping them together. "I have won, I have won," he said. He was so confident he won. It was as if I was a leaf. I just trembled to hear his words. "I have won!"

Then I was just looking at the sky again and saying, "Jesus, he can't have won. He can't have won." I didn't want to believe what the Devil was saying. All of a sudden, I could see Jesus again in the sky, with the cross of light in His hand and a dove, and with the Angel of Wrath that I described earlier. The minute I pleaded with Jesus, Jesus then took what looked like a whip or a lash.

Jesus lashed it out and it hit the head and shoulders of the Devil. The Devil just seemed to go instantly paralyzed. He sunk down into the ground. As this happened, the ground began caving in, bigger and bigger and bigger, until the hole was huge. Then the Devil was gone completely and so were the evil spirits who had been behind the Pope's chair. These were the ones who'd thrown the chair and broken it. I saw them all going down into the hole as if there was a magnet drawing them in. They were going in so fast.

I was watching this and asking. "Can they get back out, Dear Lord? Can they get back out?" Then I felt like I was floating over to where the hole was and I looked into it. I could hear these very strange sounds—screams coming from the hole and gradually fading. When I looked into the hole there was fire, but there was no trace of anything or any of the devils that had gone in. All I could see was flames . . . flames of fire. I felt much relieved at seeing this. Then I was aware of my own surroundings and everything again became normal.

⊠

According to the messages of numerous chosen souls, it is possible that there will soon be a schism in the Church and even possibly a false Pope. Perhaps this is also what Christina's messages and revelations are telling us.

⊠

My child, there are many of my children, sons, and daughters in religious life, who serve in the name of God, but the true spirit of God is not in them. They only serve God in mockery. It wounds my heart to see this. The power of darkness overshadows my Church and the world. There are many who have made themselves slaves to darkness, through money and the pleasure of the world. I love all my children. Many of them wound my heart. My love is everlasting in the spirit of God.

My child, the Purification will come. Those who have served God in His light need not fear. Those of my children who will be lost forever cause me great pain. My Son's wounds bleed profusely. My child, pray and make more sacrifices to my Son's Heart. Console my Son in love. Many of my children have become one in darkness. . . .

From all of this Christina understands the overwhelming attacks Satan has made on the priesthood. Repeatedly, she reminds people that the Blessed Mother asks for prayers for priests, bishops, cardinals, and all her consecrated souls. Our Lady says, "The religious are under incomprehensible demonic attack, and because of this we should never judge a priest."

The present spiritual warfare, Our Lady explains, has blinded priests, and it is only through our prayers that light may again shine upon them. "Prayer," the Blessed Mother emphasizes, "enlightens them in the truth and protects them for their responsibilities."

"We must ask God to give them the graces they need. Pray with love and respect your priests. Priests have many temptations and much loneliness. Try to understand. I say to women, please do not be the ticket for the Devil to steal their soul. Be for them the strength and love God desires, to bring them closer to Himself," says Christina.

Since the beginning of her apparitions, many priests have sought out the Irish seer for her advice and help. Often these priests are in the spiritual battle of their lives. The House of Prayer in Ireland is now, especially, a place where, through God's grace, priests can go to rest, pray, and find understanding in their lives, especially their missions.

Armed with a greater understanding of this unfolding spiritual war, Christina pushes forward in her special mission for priests and consecrated souls. Her personal effort, in union with Christ's suffering, in turn contribute to the welfare of the Church. On August 5, 1988, Our Lady assured her: "Your life and that of the other chosen ones is consecrated to all servants of the Holy Church. You will suffer for them, to atone for their unfaithfulness, so that they may gain the grace to raise themselves again and attain fruitfulness in their apostolate. If this is not understood by the servants of the Holy Church and the ministers of God, then nothing can save the world."

In her own words, we learn more about the future welfare of the Church and the Holy Father.

Q. The Pope was wounded in one of your apparitions. Can you tell us about the Holy Father and the Church according to what you have been told? What is going to happen to the Church?

A. The Church, as the Blessed Mother said, will be shaken, even to its very foundation. Our Holy Father is in danger in many different ways. Our Blessed Mother refers to him as being surrounded by a "Red Army of Terror." There are many who follow this command. As Our Holy Mother has said, the Church must be the one true apostolic Church of Jesus Christ. I asked Our Blessed Mother, "Is that the Catholic Church?" The Blessed Mother said, "Yes, those who follow Christ's Vicar." There are those who are no longer loyal to the Pope. There are those in authority whom the Pope leads, but they do not accept the Pope's command. Because of that, there will follow a cleansing of the Church and the world.

Q. How does the power of darkness overshadow the Church? Has Our Lady mentioned this to you? Did she explain this?

A. Yes. The darkness has entered the Church. Our Blessed Mother has said the poison has entered the crack in the rock —meaning, of course, not the Pope, the Holy Father himself, but some of those close to the Holy Father. When Our Lady talks about sin and evil, it is in different forms, but it has entered every part of the world.

Q. What did Our Lady mean when she said the Church would be shaken to its foundation?

A. I didn't know what that meant at the time, but I believe from what I'm told that the foundation is to be shaken at Rome and the Pope will be in danger.

Q. Can you now reveal the message of October 18, 1991? This is the message in which you have only revealed one part. It allegedly regarded priests and bishops.

A. All I can reveal is that it concerns priests and bishops. That's all I can reveal just now.

Q. How would you describe the gift of knowledge that God gives you concerning people, especially priests?

A. When I'm talking to a complete stranger, I am aware of details concerning that person which God wishes me to relate to the person as a sign of His gift, but more important, to help the person. I don't know when it's going to happen or where it's going to happen or to whom. Mostly, it has happened with priests. This particular priest, who was losing his sight, asked me to pray for him and ask Our Blessed Mother to help him. All of a sudden I was aware of things about him. I knew exactly the details of what happened to him. I saw where the Lord led a lady to him in a foreign country. I could see the lady; she was in her fifties. She was dark-skinned and possessed by an evil spirit. Jesus led her there to this particular priest, who was losing his sight, and was meant to help her. When she came to this priest, he became frightened. He said to me, "Christina, when I looked into her eyes, I thought I was looking into the eyes of the Devil." He said, "I thought I'd never get her out of the door fast enough."

He told me this after I had already told him about what his reactions were toward this lady. Then I told him what happened, how God sent this lady to him. I told him she was guided to him by God even with an evil spirit in her. I also told him that it had been up to him to help her and I said, "you didn't." I said, "You showed her the door and when she went out, this is what cost you your sight. She cursed you for not helping her and God permitted the loss of your sight to be part of your purification."

This suffering was permitted to fall on him because he didn't do and submit to God's will. Being a consecrated soul and being a priest, he was in a position not to be afraid of evil. He didn't have to be too brave either, but he should have known what to do. He knew the evil was there. Rather than act and do what God had guided him to do, he sent her away. He wanted nothing to do with it. So God permitted this blindness to befall him, for his own purification. He was blind to God's will when he did not respond by helping her. There's no way I could have known anything, and he didn't indicate anything of this matter to me. If someone wanted evidence of all this from this priest, I could get it for them. He will confirm the truth of this event.

Q. Do you see the sins of others? Even of priests?

A. At another time, in the same way, a priest's sins were shown to me and the sins of another priest that had come to him. I also was shown where he was in his life spiritually and where God wanted him to be. God wanted him to take a different direction in a different way. It's hard to explain that without getting into personal details. That particular priest's testimony would be available, if I asked for it.

Q. You have spoken of experiences in which you were able to see your spiritual director's room and see him doing things, although you had never been to the room or seen it in real life. Can you tell us about these experiences?

A. Yes. I was praying and the next thing I knew, I found myself looking into my spiritual director's room. I could see the desk in his room. I also could see Father and knew what he was thinking. I could see Jesus beside him, and the phone in his room. When I told Father of this experience, he didn't immediately react to explain to me its meaning. He did tell me later that those were his thoughts at the time and that it was his room that I had described but had never seen before. I have since seen the desk and yes, it was correct. Father knew it was true.

Q. What did he say when you said all this to him?

A. "Extraordinary."

Q. Was this a sign or confirmation of your experiences to him?

A. He knew that I hadn't seen what was in his room and that I couldn't know what he was thinking unless I was being shown by God.

Q. What will happen to the Church when the chastisements begin?

A. The Church will be shaken to its foundation, right to Rome. What is happening within the Church today, is that the problems are getting deeper and deeper. The souls that God has called and anointed, and those who have given themselves to God, are finding such a struggle through the darkness of sin in the world. They're finding the struggle greater and greater. But those who are consecrated to Our Blessed Mother will have the strength to struggle to the end—those who are deeply and sincerely faithful.

Q. Have there also been a lot of nuns to see you?

A. Yes, but of late, more and more priests.

Q. Are more and more religious coming, priests and nuns?

A. Yes, and it is very positive. Each time I praise God for that.

Q. Through your intercession with God, I have heard you have been able to help others. Tell us a little about this?

A. Once, my spiritual director gave my phone number to a man with a problem, and I was wishing he hadn't in one sense, because it was a very different situation. This man wanted to commit suicide. He felt he had nothing left. His wife had left him. His home was going to be taken from him and his health had broken down. He was only a young man, I suppose in his thirties. He contacted my spiritual director and Father told him to get in touch with me. He did. The first thing I thought was, "Dear God, what am I going to say to this man? Help me." The next thing I knew, I was more or less quoting Jesus to him. I told him Jesus had nothing on earth and that we are the children of God, and if we trust God, He will take care of us. This was a long, hard, stern conversation. Then I prayed with him for a good while. After praying with him he phoned me again a few weeks later.

He told me, "Christina, I believe everything you've said." He said he felt relief. He now wanted to believe. He told me nothing had changed in his life. His wife hadn't come back, his home hadn't changed—nothing in his life had altered or improved. His health was the same, everything remained the same. But he said that in his inner self his life was totally different. Not even when he was a child did he remember having so much peace. There have been many people like that, who come to me and I pray with them. Later they say, "I've received the most tremendous peace."

Q. I have heard that there have been many miracles. Can you tell us about one?

A. A woman came to me who was very distressed. Her cattle were dying and all their material wealth seemed to be going down the drain. She asked me to say a prayer. I can do nothing, so I just handed them over to God. After that, there was a feeling of great peace. A couple of days later she phoned me. She told me, "Thank the Lord," because the cattle and everything stopped dying. There had been an overwhelming amount of her cattle, sheep, and all sorts of animals that had died, and when I prayed it had all stopped. I don't say that my prayer was of any importance, but through it God must have stopped her troubles. God stopped it, not me. Many healings of cancer and other incurable conditions have been reported, published, and testified to. However, I take no credit for any of these, but I praise Our Merciful Lord and Holy Mother.

CHAPTER TWENTY-FIVE

From Mercy to Justice

LO, THE LORD SHALL COME IN FIRE, HIS CHARIOTS LIKE THE WHIRLWIND, TO WREAK HIS WRATH WITH BURNING HEAT AND HIS PUNISHMENT WITH FIERY FLAMES.

—ISA. 66:15

Christina Gallagher speaks often of God's Mercy. Yet most of us really do not understand the Mercy of God. We really don't know what it is to be merciful.

In Scripture, the word "Mercy" is so identified with God. In understanding Mercy, we come to understand His nature. "Mercy," explains John Paul II, "is the most stupendous attribute of God! It reveals to us what God is like. It is love's second name. The Bible, tradition, and the whole faith life of the People of God provide unique proof . . . that Mercy is the greatest of the attributes and perfections of God" (John Paul II, *Rich in Mercy*).

Sister Faustina agreed, "I understood that the greatest attribute is Love and Mercy. It unites the creature with the Creator. This immense Love and abyss of Mercy are made known in the

Incarnation of the Word and in the Redemption (of humanity), and it is here that I saw this as the greatest of all God's attributes."[1]

Today in the world, " 'Mercy, mercy, mercy,' is the cry that arises from many hearts as we look at the state of the world," says Father George Kosicki, a theologian and expert on God's mercy. "Strife, violence, lust for power, wars, murders, avarice, abortions, drugs, famine, poverty, disasters, and calamities abound."[2]

Indeed, God sees and knows our condition. In revelations to Christina Gallagher, we find a strong appeal to the world to take refuge in God's mercy.

On April 23, 1991, Jesus told her the path to His Mercy must come through His light and love. "It may seem as if you are surrounded by darkness, but I am your Light. I will radiate the path before you. There are many around you who live in the darkness. Be for Me their light and love. I will do all in you. Do not fear, I stand in you. You must always surrender to My will. In that way I can lead you. Reject all that the world offers you. Work only for the salvation of souls. My heart is afflicted by many. My heart is so full of love for all."

Eighteen months later, on November 2, 1992, the Queen of Peace implored all to turn to the Mercy of her Son as the world sank deeper into the night. "Beg Jesus through His Mercy that you be protected from the darkness that overflows around you."

In late 1992, even the Eternal Father, in direct appeal to all mankind, addressed Christina about the Mercy available through His Son and the Virgin Mary. "Come through the Mercy of Jesus, My Son, and by means of His Mother." Christina says, *"The Heart of the Godhead aches for the condition of His children."*

Yet this period of Mercy will eventually end and give way to the period of Justice. For God is also Justice. In September 1992, the Blessed Mother sadly informed Christina of Heaven's disappointment in the world's response to her Son's call to Mercy.

My child, my Heart weeps blood for my children who will not repent and turn away from sin. The sins of greed, pride, and lust lead to obsession and death. There are some of my children who will never see the light of God. The Evil One is deceiving many of my children. My children will not respond to the call of their Mother. I desire to give my children many graces and peace. It is God who sends me to you, to call you, my children, to repentance. I am your Mother and I love you in God for He is love. I come to you by means of the Holy Spirit of God.

The world is in great danger. It is on the brink of its destruction. I am gathering the remnant of the faithful together to help me in this work and plan of God. The remnant of the faithful who respond to my call will have peace, but their cross will be heavy, like my Heart, to pierce the hearts of those who are without the Light of God.

⊠

To help bring back some of those without the Light of God, soon the sword of God's Justice will be drawn. From the powerful experiences given to her, Christina indicates the Angel of Wrath's time draws near. Without a doubt, Christina Gallagher feels God will soon release the Angel to bring fulfillment to the times. Christina says God's Justice is an essential part of His Mercy. As the Lord told Sister Faustina, "My Mercy does not want this, but Justice demands it,"[3] and as Saint Catherine of Siena wrote of God's Justice in *The Dialogue,* "Neither civil law, nor the divine law, can be kept in any degree without holy Justice, because he who is not corrected, and does not correct others, becomes like a limb which putrefies and corrupts the whole body."

Today, it is no secret the Justice of God appears to be approaching. There would be no urgency and no limit to the period of Mercy if God's Justice was not approaching.

This is evident in the messages to Christina. The Virgin Mary's warnings announce the times are grave and short. In many messages to her, urgency as a theme prevails, almost like a train whistle heard above the cry of its turning wheels.

But has the time of Justice arrived? On November 13, 1990, the Lord admonished Christina that time was dwindling.

Tell all humanity to pray for the Spirit of Truth, the Spirit of Love. They are the one Spirit of Life Eternal. Many pray, but live in the world and by the world. They adore all of its fruits. Oh, but the day is coming faster than light, when My mighty hand will crush all the world. My daughter, you are little in the world. You are rejected by the world. Know that through this, you appease my anger. You see with the eyes of the Spirit of Truth and Love, that is why you suffer. Through it, you appease My Wrath.

Today, offer me My Divine Son, through His wounds and Sacrifice, that the world will prepare and make itself ready for the Second Coming of Jesus. As it is now, they prepare for the forthcoming of the Antichrist. Those who now live in the fruits of the world and worship thus will receive of its fruits. They will drink of its bitter cup, and become followers of him-who-destroys. Tell all to prepare themselves. Make a place in their hearts only for Me, their Lord God, Who desires to save. The battle is on. Many souls are being lost. Go in peace. Father, Son, and Holy Spirit.

Two years later on November 2, 1992, the Queen of Peace declared to Christina tough times are at hand. The times of trial, tribulation, treason, and eventually, Triumph.

My dear children, My maternal Heart is given to you for bloodshed. Your hearts are closed to me. *The betrayal of Judas through you is at hand.* There are many who are Judas. There are many among you who speak not of the Spirit of God, but of the spirit of the deceiver. . . .

My children, the laws of God are despised. Those who

deny the laws of Christ, deny Christ. The Evil One is trying to destroy my plan for Ireland and the world. In many parts of the world, its children follow deception and will be lost forever. It is you little ones who will help me bring about the Triumph of my Immaculate Heart. That is why you suffer much deception, misunderstanding, and pressure. With me, your Blessed Mother, and the weapons I offer you, we will be triumphant together. Surrender everything, even your life. Pray, pray, pray, so that you will receive grace to withstand the times of battle that are coming. Many of my children in Ireland have abandoned the sacraments and the Commandments of God. Many of the shepherds of God who lead my children have abandoned the flock. The Lord's flock is scattered. They roam about lost in the dense darkness. Love is being removed from the hearts of my children. The Martyrs cry out to God, "Put an end to this before the world is infected with evil." My Son, Jesus, and I offer our hearts to the Father in place of your hearts. That is why I cry tears of blood for love of you.

My dear child, I invite you to be little in heart. Help my children who seek your help and prayers. In responding to my children you are responding to me and, with me, responding to God. Let your heart be open to receive the graces I desire to give you. Many of my children pierce my heart each day. My children in religious life wound my heart and the heart of my Son, Jesus. My Son's hand is getting heavy, weighted down by sin. I can no longer withhold His hand. When I can no longer sustain my Son's hand, then it will fall on my children in Justice. The world fumigates the smoke of Satan. He is playing with the souls of my children, like a child plays with toys. Many of my children choose to remain blind. Look, child, see the blood of my Son's Heart. It bleeds profusely. Look at my maternal heart. It bleeds profusely in union with the Heart of my Son, Jesus. We call our children. We preach our message throughout the world.

My dear children, many are in darkness and merry in murder and bloodshed. Sin in the world is multiplying. My children who were strong in faith and prayer grow weak and dim of heart. There is much prayer and sacrifice needed to overcome the darkness of sin. Darkness and temptation are around you, my children. I plead with you, arm yourself with my Rosary, live the Ten Commandments God has given you. Each day pray for the Vicar of my Son, Jesus, . . . he begins Calvary with me. My children, I invite you, each morning, make the sign of the cross with Holy Water. Beg Jesus through His Mercy that you be protected from the darkness that overflows around you. The battle of principalities rages.

What a place the world has become! By late 1993, dozens of wars were being waged throughout the world, and the violence was growing. Likewise, since 1989, there has been an unprecedented outbreak of massive disturbances in nature. Hurricanes, floods, tidal waves, tornadoes, earthquakes, typhoons, fires, and droughts have slammed the world, and experts say more is on the way.

The Virgin Mary's and Jesus' messages to Christina indicated the same. On January 30, 1991, Jesus confided to Christina a moment of decision is approaching:

My little one, tonight I invite you to write. Be not afraid. My peace I freely give you. Tell all humanity to prepare themselves. The time has come for the cleansing of all humanity. A great darkness will come upon the world. The heavens will shake. The only light will be through the Son of God and of Man. The lightning bolts will flash like nothing the world has ever seen. My hand will come over the world more swiftly than the wind. Be not afraid.

Many tried to make you stumble. I tell you, My little one,

always unite yourself with Me, your Lord and Redeemer. I am your Shield. Through your love, offering, and tears, I tell you I have set free many souls who were bound in the slavery of sin and evil. Yes, you are nothing, but the work you permit Me to do through you is beyond your comprehending.

Tell my son and brother . . . be not afraid of My words to you, My little one. My words will come to pass. Each day I bless your work. The Light of My Sacred Heart will fill you in the days that are to come. Each day I work through you in the Light of the Holy Spirit. I flow through you.

The battle between Light and Darkness is great. I thirst for the little souls who will abandon themselves to Me. I thirst for the souls out of love. The demons rage upon the earth. They are loosed from their pit. Tell all humanity of the Seven Seals of God! Tell all humanity! Pray! Confess! Seek you only the Kingdom of God. I will bless you, My little one.

While minor purification is one way God's Justice can be served, the Lord is not limited. On July 8, 1992, Christina received a message from Jesus and witnessed an apparition of perhaps more of the coming of God's Wrath, a wrath that could also strike like lightning.

"Oh you sinful people of this generation. Now I destroy all of you who have abandoned Me." Upon this utterance, suddenly Jesus appeared in the sky with His right hand raised and His palm facing forward. The Lord approached Christina with great speed. Suddenly, she saw big buildings crumble, topple, and disappear into a chasm. Then she saw a flash of exploding light. As the Lord approached another area, she saw a woman clutching a child while crying, "Save us! Save us for the sake of the children!"

Then Christina saw a landslide, taking trees and everything with it. "Pray for this sinful generation," Jesus told her, as the frightening apparition faded.

Three days later on July 11, 1992, on a balcony overlooking the city of Los Angeles, Christina had another experience. She was alone that evening as Jesus appeared. "Welcome back to My sanctuary," He said. Speaking of Los Angeles, He disclosed, "The sins committed here are beyond your comprehending."

Later that evening, the Lord again appeared to Christina in the sky and beckoned her to the end of the balcony. He was dressed in white with a cincture around His waist. He extended an invitation to her, "Come walk with Me." She did not fully understand His meaning. After this, He came close to her and touched her face with His fingers. When He came close, says Christina, He seemed sad but not angry. When He went back into the sky He became firm. To His left appeared the Angel of Wrath, dressed in red, holding a sword. Beneath the angel was a dark cloud that rested over the city.

Instinctively, Christina pleaded with Jesus to stop the angel. For she somehow intuitively sensed his mission. With this, the angel retreated. Then Jesus invited Christina to read a large book which He held open in His hand. Although the print was legible she refused to read it. She trembled before the book. She later said she couldn't look at it. Then above and to her left, the Virgin Mary and Saint Catherine appeared. Although she appealed to them for intervention, they failed to respond. Christina understood the time of Our Blessed Mother's call to repentance would be giving way to God's Justice.

Suddenly, flashes of lightning came from the cloud beneath the Angel of Wrath and the city below was covered with blood.

After this, angels appeared and hovered over the city. Curiously, these angels were not sad, nor disturbed over what had occurred. Like the Virgin Mary and Saint Catherine, they seemed to understand God's will for this city.

Although this entire happening lasted only fifteen minutes, it left Christina shaken. For days, shock and horror filled her. Later her spiritual director concluded it must have been the Book of Life contained in The Apocalypse, which Jesus wanted to show her as justification for His actions on the city. "The Book of Life, we know from Scripture," said Father McGinnity, "contains the sins of the world." Anyone whose name is not written in the Book of Life will not be saved.

To some, this apparition is disturbing. But to those who know Scripture and God's love for His people, it is consistent. Sin is the culprit, not God's Justice. Christina says that God does not inflict pain, but our sins allow sufferings to happen. Sin has its consequences. God acts, but never before He exhausts His Mercy. On March 12, 1993, Our Lady again reminded her of this reality, "The Justice of God awaits those who do not want to respond. Pray for them with Me your mother."

All indications dictate that mankind is approaching the end of God's era of Mercy. And here lies the delicate and confusing matter. Does God's Mercy ever end? If God is a God of love, how could He do terrible things to us? How could He allow chastisements to strike us?

On March 23, 1993, the Queen of Peace tearfully explained to Christina a little of this mystery and confirmed God's Justice would now come.

> God has permitted this time of my call with love, in His Mercy for you, to receive His Holy Mercy, before entering into Justice, the Holy Justice of your God.
>
> My children, you must now choose to live the messages I call you to or remain in silence and laziness, or scoff at my messengers.
>
> My children, hear my words to you! Those of you whose desire is to live by the world, will die by the world. For those of you, my children, who choose not to change your ways and turn away from sin, I tell you, you will have to go through the Justice of God.
>
> My children, if you were to understand a little of the meaning of the Holy Justice of God, you would die of shock. For those of you who do not desire God's Mercy will go through His Justice.
>
> My children, it is sin that is drawing God's Justice.

My dear children, if only you could realize the greatness of God's Love, Grace, and Mercy. He desires to give you the value and greatness of the call of your Mother.

My children, my tears are many, my tears I have shed throughout the world for love of you. You are my children and I must tell you the cup is overflowing and is about to be poured out upon you. You will cry bitterly for refusing to respond to the message of your mother's heart. My Heart is in union with the Heart of my beloved Son, Jesus.

In the Old Testament the Jews were brought into the land of Israel on a promise by Yahweh. While on this journey they traveled under the Shekinah Glory, which was God's physical presence among His people—a cloud by day and a fire by night. What should have been a very short journey took forty years because of their sinfulness.

From the beginning, man has been given a free will to do as he chooses. God has never forced His will upon us, nor did He force His will upon the Israelites. When they chose not to obey, God withdrew His protective graces, and they were left to their own devices. The result was chaos.

As Scripture tells us, "It has been your sins which have separated you from God." (Is. 59:2) From sin, the mantle of God's covering became absent. Thus, calamity often struck in the desert as a result of disobedience to God. The Israelites thought they knew a better way and ignored every opportunity to repent.

Our world is no different today, which is why God sends His Mother. This is the greatest sign of His Mercy. In Our Lady, we find the greatest advocate of God's Mercy the world will ever know.

As the Blessed Mother told Sister Faustina, "I am not only the Queen of Heaven, but also the Mother of Mercy and your mother . . . I am the Mother of you all, thanks to the unfathomable Mercy of God."[4]

Our Lady also told Christina that our mothers are the mothers of our flesh through the gift of God and she is Mother of all of our souls. Christina tells us, "If all mothers were to unite their prayers for their children to the prayers of the Blessed Mother, then their prayers would be raised in union with her prayers through the heart of her Son, Jesus, to gain the grace and enlightenment of the Eternal Father."

In her own words, Christina explains more of what she learned of God's Grace, Mercy, and Justice:

Q. Christina, are we living in a special period of grace right now?

A. We are living in a time of grace, but also a time of great darkness. Because of the darkness, the hearts of people are closed to the graces. There are an awful lot of people with their hearts closed. It's not that God does not want to give the grace. It's because our hearts are closed and we don't even know how to receive the graces being given to us. That's why prayer from the heart, for those who do not pray, is so important.

Q. You have said that sin is the reason for all disaster, illness, and suffering.

A. Yes.

Q. Many today do not even believe in sin. Can you tell us what you know about sin?

A. Sin is the cause of all the disaster, illness, and suffering. Sin is what draws down these things upon mankind. How do I describe this? Because of sin, we're all in this disaster and God permits it. In other words, God permits the Devil and the sin that causes all the suffering to fall on His people. He allows it, not because He wants to, but He uses it as a source of purification.

Q. What does sin bring upon us?

A. Oftentimes, there's great suffering. People sin in so many different ways, shapes, and forms. They cannot help but see, no matter how blind they are, the reality of sin through the suffering.

Q. What can we do about this suffering?

A. We must turn to the sacraments, prayer, fasting, and sacrifices. That is what Our Blessed Mother is asking of us.

Q. You have said that by the end of the twentieth century, all will be fulfilled. What does this mean?

A. From what Our Holy Mother has said, I have been led to believe that by the year 2000 or before all will be fulfilled.

Q. Have you been told about secrets like other chosen souls at Garabandal, Medjugorje, and Fatima?

A. No, I wouldn't call them secrets. Sometimes you cannot talk about things because it isn't the right time, and private things about the Church are revealed. The important thing is to pray.

Q. What should Protestants do, who do not recognize the role of the Virgin Mary or her apparitions, especially since most of them are not receiving the Blessed Mother's messages of conversion directly?

A. It's like any religion. They've first got to recognize there is a God and pray to Him with love.

Q. Our Lady says there are dreadful times ahead in battle. What is she talking about?

A. The battle between good and evil.

Q. Is this battle raging now and will it become more intense?

A. Yes.

Q. Has Our Lady spoken any more about this battle?

A. No.

Q. Do you think there is any importance to these messages from Jesus and the Blessed Mother that goes beyond our human comprehension?

A. Yes, Our Blessed Mother refers to them as being "urgent."

Q. Our Lady says that those who carry out her messages have nothing to fear. What does this mean?

A. Those who heed and live Our Lady's messages have nothing to fear.

Q. Does this mean we will be spared the chastisement or does this mean we will be saved and go to Heaven?

A. The chastisement will come and those who are lost will be lost in the chastisement. But those, Our Lady said, who have turned back to God have nothing to fear.

Q. Did Our Lady say those who convert now will have it easier during the chastisements? Will they have less suffering?

A. A lot of people are going to find it hard to convert and remain converted. Those who have turned back to God, Our Lady said, have nothing to fear. Our Holy Mother has said there is a lot of sin in the world. Where hearts are open we need to help those who are now involved in every kind of bad situation. The Devil is tempting the flesh more and more. In one of Our Lady's messages, I think she said, "It is the sins of the flesh that draw many to Hell." More and more, I am becoming aware of all of this sin around me. We are hearing about it here, there, and everywhere, and even of babies being sexually abused. Recently it happened that Our Lady made me more aware of this horror. It was like a knife going through my heart. I don't know . . . how someone could do these things. I just say, "Please Lord, help them . . . because they can't know what they're doing. Surely, they wouldn't do this if they knew what they were doing."

Q. There are millions of people on the earth who are not Christians. What do Our Lady and Our Lord want of them? Have Our Lady and Our Lord ever spoken of them?

A. Our Lady has never referred to any particular religion. Our Blessed Mother says all people belong to God and Our Lady has said she respects people of all religions. Our Blessed Mother doesn't condemn any particular religion. Before anybody can say that they are Catholic, Protestant, or Jew, or any other religion, they first have to love God. They first have to have this love in their hearts for God and an awareness of believing in God. They can be any religion or no religion. But they must believe in God, and by believing in God you must talk to Him in prayer. If you don't do that you are totally opposed to God, which is anti-God or antichrist. Most people, I think, if they're anti-God, know it and are aware of it. So I think it's not so much what religion as it is what kind of person they are in their particular religion, if you know what I mean.

Q. Have Our Lady or Our Lord ever spoken to you about the Three Days of Darkness?

A. No. I've never received anything about the Three Days of Darkness, but yes, I have gotten a message regarding the "time of darkness," which will come upon the world. That's in the messages. But they have not spoken about Three Days of Darkness in particular, only that a darkness would come upon the world and the light of the world would be Christ.

Q. There are some prophecies that say three-fourths of the earth's population will be lost during the chastisement. Have you heard anything like this or have you had any messages like this?

A. No. The Blessed Mother just said many will be lost for their sins of the flesh and of the world.

Q. Has Our Lady spoken to you about other visionaries in the world?

A. Yes, about a number of visionaries. In recent times, Our Blessed Mother has warned me of false prophets. Our Lady has asked me to remain by myself. This way, I would not be drawn into connection with people who were not telling the truth. They were false prophets.

Q. How do we know which ones are false?

A. Our Holy Mother said that the way to recognize this is when we see those who want and seek popularity or money, they are not true instruments of God. Also, anything that is in contradiction with Holy Scripture. The false prophets force their way in a sensational way.

Q. Did Our Lady reveal names to you of false prophets?

A. Yes, I was given awareness of quite a number of whom I was very surprised, some of whom I actually thought were genuine. I never like to see the negative in anyone. Then I thought that some of those, who perhaps did not have apparitions, had an inner experience of some sort. However, through a recent experience, God permitted me to know any such claims by these people were false.

Q. Were any of the false visionaries from America?

A. God's desire for me was to pray for them and not judge them. It is not my function to comment on any of those given to me.

I just pray for them and remain apart from anyone authentic or otherwise.

Q. In the November 2, 1992, message, you talked about betrayal.

A. There are many Judases around now. There have been many betrayers since him. We all betray Jesus constantly through one another in our weakness.

CHAPTER TWENTY-SIX

The Matrix Medal, the House of Prayer, and the Prophet Elijah

I WILL LAVISH CHOICE PORTIONS UPON THE PRIESTS, AND MY PEOPLE SHALL BE FILLED WITH MY BLESSINGS, SAYS THE LORD.

—JER. 31:14

God is generous. In His generosity, He is always sending us gifts through the Virgin Mary, gifts that have special blessings for His children. These spiritual gifts include medals with powerful graces, hidden springs where the sick, through faith, find waters that heal; special instructions for new chapels, houses of prayer, churches, and even basilicas; all of which, when used by the faithful, spiritually and physically heal and enrich their lives. Probably the most well known of these gifts was the spring at Lourdes in 1858 and the Miraculous Medal Our Lady requested of Saint Catherine Labouré at Paris in 1830.

In Ireland it has been no different. In March 1988, the Queen of Peace requested of Christina Gallagher that a medal be struck. Our Lady said this medal was to be called the *Matrix Medal*. On one side, this medal depicts The Cross with Our Lady on her knees before it, with her arms and hands extended, pleading for her children.

On the other side are the two hearts of Jesus and Our Blessed Mother, weeping blood. As a request by her spiritual director, Christina inquired why the medal was to be called the Matrix Medal and Our Lady replied, "Simply call it 'THE MATRIX'; My Son wishes to mold." This made sense, for God has always spoken of molding souls.

By definition, to mold means to shape, to shape us anew. In Scripture (Rom. 8:29), Saint Paul says God destined us to be molded into the Image of His Son. Therefore, God's plan is to restore His Divine Image in us, which was distorted by sin. Jesus then places us in a new mold which is His mother. Christina says the Blessed Mother fosters her Son's life in each of us. Afterward, Our Lady protects that Divine Life within us.

According to Father McGinnity, "This medal, therefore, is for protection. Protection against sin and Satan's attacks. Sometimes reshaping, remolding is painful and awkward. It's done with a cross, but always out of love. God frequently uses suffering to reshape us. Because He is a God of love—He is Love itself. He always acts from love, even when He corrects or chastises His children. That's why Our Blessed Mother obtains the grace of conversion through the merits of her Son's cross. That's why Our Lady pleads in front of it every day for sinners and invites us to assist her work through fasting and prayer." Christina says, "Our Lady desires that her children *wear the Matrix Medal and the Brown Scapular.*"

Since 1988, over 1 million of these Matrix Medals have been distributed throughout the world. Requests are endless and God has kept up with His promises. Countless letters attributing special graces, blessings, and healings have been received. Over and over, those who wear the Matrix Medal write informing Christina of their personal miracles.

Not surprisingly, several reports of cures have emerged. From mysterious healings of bone fractures, leg ulcers, and migraine headaches to the sudden vanishing of rheumatoid arthritis and cancer, the Matrix Medal is repeatedly cited as the means used by God for these miracles.

A pregnant woman, enduring a long, painful labor, attributed a quick, happy resolution to the ordeal after someone placed the medal in her hands. One grief-stricken mother, who prayed for fifteen years for her son's deliverance from alcohol and drug dependency, reported that within one week of "asking her son to wear it, or at least carry it in his wallet," he entered an alcoholic program and turned his life around. Another woman, with cancer of the bladder and extremely jaundiced from the ravages of the disease, reported that when the surgeons opened her, "no cancer was present," and suddenly her "skin color was perfect." A little boy, on life support and given no hope, was healed when his mother attached a Matrix Medal to a photograph of him.

The healings of souls has been no less. Many spiritual conversions have been reported. A man wrote to tell Christina that after wearing the Matrix Medal he went from a nominal Catholic to a "devout believer in Jesus Christ." Another man said he went to confession for the first time in thirty years. His daughter, two hundred miles away, reconciled after an absence of fifteen years. One family, torn apart by scandal, separation, and numerous legal and financial problems, reported a miracle healing of all their difficulties after receiving the Matrix Medal. In a special sign of the medal's power, one young boy from Dublin, healed from a terrible suffering, reported his Matrix Medal wept blood.

As months go by, more and more stories of conversion and healing arrive. Responding to it all, Christina says Our Lady is very happy to help answer the prayers of her children. The Blessed Mother told her, "Healings bring glory to God." Indeed, Father McGinnity reports one story that did just that:

> A pilgrim to Our Lady's House of Prayer in summer 1993 acquired Matrix Medals for her family connection. A few months later a nephew, who had received one, tragically committed suicide. Needless to say his relations were shattered. Christina was thinking about the pathetic situation and feeling such a horror at the notion of suicide that she did not

wish to even ask Our Blessed Mother about the young man's soul, but Our Lady then spoke to her. Our Blessed Mother asked Christina to tell the young man's aunt that he was in a higher level of Purgatory. Our Holy Mother added he would have been damned, but "because of her Matrix Medal God had permitted her to inspire him to say the words necessary to enter the Kingdom of God just before he died."

A few weeks later, just as the Midnight Mass on Christmas Eve was about to commence, Our Holy Mother while speaking to Christina said that if the young man's soul were offered in that Holy Mass he would be released into Heaven. During that Mass Christina witnessed a good number of souls, the first of whom was this same young man, being received by Our Blessed Lady into the blinding Light of Glory.

Christina was delighted by one healing. As she expressed her gratitude and joy to Our Lady she was told, "I have given many signs and you (my children) have not noticed them." The Virgin Mary's response was a confirmation that many were being touched by God through the graces of this apparition but not acknowledging it. That includes many more than just those who have met or heard of Christina Gallagher.

The Matrix Medal is available through
Our Lady Queen of Peace House of Prayer
Achill Sound, Achill
County Mayo
Republic of Ireland

The Matrix Medal is not the only gift God gives His children through Christina. The Queen of Peace also asked that a House of Prayer be opened.

In Ireland, Our Lady Queen of Peace House of Prayer was officially opened on Friday, July 16, 1993, the Feast of Our Lady of Mount Carmel, at Achill Sound, Achill, County Mayo, Republic of Ireland, by Archbishop Joseph Cassidy. This is approximately fifty-seven miles from Christina's home in Gortnadreha.

The Queen of Peace requested this House of Prayer be especially used for the recitation of the Rosary, Eucharistic Adoration, and as a sanctuary or retreat house for priests. At the Blessed Mother's request, Christina is to be there and pray the Rosary the way the Virgin Mary instructed her, with pilgrims and priests. The House is open on a daily basis with Mass at 11:00 A.M. when a priest is in residence, and the exposition of the Blessed Sacrament is daily from 10:00 A.M. until 9:00 P.M. On occasion there are night vigils at the request of groups of pilgrims. Our Lady recently said to Christina, "If people only knew the amount of graces received from even a single visit." Our Blessed Mother also told Christina that if anyone helped with her little House or Prayer, even in the smallest way, she would reward them abundantly. The Rosary is recited along with prayers and devotions daily while confessions are heard when priests are available.

Primarily, the House of Prayer in Ireland promises to be a sanctuary where God will help those who come to pray, especially priests. The Queen of Peace's references to her plan for Ireland appear to involve this House of Prayer. On August 22, 1991, Our Lady gave a special message concerning this plan.

"I am your Maternal Mother and I desire my chosen Children of Light to be united with me in prayer from your heart. You are my dear children of peace and love. Through you, my little ones, I desire great work for the salvation of the world. You little ones of the Lamb will be triumphant in my Immaculate Heart."

The Virgin Mary then told Christina:

I desire to gather my children together. You, my child, pray the Rosary with my children, as I have taught you. I entrust you with this. Do not be afraid, there is no place for fear. I will be present in this house with many angels, praying with all my children. There is to be love, no disunity. I will disperse darkness and surround you with light. Yet my children must be alert. Be pure in heart, and love one another and pray my beautiful Rosary with love from your heart. . . .

My child, look at my many priest sons who are living in such darkness. Will you help me? I desire to bring them into the light of salvation. My child, you must pray, pray, pray. That way, I can draw you into the grace of my Immaculate Heart.

❖

Shortly after this, a man who had frequently, but indecisively, spoken about helping with Our Lady's House of Prayer called to discern if he should help with the House of Prayer and if it was to be for priests. When Christina inquired, Our Lady replied, "My child, do you not understand? All my children who call on you are sent through my invitation and my maternal grace. You, my child, speak only as my Son, Jesus, desires." Our Blessed Mother has requested that the names of all who help, no matter how little, with her little House of Prayer be kept in a book at the House of Prayer.

As time passed Christina was given different experiences concerning the House of Prayer.

❖

I was shown the House and in different scenes; I saw evil being cast from the island. I was shown some of the things that would take place there. I also saw darkness coming as in what people might call the three days of darkness, but I wasn't told at any point it was three dark days. I was told that a darkness would come upon the world. The only light will be through the Son of God. In one particular apparition, I saw the House of Prayer with many, many people surrounding the House. The Holy Eucharist appeared above the wall outside the House of Prayer.

It was close to where we were. I could see, in the very center of the Holy Eucharist, a trickle of blood. As soon as this appeared instantly everything went totally dark. As it went dark, I could still look through the darkness. Then I saw many souls coming from many places. They were souls from Purgatory. They were all going into the Holy Eucharist, into the Light of God.

The souls on this occasion looked gray—nearly human form, but in some ways you could look through them because they still weren't exactly human. I saw their hair, face, and clothes. They looked like transparent gray figures. They were like statues frozen in a kneeling position. They were pleading, with hands joined together, as if praying and begging. There were many souls coming from all directions. They came from the rocks and the sea. They were all going toward where the Holy Eucharist was. I could see this as I was looking through the darkness.

They were floating toward the Holy Eucharist. For some reason, the souls were pleading with Jesus in the Holy Eucharist. The Holy Eucharist was above us but not in the sky. It was above where the crowd was at the House of Prayer. It must be some kind of sign that will be given to the people at a particular time. It must be a sign drawn close to the chastisement.

Father McGinnity describes another apparition that Christina received in 1993 concerning the House of Prayer and how it is to be a place of refuge during the times of chastisement. This time, Christina was shown the prophet Elijah and a striking scene from the Old Testament that has meaning for us today.

Christina, since the opening of the House of Prayer, which, of course, happened on the Feast of Our Lady of Mount Carmel, was shown the scene of Elijah's Triumph over the false prophets at Mount Carmel in Israel at the time of King Achab and Queen Jezebel. Christina, who has no familiarity with the Books of Kings in the Old Testament, saw in this apparition of Elijah the soil being scooped out with a crude trowellike instrument and then filled up with water to surround Elijah's altar; she was conscious of the great threats on Elijah's life, even the hatred of Jezebel and, indeed, the preparation of a gallows on which to kill him. Then she saw the fire in a swift instant come down and consume the sacrifice.

At the same time, Christina was given a consciousness of the message already given in relation to the House of Prayer of the waters around the island (of Achill) having been blessed and of the promise that evil would be cast from the island, and that the House there would be a refuge in the time of Chastisement.

Christina was also conscious that the water in the trench when Elijah proved victorious over the false prophets was God's means of protection to exclude evil, and so for the time of purification the waters blessed around the island would safeguard this place of refuge (The House of Prayer).

The false prophets opposing Elijah were misleading the people with their false assurances that everything was rosy in the garden while Elijah conveyed a message of penance and the need to change and repent. . . .

All of this related so powerfully with Our Lady's request, just after the opening of her house, that her children be blessed and enrolled in her Brown Scapular.

Just as the Queen of Peace and Jesus foretold, the House of Prayer is today a special place where Christina and priests, as well as laypeople, gather to pray and adore God. Through prayer, she understands her spiritual calling to help priests will be enhanced by the House of Prayer, especially during the upcoming trials.

It is also evident from her messages that the spiritual benefits from this House of Prayer will affect Ireland and the whole world. The Queen of Peace promised Christina that she will always be present, along with her angels, who will constantly intercede for the intentions of the people.

The actual building was a former convent that the Queen of Peace said God had chosen. It was purchased through the help of donors. According to Father McGinnity, donations are still needed to expand the facilities and for the upkeep of the House.

On June 29, 1993, the statute of the Angel of Ireland for the House of Prayer was blessed during Mass. Before the consecration of the Mass, Christina saw a light grow more and more intense until, between the consecration and communion, it formed a great ball of light that came toward her and struck her, especially her head. Although stunned, she mustered strength to get up for Holy Communion but felt entirely exhausted. She later saw the Angel of Ireland, who conveyed to her a feeling of great power similar to that of Blessed Michael. She was then told that the people were to pray to the Angel of Ireland.

In October of 1992, Jesus confirmed to Christina it was He who desired the House of Prayer for the coming battle. The Lord said,

> The godless men multiply in number. They fight against My might. Thou hast seen the might of My hand to put to flight the godless man. Thou art My little one, safely guarded in My hand. The godless who try to strike you down, I will strike down beneath My foot, for it is I, your Lord, who has deigned you to act for Me in the manner you effect. Thou art My little one of My heart. Do not fear and do not cry. Proclaim My words to all people, to the godless as to the godly. Those who hear your call will hear but My Words. Many will try to find fault with you. Have no fear, for I am with you.
>
> You will see great progress of the godless. They will grow faster than wild weed. There is sin on every side you turn your head. I will show thee the might of My arm. I will strike cities that despise Me. I have shown to you that godless sinful pit . . .
>
> . . . leading to many parts. I tell you. I tell you I will destroy the sinful godless who dwell there. You will hear of

wars, disasters, and yet the godless grow. They have filtered into the cracks in the Rock, their venom full of poison.

It was I who desired a house for prayer. My words have been spoken through the heart of thy Mother, for she calls her children, but they do not hear. Thou, My little one, take heed. This house will be a refuge for the remnant who hear and follow the cries of My Mother's Heart. You be steadfast in My call, for those who hear the cries of My Mother's Heart will come to you. Make available your time in life and pray with them.

Jesus also gave Christina a wonderful experience, which revealed that, indeed, His coming victory would be furthered by the House of Prayer. Her spiritual director explains:

"While praying before the Blessed Sacrament just before the purchase of the former convent as the House of Prayer, and while 'offering all to the Heart of Jesus,' Christina could see Jesus in a younger than usual appearance on a White Horse moving forward, His hair blowing in the wind. He seemed solemn but victorious and giving great peace, holding something like a flag, part of which was red. According to Christina, Jesus wore red and was surrounded by a lot of light."

Father continues,

After the deal was concluded and while traveling home, Christina could see Jesus again in the uncustomary position of being on the White Horse. Then she could see Holy Souls reaching up from a cloud of mist, bobbing up and down, eager to be released from Purgatory before the coming event signified by Jesus Triumphant Warrior on the White Horse —almost with an urgency equivalent to that of souls on earth needing to be saved.

Christina goes on to say, "While the White Horse was visible, devils were also visible. Jesus looked upward and four huge angels (with transparent faces, huge red wings, very authoritative in appearance) appeared as if summoned at Jesus' request by the Father. Then the demons below the horse fell and disappeared. After this, the four angels went in the shape of a cross—North, South, East, and West. Then Jesus raised a sword upward and fire appeared swirling throughout the sky, becoming more and more widespread."

Christina could then see Our Lady at a distance wearing a white gown and loose blue shawl. Our Lady's hair was blowing in the breeze. Our Holy Mother was weeping but explained to Christina "these were tears of joy." Our Lady told her, "Many souls will be released from Purgatory on this day of the opening of the House of Prayer. If only you could comprehend the enormous victory of this day [referring to the House of Prayer]." Our Holy Mother's heartbeat within her body could be seen and exploded from her chest in white light, flowing to her hands and from her hands downward (to the House of Prayer).

On July 16, 1993, Archbishop Joseph Cassidy of Tuam, who officially granted permission one year before to Christina for the project, blessed and dedicated the new House of Prayer to Our Lady Queen of Peace. The Archbishop thanked Christina and prayed God's blessing on her and her family and the House of Prayer.

Quoting G. K. Chesterton, the English convert to Catholicism, Archbishop Cassidy said he shared in Chesterton's devotion to the Virgin Mary. "I share his love for the Blessed Mother, his faith, and his conviction as I know all of you do, and so let these beautiful lines be our common tribute to Our Lady as our advocate as we dedicate this house to Our Lady Queen of Peace." The Archbishop prayed, "May this House of Prayer be always at the heart of the Church. May it give glory to God and honor to Mary the Mother of God. May many a troubled soul find peace here and many a tired soul be revived."

On Friday, September 10, 1993, Christina received a very special message from the Queen of Peace concerning God's plan for the House of Prayer. Our Lady told her: "Pray that the plan God desires for the House of Prayer will be accomplished."

Christina then asked, "Holy Mother, what is the plan of God for The House?" The Queen of Peace replied,

My child, it is so great, if you were to know its depths your heart would burst, for you would not be able to comprehend its greatness and the wonder of God's goodness to you, little soul.

My child, let your every moment be united in prayer. Offer in prayer all your trials and sacrifices to God for poor sinners, for many hearts will be healed through the works at my little House of Prayer. Pray, pray, pray that God's plans will prevail, for God desires to save many souls through its fruits. Offer your every work and prayer to God for God's priests, bishops, cardinals, and nuns—all the religious. The deceiver is destroying the hearts of many of my children. There is more evil in the world today than at any time in the world's history. Mankind is multiplying evil through sin . . . sins beyond that of animals' behavior. My child, you do not understand why you are suffering and tormented. It is best you do not understand, for God draws many souls to Light and Mercy through your trials and suffering. . . . God saves many souls; even those who were lost permanently. Mercy is granted. Your cross will get heavy. It can become light through your offering in love. Pray for Christ's Vicar. He Ascends Calvary with me. God is awaiting his Sacrifice. The Church will have great pain. Pray, pray for poor sinners.

Several months later, on Christmas Eve, the Queen of Peace told Christina that those present at the Mass had gained, by their effort to be there, "the same as the shepherds on the first Christmas

Night." When Christina inquired of Our Lady what that was, she was told, "The same as the good thief gained on the cross."

Thus, Christina has begun her mission through Our Lady Queen of Peace House of Prayer. People from all over the world now come to the new House of Prayer in Ireland. Together the Virgin Mary's children of light, through prayer and good works, respond to the call of their Heavenly Mother. It is the response to the grace of God that continues to pour out of County Mayo to the whole world as many heed the words of the Virgin Mary, "I am your mother, I am leading you to perfection, to be ready to meet my Son, your dear Lord."

CHAPTER TWENTY-SEVEN

"My Beloved Children of Ireland"

PRAISE THE LORD, ALL YOU NATIONS; GLORIFY HIM, ALL YOU PEOPLES! FOR STEADFAST IS HIS KINDNESS TOWARD US, AND THE FIDELITY OF THE LORD ENDURES FOREVER.

—Ps. 117:1–2

Why God has chosen Ireland for so many blessings is uncertain. What is certain is that He couldn't have picked a more beautiful and fascinating land to make His presence known.

More than anything else, Ireland's Catholic history and tradition are unparalleled. Numerous churches throughout the world are under the patronage of Irish saints.

As author Michael Brown observed in his book, *The Final Hour,* "It was as if Ireland, a nation of missionaries, where abortion and divorce were still against the law, was in Our Lady's plan as a beacon to the rest of Europe and perhaps the world."[1]

In 1979, the Holy Father himself expressed a similar view. Before reaching the shores of Ireland, Pope John Paul II observed, "Ireland was one of the three countries in the world that deserved a visit from the Pope, a visit earned by their suffering for the faith and because of their spreading of it."

Indeed, for a country so small, the Irish people have made the greatest impact in Christian evangelization of any nation in the world. No one has done a better job. In the United States alone there are an estimated 39 million Irish descendants, many of whom are baptized Catholic.

From her revelations, Christina Gallagher was told that God is pleased with the effort the Irish have made over the centuries to spread and live the faith. Although lacking official Church sainthood, many who today are unknown worked courageously to spread the faith. It is in this spirit that God again calls upon the people of Ireland.

Christina stresses that Our Blessed Mother and Jesus are not just calling Ireland, but the whole world. Ireland, still a strong Catholic nation, has been singled out by God for an important mission. It is to be a catalyst, says Christina, in God's plan for the salvation of the world. Christina tells us, "Our Lady wants Ireland to do God's work for her. Our Blessed Mother desires that her messages in Ireland be allowed to go out to the whole world."

On February 22, 1988, the Queen of Peace told Christina of her wishes for her beloved Ireland. Once again, an urgency was intoned: "I hold Ireland in the palms of my hands. I am the Virgin Mary, Queen of Peace. I want them to act on my messages for Ireland. It is urgent. Please do not waste any more time. The cup is overflowing. There is no time to waste. It is urgent."

One month later, Our Lady reminded Christina of her longing for the people of Ireland to act on Heaven's behalf. "I want my children to help me. I have a plan for Ireland. If my children will not listen to my message, they cannot help."

The following year, on May 30, 1989, the Virgin Mary issued a warning. Ireland, the Blessed Mother said, needed to respond to God. As in Scripture, it seemed she was saying much had been given to Ireland and much would now be expected. Our Lady even implied severe consequences. "My children, the purification is on the way. How my Heart bleeds for my children, who are blind and deaf. So many try to find all sorts of excuses not to believe. Ireland will not be saved if my children do not become my messengers. There are so few in Ireland who fast; and prayer —that, too, is like a burden to them. My child, I want to help my children, but they reject me every day."

To go with these requests, Christina relates what was shown to her in 1991. This apparition was a strong warning to the Irish people.

Our Blessed Mother showed me the map of Ireland, very distinct and clear in black, with a black cross over it. Then tiny little specks or dots of light came on the map of Ireland. Then there appeared a tabernacle, indicating the importance of honoring Jesus' Eucharistic presence in the tabernacles of every church.

What it was showing me was that if the people returned to Jesus, then the little tiny lights would get greater, and the darkness of sin in Ireland would come into complete light, be disbursed and Ireland would be renewed into the great Light of God, and the light would reach up to the black cross of sin.

In other words, the hand of God is hanging over Ireland, because it is steeped in sin, and if the people do not make reparation, then in the purification, not only is the suffering going to be intense, but Ireland will be no different from anywhere else. There are awful times ahead of us and anyone should be able to see it. This invitation to save Ireland through Eucharistic adoration was issued by Our Blessed Mother prior to the Maastricht Treaty Referendum. The people, sadly, did not generally respond. Refusing to listen to the dangers inseparable from this Treaty, they accepted it. Shortly afterward, many realized the moral dangers they had brought upon themselves, but it was too late.

During a controversy over abortion in Ireland in 1992, the Queen of Peace tried hard to help her Irish children make the right decision. On April 8, 1992, the Blessed Mother delivered to Christina another message to help them find the light:

My children, how many times will my Immaculate Heart have to plead before your blindness? Your hearts are closed to me, your Mother. I desire to lead you, my children, out of darkness and into the Light of my Divine Son, Jesus.

My children, the law of God never changes. It remains the same forever. It does not change like your fashions. I desire that you live the Ten Commandments of your God.

Pray, pray, my children, that your country be saved from the deceit of the Devil. He wants to destroy you and my plan for Ireland.

My children, unite before my Son, Jesus, in the Holy Eucharist and pray the Rosary from your hearts. God desires peace, not war. My child, there are many different wars now —war with life, war with death eternal.

This was a spiritual war, said Christina, that would be fought for the soul of Ireland. In June 1992, just before the Maastricht Referendum in Ireland and after many of the faithful prayed and called on God to protect Ireland, the Blessed Mother reassured the faithful who had responded, knowing that they would be disappointed by the outcome shortly to be disclosed. Our Lady acknowledged their prayers and sacrifices and gave the following message:

My children, in this hour of darkness and distress, you, my dear children of Ireland, are in the folding of your Mother's arms. Never let your hearts despair. Let the light of God inflame your hearts to be the light of the world. I, your Holy Mother, desire to thank you and bless you for your response.

My dear children, continue to respond to the call of your Mother. My love for you is beyond your understanding. You have brought great joy to my sorrowful heart, now I offer it to God and plead with you. Be not afraid of the cry of distress you see around you. Always offer poor souls to me in the folding of my arms. Offer me your prayers and sacrifices. I will plead for your needs. Be at peace my beloved children of Ireland—My peace be with you.

Five months later, in late November 1992, she had another powerful experience concerning the future of Ireland. During a television debate, prior to the Abortion Referendum in Ireland, she saw a tearful Virgin Mary with a red dress and mantle dripping blood. Christina said, "Then I could see devils grabbing at people and the people looked as if drugged in slow motion. Then I could see a black beast growing up from the ground." At this, Christina heard the following words: Immorality, Impurity, Greed, Self-Will.

As the apparition unfolded, the Irish seer saw little pockets or areas on the beast become clear. The people seemed as if on drugs in one area and, in another area, she saw screaming babies in their mothers' wombs.

Later, Christina intuitively understood the spectacle better and its meaning to Ireland and the Church. "The uniting of the currency through Maastricht would result in control of the people; those who would not obey would be suppressed—a work of the Devil—not that they would have a choice. There would be no money to keep the old or the handicapped. Only those who could support themselves would be able to live. The world would become a living Hell of sickness, death, hunger, mourning, and tears."

That same night Christina was shown more. Again she saw the danger approaching Ireland. "I could see Our Holy Mother crying and looking at the voting paper, and she said 'No!' three or four times. Then she was as if falling on her knees. At that I could see a spear of fire come from above and from behind Our Holy Mother, and go through the voting paper and burn it. Flames were all around. Then I could see the map of Ireland, and the flames fell on parts of the map and burned the parts out of existence: Northern Ireland; the middle, which I took to be Dublin; and the bottom, which I took to be Cork. The blobs of the fire fell on different parts of the rest of the map."

On November 29, 1993, Christina received a stern message from the Queen of Peace concerning the world, especially Ireland. It was an urgent plea from a mother for all her children:

My child, I desire you make known my message to the world. My tears are many upon the earth for my children. Many of my children are in great darkness. The dangers that are upon them they do not see.

My children, you do not see the damage you are doing to your souls, and the wrong that is committed against God.

The powers of darkness blind you from the Truth. Your desires for power, money, lust—fulfillment of the world through your flesh—are deceptions that are like poison.

So many suffer from cancer, a cancer of the soul. My children drink of the poison and feed it into their souls.

How long will my children wait before they awaken from their sleep of death?

Ireland is like a jewel in my crown that once shone brightly. It no longer sparkles. My children, you sleep while you are being robbed of your inheritance of glory.

My Immaculate Heart is surrounded by thorns. My child, be ready to witness calamity after calamity throughout the world. You suffer as you do for those whose hearts are full of greed. The pain you endure in silence has won many souls, through Jesus, my Son.

As she does for priests, Christina now prays and suffers constantly for the people of Ireland and the world. She intercedes for their conversion, especially for peace.

CHAPTER TWENTY-EIGHT

Abortion and the Century of Death

I SET BEFORE YOU LIFE AND DEATH, THE BLESSING AND THE CURSE; CHOOSE LIFE, THEN, THAT YOU AND YOUR DESCENDANTS MAY LIVE.

—DEUT. 30:19

Communism and Fascism, Stalin and Hitler, and Auschwitz and Hiroshima are all synonymous with murder—mass murder.

In the past one hundred years it is estimated that there have been as many as 200 million terroristic and state killings, some say many more. Although unofficial, this statistic truly confirms the twentieth century as the century of death, the century of unspeakable decimation, massacre, and slaughter of human creation.

But what about the number of lives terminated by abortions and contraceptives? When added to the genocide, the number of deaths in this century of Satan is incomprehensible.

Experts estimate there are an approximate 50 million abortions a year worldwide. If this estimate is remotely accurate, then surely the Blessed Virgin's messages to Christina Gallagher concerning abortion and the coming Justice of God are extremely serious. It appears the slaughter of the unborn is the single most threatening danger to the future of the world.

The great crime of abortion has been repeatedly denounced by the Queen of Peace to Christina. Our Blessed Mother made it clear to her on December 28, 1992. "Abortion is the greatest sin against God. It permits the Devil to work like never before." Yet Christina says, "God forgives even the sin of abortion."

Moral theologians today say that the massive taking of innocent life blinds men to their actions. This is, as Scripture indicates, one of the results of sin. These theologians say this blindness, in turn, could lead to a disaster.

The tragedy of abortion has been shown to Christina several other times. Repeatedly, the disclosures leave no doubt in her of God's displeasure from the slaughter of the innocent. As Our Lady told her, "The Martyrs cry out to God."

The memories of those experiences have stayed with her. She had not understood the full reality of abortion prior to the first of these. Without hesitation, she straightforwardly confesses her previous lack of awareness:

> I didn't realize what abortion actually was. I knew it was the taking of life, but I heard people speak and they referred to it as something undeveloped, and I believed this.
>
> Once I was permitted to see just one day's killing by abortion and that was something that shook me up, maybe because I didn't pay too much attention before to abortion and even the word "abortion" didn't have enough meaning to me other than it was something that should not be done. I didn't take any more serious notice of it than that.
>
> Then I was shown thousands and thousands of little babies. They were all little, beautiful babies and they were curled up in little cocoon positions, which obviously was the womb. Some of them were bigger than others. Some were ready for birth. I could see their heads, bodies, legs, and arms. I could see them moving their hands, their heads, and their legs and I could just see them twitch. It grieved my heart so much because this wasn't something undeveloped. This I found

painful. I couldn't believe any real mother would do something like this, or that a doctor would do something like this.

Again it made me realize it was the work of Satan. To save them, the Blessed Mother asked me to offer up the Holy Contents of the Mass, to pray the Holy Rosary to her Immaculate Heart and pray the Prayer of Baptism. "And that way," said the Queen of Peace, "I will be able to take each one of my little babies into the safety of my Immaculate Heart."

So I prayed. I didn't know what was going to happen—if the babies' parents or the women involved would change their minds about abortion. I honestly didn't know what was going to happen until the next day.

On the next day, I was going through the most unbelievable suffering. How do I describe this suffering? If you had two children and you were to see those two children dying, how would you feel? That's how I felt. A deep sorrow and helplessness. It caused such an anguish in my heart and mind. I just couldn't stop crying. My back was burning from what felt like lashes.

To this day, whenever I hear a girl is pregnant, I think a woman should be there to protect the girl and the baby. People need to help others see the reality that only from God's gift of life can a man and woman create the flesh of a child. *Only God can give the soul to the child*. I felt love for those little babies and their mothers and yet a helplessness. After this revelation, abortion took on a totally new image—a new meaning for me. That word "abortion" now tears my heart apart.

To enhance the meaning of what she was shown, Our Lady explained, in no uncertain terms, what Heaven considers abortion: "My child, my heart weeps blood for the abomination, killing of the unborn—murder, murder. What punishment it will draw down on my children." Christina says,

There is more to all of this than meets the eye. For myself, it always brings me back to the time of Jesus when the people shouted "Crucify Him. Crucify Him." Yet he was innocent. In the same way, the little babies in the wombs of their mothers are also the innocent victims.

Yet again, through compulsion or situation or whatever, our world today claims a woman has a right over her body. Yet in that act of lust in which she takes part, and through which the baby is conceived even though the baby is not herself—it is distinctly new life—that person feels she can crucify it. She says, I have the right. No, God gives man and woman the gift to create life but only God has the right to take it away.

Christina stresses the Blessed Mother's prayer request for mothers who may make decisions that will terminate the life of their unborn baby. Many mothers who have had abortions may not be practicing within the Church and, through guilt and suppressed fear, may not desire baptism for their aborted babies. This Christina confirms after speaking to many such women.

The Church has already taken account of the fact that many people who cannot receive actual baptism would, if they knew, desire it. Others who die for the truth, receive baptism by blood. We can express, through the communion of saints, *desire* for baptism of the unborn by saying the baptism prayer for their benefit.

According to Father McGinnity, some form of baptism is needed for the Kingdom of Heaven. It was in this connection that the state of Limbo used to be mentioned for children who died unbaptized. Limbo was never a defined truth of faith—i.e., it was never compulsory to believe it—but it is worth noting that the very theologians who proposed it also said the parents could spare the child Limbo by desiring its baptism and through prayer. Because of the widespread sin of abortion, which together with genetic experimentation is surely bringing a chastisement on the whole world, it would be good to offer Mass, the Rosary, and the Baptism of the unborn each day. Here is one such prayer we should offer for the aborted babies, their parents, and the medical personnel who carry out the abortion.

> N.B. This is not a remote use of the Sacrament of Baptism but an intense plea so that any aborted babies whose parents are unrepentant, linked with evil, and do not desire salvation for their aborted children may not be held bound in any way. Through the communion of saints we try to express the baptism of desire on their behalf by this prayer.
>
> Baptism of Desire
> Prayer of Baptism
>
> At first, pray the Apostles' Creed. Then take the Holy Water and sprinkle it in all directions, saying:
>
> All of you who were born dead and are still to be born dead, by day and at night, all of you who were killed in the womb of your mother and are still to be killed, so that all of you will be given eternal life by Our Lord, Jesus Christ, I baptize [give the child a baptismal name, generally the name of Mary, Joseph, John, or the name of the saint whose feast happens to fall on the day] in the name of the Father, and of the Son, and of the Holy Spirit.
>
> At the end, pray the Lord's Prayer, a Hail Mary, and a Glory Be to the Father. . . .

Through prayers, Christina was shown minds and hearts can be converted. Special graces can be received. On September 26, 1992, while in Scotland, Christina was given a special apparition which enlightened her regarding this very special grace.

At Mass during Holy Communion, Christina saw Jesus fallen with the crown of thorns on His Head and His Heart visible, blood dripping from the wounds in His head, and little babies could be seen entering His Sacred Heart. The Lord then asked the people to offer the contents of the Holy Sacrifice—Himself—in reparation for the sin of abortion. However, Christina adds, "The people must decide of their own free will to make reparation for all the sin in the world, especially the sin of abortion."

By choosing to offer *every little thing* in reparation, Christina says we are responding to God's plan for the salvation of the world at this time, but we must choose to do so.

God's recognition of our free will, His gift to us, is ever-present in Christina's messages and revelations. She insists that God will not violate our free will, even in the matter of abortion. She adds, "We must be prepared to pay the consequences of our misuse of this gift of sexuality."

PART IV

Mystical Experiences in Union with God

CHAPTER TWENTY-NINE

The Real World

I WAS IN THE CITY OF JOPPA PRAYING, AND IN A TRANCE I SAW A VISION.

—ACTS 11:5

Jesus has shared with Christina Gallagher many scenes from His Passion as well as requesting permission to suffer in her, and has permitted her to see the wounds inflicted during His Passion. Through her own words, Christina gives us more insight into these mysteries.

Q. You have said that you have seen Jesus crucified. Will you share that with us?

A. I have seen the Sorrowful Mysteries of the Rosary. It was during the Sorrowful Mysteries of the Rosary that I first saw Jesus.

Q. Can you tell us about the Sorrowful Mysteries, starting with the Agony in the Garden?

A. In the first scene, Jesus was thrown across a stone. He didn't seem to be in great pain but as if in deep prayer to God Our

Father. Then I saw Jesus in great agony. In the next scene, He seemed to be on the ground kneeling down away from the stone. There was no grass. There was just hardened clay. Jesus had His hands down on the clay. He was kneeling down. As Jesus was left in that position, I could hear a lot of mocking noises and ugly sounds going on. I remember looking upward and I saw the most enormous crowd of angry devils. They were heaped up as if like a mountain. They were all mocking Jesus and making angry gestures toward Him. Jesus got up and then an angel came with a chalice. Jesus turned away from the chalice, in the opposite direction, to where the devils were. Then I saw a wide conveyor belt. It was coming along with loads and loads of people like dots, coming and going past Jesus.

For a minute, Jesus would look at all these people of the world coming and going. It was as if generation to generation of mankind was going past Him. That's what the conveyor belt was symbolizing to me. After the minute Jesus watched the people, He turned back and received the chalice. The moment Jesus received the chalice, the devils were silenced totally. There was not a sound from them. Then came a gray-black slime from the devils and it just flooded down from the mountain and came over to where Jesus was kneeling. It came over Jesus' knees where He was kneeling down. Jesus began to tremble and then put His hands upward to His Father as if to look and pray or talk to His Father. I didn't hear what He was saying to God the Father.

The next thing I saw was Jesus' face getting all sweaty and wet. Then the sweat turned into blood as if the blood was coming through His face. Then you could see the blood on His neck. You could see it all over Him. When Jesus was in this state, He was trembling. I found myself looking at the whites of His eyes. The whites of His eyes, in fact, had turned bloodshot. It got to the point that I thought Jesus was going to go into a convulsion. Personally, I get afraid sometimes because I see all this as the result of sin. It's a horror. That was the end of that particular scene of the Agony in the Garden.

Q. Can you describe for us the Scourging at the Pillar?

A. The Scourging at the Pillar was when I found myself going down the steps into a cellar. I could see a big, ugly black beam across the room. The steps were on one side and on the opposite side of the room there was this big beam. Jesus had His back to me. His back was bare and His hands had bands and chains around them. His hands were stretched upward as far as they could go. There were two ugly fat men, with very little clothes on them, with Jesus. One had a whip, the other one had a set of cat-o'-nine-tails. These tails or lashes coming out of the end of it had lead at the tips of them. There was another cat-o'-nine-tails, with cone-shaped lead pieces at the end of each strand. These men took these whips or whatever, with the lead at the end, and used them to strike Jesus. The whips would wrap around His ribs and you could hear a sound as if His very ribs were cracking from the noise of the wallops. They would take the whip and lash and lash His back. Jesus would collapse and then sort of struggle up again by pulling Himself up. His toes barely touched the ground. They would lash Him again until His shoulders, His whole back, were just in bits—all kinds of strokes of every description. When they drew back the whip at times, I could see bits of His flesh flying back with the whip.

Q. Upon seeing all of this, how did it affect you?

A. On one occasion when I saw this, I couldn't bear to see the extent and horror of each time they hit Him. To live through this was beyond words. Once, I thought maybe I'd be able to run in front of Jesus' body in some particular way. So I threw myself as if around Jesus. I said, "I deserve this—you don't." Somehow, immediately Jesus was released from where He was being tied. His hands were free. Don't ask me how this happened. It wasn't in physical terms He was freed, but it was very real what I was going through. I got Jesus over to where there was a grid of planks on the flood. I placed Jesus there, His back upward. I was heartbroken because His back was cut in so many pieces. I was crying. I wanted my tears to heal the wounds of His back. I desired it so much. After that, I myself started to experience the lashes on my back from time to time. That was all I saw regarding the Scourging at the Pillar.

Q. Tell us about the Crowning of Thorns.

A. I saw the Crowning of Thorns. I was always led to believe, in my life, that the crown of thorns was just a band of thorns around the head of Jesus. On this occasion, I saw Jesus being brought out. He was pushed and slapped and punched. Jesus was brought to a little pillar and a little seat. These two ugly men were still there, and they pushed Jesus down on the seat. He looked so weak and His body so raw with blood all over Him. He looked as if He was nearly dead. One of the ugly men had a crown of thorns in his hands, in the shape of a hat. The crown was dark brown to black. This man went up to Jesus and, with his hands high in the air protected by what looked like animal skins while Jesus was still partly swaying and the other man held Him, crushed the crown of thorns down onto Jesus' head. When they crushed the thorns down onto His head, I was permitted to look away for a split second. Then I looked back and could still see Jesus. He was going down, collapsing. It was awful to see. Again they beat Him. There were slaps and punches and pushing. Words can't begin to describe it. Jesus was in some horrific pain. It looked like He couldn't be fully conscious because His face was covered in blood and His back was covered in blood. He wasn't just stripped of His clothes, He was stripped of His flesh.

Q. What did you see during the Carrying of the Cross?

A. There was a road where I saw the carrying of the cross. It was a well-worn path. The ground was hardened earth and you could see the stones coming up through it. Jesus was going down this road. The cross He carried was just two planks. They were first tied together and laid across his shoulder.

That's what drew my attention to His shoulder. I don't know what two bones they were, because I don't know the inside of a person's shoulder. I could see two bones on His shoulder that were going zigzag, because there was no flesh over them. The cross was down over this part of His shoulder and tearing into the bone, not just the flesh. When Jesus stumbled and fell, the cross fell across His back. Every time He tried to get up, they would kick Him and punch Him. He would fall again. Then He'd struggle to get up again.

Jesus couldn't walk step by step. He just pushed His feet along the ground. He pushed them, little by little, to make about quarter-size steps. He'd proceed a couple of inches at a time. He was really struggling to go on. Then I saw Our Blessed Mother coming down the road. Our Lady approached as if she had come from the opposite direction to meet Him. The minute she came to meet Him, they both stopped, which seemed to be for a few seconds.

There were no words, yet everything was said in the expression between them. He was so grieved for Our Blessed Mother seeing that she would have to witness this. Our Blessed Mother was grieved and helpless as if only she could take His place, but she knew she could not. The pain expressed in their eyes was beyond understanding. For a long time after that as I remembered the horror it would break me. Then God did something and erased the horror from my memory. The horror of that scene doesn't continually live with me anymore. I can now talk about it, though not always. The majority of the time I'm now without that terrible feeling. For a long time I couldn't function. For me, that was where I believe Our Lady's heart was truly pierced—through and through with a sword.

Q. I know this is difficult, but please describe for us the crucifixion of Jesus.

A. During the crucifixion, I didn't see the two other men who were crucified. I just saw Jesus. The planks of wood were thrown on the ground so abruptly. Then Jesus was also thrown roughly down on the cross. That's when, for the first time, I saw Jesus pierced with the nails. They were like steel pins. The nails were thick and long. One of the men pulled the hand of Jesus and he stamped his foot across His hand. The other man had some kind of a bar and swung down on Jesus' hand. At that moment I felt I was permitted to look away. I couldn't bear to look at it. When the nail went in His wrist, it wasn't really straight. I know the men were discussing with each other that it wasn't straight. You could see the pin where it went in. It wasn't upright. Whatever they said, they then decided to leave it there, seeing it was secure.

Then they went over to the other side of Jesus. They just took Jesus as if they were going to tear Him apart. They just pulled Him and then the other man again put his foot on this hand. The same man pounded the nail into His wrists both times. Then they did the same with His feet. There was a hole in the ground and stones beside it. Then the two men lifted up the cross with Jesus on it and just let it fall directly into the hole. When they did this, His body was nearly wrenched off the cross. But it was held securely by the nails pinning His wrists and feet to the Cross. Jesus looked to me as if He was dead. Then I could see a slight movement. Then that scene was over.

Q. Have you had any other apparitions such as this, of Christ's suffering?

A. In December 1994, during afternoon prayer in the Chapel at the House of Prayer, I saw Jesus on the cross, head bent down, blows and cuts on His face, congealed blood, welts, and marks of blood *all* over His body. Now and again, He would raise His head with a great effort as if dazed yet talking to the little group praying in the chapel. I saw angels, about fifteen of them, come in turn to wipe—ever so gently—blood from the wounds, but pathetically and not daring to look. The one wound they did not touch was the wound in the Sacred Side from which blood was streaming. I was affected deeply and suffered aches all over my body, especially in my head. Over my left eye felt the worst.

Q. What is sin doing to Our Lord?

A. Sin is tearing Him apart. Jesus has redeemed our souls . . . set us free. In being redeemed by Christ, we have become the Mystical Body of Christ. What we're doing to Him, through division, hatred, violence, whatever form the sin takes, is literally pulling the body of Jesus—His Mystical Body—apart. We need to offer up with love to Jesus our suffering. In other words, we can do nothing by ourselves, only when God gives it. If we offer it up to Him, then He gives it to another, and brings unity and love and peace to others. When we get, as it were, a slap across the face or a cross, we need to accept it for love of Christ. Then it's as if you close the wounds of the body of Jesus. Jesus wants us all to become holy and purified. He will continue to suffer in a great way as on Calvary through each one of us for the purification of us all. When we are all purified we will become perfect in Him.

Q. Christina, you have said that you suffer pain in mind, soul, body, and heart. These are all different sufferings. Can you describe them to us?

A. When I suffer in mind, it's like a torment; I never know peace. I am in anguish and can recognize it as being that. I am really mentally distracted to a point. I become so upset that it doesn't go away. Sometimes when I'm permitted to go through inner suffering or when I see a lot of sin, if God permits it, the sin causes an anguish and a tearfulness. The pain of heart is like deep sorrow, but it also afflicts the mind. The pain of the body can or cannot be bearable—it is very difficult to express in words. It is a feeling of being abandoned and in darkness. No earthly person can remove this void until God decides to fill it with His grace and the light of the Holy Spirit.

Q. When you say, "If you're permitted to see a lot of sin," what do you mean by that? Are you seeing people commit sin?

A. Yes, I've been permitted to see people commit sin and as Our Blessed Mother said, "Do as I have done, ponder all in your heart and pray."

Q. Christina, as a victim soul, your suffering is united with Our Lord's. Can you tell us about this suffering?

A. From what I've seen, I now realize that all the sin of the world and all the sins of the flesh are tearing the Hearts of Jesus and His Blessed Mother apart. For me, that's a part of the suffering of my heart and mind. Sometimes I feel deep physical pains in my wrists which are the wounds of Jesus. The pain extends down to the palms of my hands, where I experience a burning sensation. I don't like talking about this too often to be truthful to you. For example, today I felt pain going down through my hands a number of times. I'm glad when the Lord doesn't permit it to be seen. Sometimes the marks come out. Sometimes I feel like running away from the marks. The reality of them comes and stays with me. I can surrender and accept the pain but not the visibility of it. I get pain in my hands, my feet, and my head. On three occasions I experienced it through my heart. That's one form of physical suffering. But when I try to explain the suffering of my soul, it is beyond suffering of mind or body. The inner me is crushed completely. It's worse than the other types of suffering. Suppose your heart is sensitive and there's a Band-Aid over your heart closing a wound. If someone was to come along and rip that Band-Aid off quickly, you'd be in so much pain.

It's the same for my inner soul, it's like being stripped and stretched. Then there is an inflow of light. When this inflow of light comes, it's beautiful, but it burns right here in my heart. I don't understand this. I don't even know what I am talking about, except I know it happens to me. I'm not great at expressing it, but I don't know any other way to explain it other than what I am saying right now.

Q. Do you presently suffer the stigmata pains in your hands and feet? Are the red marks still visible?

A. They have bled at times. It's as if a great heat comes from them. They get raw and then go away. Sometimes I have pain from the marks when they're visible, although I sometimes have the pain even more severely without the marks showing at all. I've been begging and praying to God that He won't let the marks be visible because I don't like them to be visible. Then again, this is my will conflicting with the Will of God. So I just say at the end of the prayer, "Lord, please help me in my weakness, and not my will be done, but Yours."

Q. Are there also visible marks on your head when you have the pain around your head, the pain from the crown of thorns?

A. Yes. The visible marks can come and go. Sometimes the pain can be there even when there are no marks. It's as if there are holes there. I can feel as I said sharp thorns going down into particular areas on my head. I can feel this whether the marks are there or not.

Q. You have spoken of the value of suffering. Can you tell us what the Lord has taught you about suffering?

A. The Lord has taught me about suffering as a victim soul. The only way I can really explain it is I am not the Mystical Body of Christ, I am only a tiny part of it. We all are. Let me explain my suffering like this. As the left hand is one part of our body, the right hand is another. Let us say the left hand represents someone who is asked to work extremely hard. This hand is a person who's responded and is open to God. God can then pour His grace into the heart of this person's soul. So his heart is opened to respond to God's spirit and grace. This person is like an open hand to do God's work. The person that's closed to God and not aware of Him is like a paralyzed hand. The more God gives to this person, the more the Evil One wants to attack him because of his value to the Mystical Body of Christ. This is what Jesus does through the surrender and suffering of the victim soul. Jesus lets His grace flow freely from the left hand's work through to the right hand. This brings life into it. This is called conversion. Anyone who loves Jesus will love suffering because Jesus draws good out of suffering for the conversion of others.

Q. Can you tell us about seeing your own death?

A. I have been shown my own death. I was shown my death in one way and I pleaded with God, at that very moment, that what Jesus showed me seemed too easy. I inwardly yearned, at that moment for something much more difficult. Normally speaking, I wouldn't ask for something more difficult, only if God inspired me to desire it this way. So when I desired a more difficult death, Jesus said to me that He didn't desire me to suffer so much. Then I said, "But Lord, only in this way can I be of any value. Anything I would have to suffer, I know will be in union with you."

Q. So you were shown how you would die. Does this mean the type of death? Were you shown your soul leaving your body?

A. Yes. I was shown my soul leaving my body, and Jesus and Our Blessed Mother coming to meet me.

Q. Then what happened?

A. That was where I pleaded for extra suffering, for the more difficult type of death, and Jesus didn't let me know which one then it would be.

Q. During your death, which the Lord showed you, did you see yourself in a bed suffering or was there an accident? Did you see how you died?

A. I prefer not to talk about it. I shared it with my spiritual director.

CHAPTER THIRTY

A Time for Pillars to Crumble

I TELL YOU TRULY YOU WILL WEEP AND MOURN WHILE THE WORLD REJOICES. YOU WILL GRIEVE FOR A TIME, BUT YOUR GRIEF WILL TURN TO JOY.

—JOHN 16:20

The revelations of Christina Gallagher concerning the future of the world appear to predict an era of peace preceded by some dire events. However, the evils of the present world are caught up in the drama of the meaning of these revelations and, therefore, many people focus on an uncertain future. They become filled with anxiety and fear. The early Christians expected to see the Second Coming of Christ at their own death. (1 Thess. 4:13–18)

Even though there are many sorrows in the world, nothing can take away peace from those who know God. This is the advice of the Queen of Peace and her promise to her children who respond to her call regardless of world events.

With all this in mind, what Christina Gallagher has received of the future is put into the best perspective. More than anything else, these are signs foretelling that God is active in our lives and in the world. The outcome of this world is already decided as we know from Scripture. The function of Christina's revelations are no different than any of the other messages or signs the Blessed Virgin or the Lord have brought to the world. They are an invitation to a healthier relationship with our Creator, based not on fear, but on love, trust, and acceptance. Those who live by God's rules and grasp His message of love and His invitation to peace are truly part of His Mystical Body, and live with great confidence in His Mercy. As Christina has stated, "Don't feel frightened when you hear of chastisements, because that is the call of your Mother through the Most Holy Trinity—a call of repentance, a call out of love to prepare yourself."

With that in mind, the messages of Christina Gallagher can best be understood. Once again they are best professed in her own words.

Q. Have Our Lady or Our Lord said exactly what this means?

A. The end times—the end of sin—when God is going to purify and cleanse the world of sin. I've been given to understand there are to be three stages. The first stage is when the world, or the people of the world, will suffer more and more. The suffering in the world will get greater and greater. This will be the purification of the world through the process of suffering. Although it may seem awful to some people, they will be purified through it. The suffering draws them to God through the cross. In other words, it purifies them.

Stage two is when Our Blessed Mother is saying, "pray, pray, pray," and when God is permitting Our Blessed Mother to give grace to the world. A lot of people are closed. In the second stage, everybody in the entire world will come to be aware of God's existence. That may mean, from what I gather, even people who had never heard of God will automatically become aware of God. God and Our Blessed Mother are both going to empty out a storehouse of grace upon the world through the power of the Holy Spirit. Hearts will be totally converted. As they're totally converted, they will have a realization of God. But they will still have their free will to drift back into their old sinful ways. For those who do drift back, the storehouse of special grace will have become empty, because they will have known about God and will have no excuse.

Stage three is when those who did not respond to the call of Our Mother, before the storehouse of grace was poured out upon the world by Jesus and our Blessed Mother, will not have the strength to resist sin and will drift back into their sinful ways. God will then do as He said as Jesus has said. His hand will come over the world more swiftly than the wind. A short time after that, the chastisements will come upon the world.

Q. When will the sign you have spoken of come about?

A. I don't know the full details about that and, even if I did, I don't say I would have the authority to disclose it. I was told that in the year 1992, many will begin to cry out to their Lord and He will not hear them. So I feel, from what Jesus has said to me, that the time of His Mercy is about to be over. The time of His Justice is about to begin. I feel that the suffering time could be part of the Justice of God. The deeper level of suffering will be the beginning of the Justice of God.

Q. So what you're saying to me is that you are being given things that are critical in the events of the world, but may not make newspaper headlines at the time they occur. Behind the scenes they are important stepping stones to the Triumph of the Immaculate Heart. Is this correct?

A. That's right. Once it was revealed to me that there were secret talks going on. Underground talks going on between top leaders, and there was a danger to the world of a nuclear war between Russia and China.

Q. Has that threat passed or is it still there?

A. I understand it's still there.

Q. Many people have talked about a nuclear war between the United States and the former Soviet Union, but you said China and the Soviet Union?

A. Yes, Russia and China.

Q. Can you tell us about the experience you had concerning the Holy Eucharist and the Bible?

A. Yes. On one occasion I saw a church. The church was in total blackness. People and demons were together with the Holy Eucharist. . . . The people and the demons were mocking the Holy Eucharist and Bible. I was very saddened by this. I felt myself very frightened. It was as if I were living in this particular area or stage where this was occurring. Then I could see automatically a cross of light and Jesus was upon the cross of light. Blood was coming from His Heart and His side. The blood was streaming down. I could see the world beneath where Jesus was on the cross. The minute the blood hit the globe of the world, there came a most blinding, enormous light. This light came from the Eternal Father in Heaven, who was above Jesus. His hands were drawn over the world. This light that came from the hands of the Eternal Father then hit the globe of the world as did the blood of Jesus from His heart and His side. The light and blood together hit the world. Then you could see the globe of the world illuminated as if there had been a light switched on inside the globe. I then found myself down where the people were again. This time there was no trace of any people in darkness or any demons. Everything was gone. The Church that was in darkness was gone and there were now people there in great joy and happiness and peacefulness. Everybody there was going about their work in total joy. I could see angels. These particular angels were formed in shapes of Light. They were in every color possible and they seemed to have direct communication from Heaven. This was from above the globe where Jesus and the Eternal Father were. The angels seemed to just go into the globe and go up or down anyway they wanted. It was total beauty.

Q. What do you infer all of this to mean? Is this the way the world will be after the purification, or the way the world will be after the great sign? Is this the way in which the world will respond?

A. I feel it will be after the time that God cleanses the world of all its sins.

Q. So this apparition you received doesn't necessarily mean that the world will immediately be good after the great sign that is to come.

A. Not immediately. Because people shall still have the free will to drift back into their old selves and this isn't the chastisement. This is why Our Blessed Mother wants the consecration of Russia, to lessen the chastisement.

Q. Have Jesus or the Blessed Mother talked to you about the warning?

A. They have talked to me about the warning in the sense that everyone would receive the knowledge of the Reality of God. Everyone would know God was a Reality, not a myth, and how they stand before Him at the particular time the warning would come. I was given the understanding it would come from the hand of God.

Q. Did they use the word "warning" with you?

A. No . . . sign.

Q. What will happen to those people who won't convert?

A. I don't know what's going to happen to them. That's why Our Blessed Mother keeps saying, "*pray, pray, pray, make sacrifices, and fast,*" not only to prevent disasters, but for our own protection, purification, and guidance. Our Lady also desires all of this for those who have strayed from God. Our Holy Mother is a mother to all and loves them all. Our Blessed Mother's concern is for those who are spiritually blind. Our Lady desires us to be active members in the Mystical Body of Christ. If we see our brother or sister stray, it's our duty to pray for them and our duty to pray for the priests, bishops, cardinals, nuns, and our Holy Father. It's not something Our Lady is just asking. Our Blessed Mother is making it clear that it's a duty.

Q. Has Our Lady spoken to you about unbelievers?

A. The Queen of Peace has spoken to me about her lost children and she showed me when she came that she's crying for her lost children. Our Lady has spoken of some of her children being lost—some forever—and they cause her great pain. But she never judges anybody. She just shows me the pain to an extent, and I feel a great suffering, inwardly, when Our Blessed Mother is crying for her lost children. I would gladly give my life a hundred times over just to wipe one tear away from Our Lady's eyes.

Q. Can you tell us about what Jesus said in his message of October 18, 1991, in terms of His Justice. What does it mean?

A. The Justice of God is when His Mercy ends. It is when He won't be as sympathetic toward His people anymore. They will feel the pain of His rejection as He turns away from them to the point that they will have to realize and feel the depth of their own sin.

Q. Were you shown any other catastrophes in America?

A. I knew what I had seen of Los Angeles, but then Jesus showed me a number of other places which seemed to be in a kind of streamline from Los Angeles into different parts of America. I could see the seaside on one occasion with water washing over houses and dead bodies on the ground. There were a number of different calamities that Jesus showed me that I then realized was the Justice of God. I knew and became very much aware that there were many different parts of America that were going to be hit by what people would call "natural calamities." But, in fact, it was actually the Justice of God in the action of the calamities.

Q. Did the people recognize this was the Justice of God happening in America?

A. I understood this would occur until it would reach a particular level when people could no longer call them natural calamities or things that would just happen. They would finally know the calamities weren't natural when they would eventually reach a peak level. Then people would begin to become aware there was something very wrong.

Q. You said that America would go through multiple sufferings to the point where people would start to realize that all of this was actually coming from God. How do you know the people will come to that awareness? Were you lead to understand that the people would eventually have this awareness?

A. Yes. They would finally become aware. They will try to explain everything away as natural calamities or weird happenings in their own rite. They will also try to attribute the cause of the events to natural, scientific reasons. They will say such things as "freak storms" or "freak this" or "freak that." They won't want to accept that the sins of mankind are drawing this down upon them. Then Jesus spoke to me about the people not being able to understand how the sins that took place in the particular city, Los Angeles, caused certain events. Jesus said that even I wouldn't understand the kind of sin that goes on there.

Q. Were you given an internal understanding that the people will begin to convert and turn back to God?

A. From what I saw, the people did not necessarily convert. They got afraid because they knew it wasn't natural calamities, but they couldn't prove it. Then this unnatural something that was happening kept getting bigger and bigger until it finally was something that they became afraid of. It then got to the point that they became aware. They knew there was something not right here, but "What is it?" they asked.

Q. Were you given this understanding through an internal knowledge that the people would eventually know these events were unnatural?

A. Inwardly I became aware of it.

Q. Has Our Lady said anything about war or future wars?

A. Only about the danger of a nuclear war between Russia and China and that we were to pray about this.

Q. Has Our Lady mentioned the United States being involved in the war?

A. No.

Q. You said that starting in the year 1992 many would cry out for the Lord and the Lord would not hear them. Can you explain what you meant?

A. Yes, because the Mercy of God will begin to be over, I was told, and the Justice of God will begin.

Q. Do you know more than you are saying about this?

A. I don't want to answer that.

Q. Have you received anything else on war or future wars?

A. Our Blessed Mother said it was up to us, the people. Recently, Our Holy Mother said that there will be a third world war if the people do not respond to her message. That was in February of 1993.

Q. Was there anything else said to you at this time?

A. Yes. Our Holy Mother said Jesus did not desire this. Our Blessed Mother said it was the Evil One that wanted to use the youth to be instruments of destruction, but that God does not desire this.

Q. What does the Blessed Mother mean? Does Our Lady mean the sins of the youth will bring about a third world war?

A. Obviously, the youth seem to be manipulated more easily and used by the Evil One more so than the adults. The youth seem to be the ones the Devil wants to use, in a greater way. Our Holy Mother desires that the youth of Ireland and the world be consecrated to her Immaculate Heart. This is the only way to permit her to protect them. She desires that in their own free will that they consecrate themselves to her Immaculate Heart.

Act of Consecration

O Mary Queen of Peace,
Today I consecrate myself to your Immaculate Heart.
Cover me with the protective mantle of your Motherly Love
And place me in the open wound of your Son's beating Heart.

Wash me in the Precious Blood flowing from your weeping
Hearts united in perfect love.
I abandon my entire life into your Hands to be united in your
Love and grace by means of your
Matrix Medal which I lovingly wear as a sign of my surrender
To your care.

Mould my heart to reflect the image of your Son until I, too,
Have learned to love Him, as you do, with a true and perfect
Love. Amen.

(Rev. Dr. Gerard McGinnity)

Q. Did Our Lady also say this in February 1993?

A. Yes.

Q. Has Our Lady said anything recently about a nuclear war?

A. No, Our Blessed Mother hasn't mentioned a nuclear war recently; nothing about any particular kind of war. I have been told there would be, in many parts of the world, pockets of war, wars here and there; that there would be different diseases spreading in different parts of the world; and that we would be seeing more destruction again, coming not only in calamities, but by disease and hunger. I was told this in October or November 1992.

Q. What else did Our Lady tell you?

A. Our Lady also said that I would see this spreading more and more. Recently, in an inner awareness, it was made known to me about the future situations in England. I understood England would go down because of its lack of morality and faith in God. It would go down to such an extent that the Queen and the Monarchy in England would disappear. Work will be practically nil. There will be many, many situations of crime growing with poverty, striking in many, many locations. Again, this will be for the welfare of the people's spiritual lives. In the depths of their sufferings, they can find God. This was like a total awareness given to me.

Q. So you have been led to understand that the Royal Family would lose its power and privilege?

A. Yes, power, respect, and then they would just disappear. In England, everyday people would find the struggle greater and greater, to the point they would be living on bread and water or practically starving. Then through that suffering, many would turn back to God.

Q. So, in a way, this is similar to what America will go through, only suffering of a different nature.

A. Yes.

Q. What will happen in the rest of the world?

A. In many parts of the world, different areas will be stricken by wars through its leaders. It was given to me that Russia and China have underground talks going on. It was in the underground talks that the danger would lie. If we see any kind of war breaking out between Russia and China, then we can be prepared for very serious consequences. Our Blessed Mother wants us to pray that this will not take place.

Q. You have mentioned England and America. Have you seen or received anything about Europe or any specific nation?

A. The only other thing was when I went to Hawaii. I became aware of Hawaii being a very godless place. The Church was as if dead in Hawaii.

Q. Hawaii did suffer a terrible hurricane last fall. Was this part of what you saw?

A. That was a very coincidental thing as well, because a lady invited me and my spiritual director to her hotel in Hawaii. When we went there I knew and was very much aware that this woman didn't believe one word of what was happening to me. I felt it very difficult, a struggle within me, to keep a straight face and pretend I didn't know this. I had to act as if I knew nothing. But she was extremely nice to us.

Later, the lady told my spiritual director, after the hurricane came, that she had prayed to God about us. She said, "Dear Lord, because Father McGinnity and Christina Gallagher were here, surely you'll protect this place!" She then told him nothing happened to their hotel during the hurricane. Everything was left perfect. The little bungalows around the area and all around that particular place had their roofs torn off and horrific damage was done. Yet their hotel, which was sitting on the sea and towering into the air, wasn't damaged. She proclaimed this openly afterward and told many people, you know, that it was in her estimation some kind of power from God for protection for their hotel.

Q. On December 26, 1992, a Saturday night, you said, "I could see Boris Yeltsin's face and he looked awful as he was very mad and hateful. Then I could see people running out of the fire and they were on fire."

A. Yes.

Q. Can you tell us about this experience?

A. I could see the flames of fire going higher and higher with devils surrounding it. I could see Yeltsin's face. Then I could see people running around fire and I could see Yeltsin's face in the fire. I could see people were screaming. Yeltsin's face was so hateful and cold. It was horrible. The people were on fire, and at that time, I remember being very shaken.

Q. In this apparition of Russia, was there chaos in Russia?

A. In Russia and later in a different place, or it seemed to be a different place, I saw trucks, tanks, and jeeps. The boys that were in them were in the army and had some kind of greenish uniform on. I remembered I could only see their backs as they were marching. I saw one young lad, he was so young to me. He was like a child in a sense—maybe sixteen or seventeen. He looked around and directly at me. He was Oriental. I remember him looking directly at me. He had yellow skin.

Q. Is the Philippines the first country where the Triumph of the Immaculate Heart will begin?

A. Jesus said the Triumph of the Immaculate Heart of His Mother would take place there and spread from there throughout the world.

Q. It is now August 1993. What's going to happen to the Church during these hard times ahead?

A. The Church will deteriorate for its purification and then be renewed. What we are looking at now is nothing compared to what we will be looking at regarding the Church's decline and deterioration. Also, we will look at the deterioration of faith and morals in every country worldwide, much more than it is now, although you would think that it can't get much worse.

Q. What else will happen?

A. Our Blessed Mother said there will be pockets of war in different places throughout the world and this would spread. Atheism and disbelief in God would grow from this and the despair that will come. Jesus told me sin will grow faster than wild weeds, and those who believe should pray for those who don't. The disasters that will happen, Jesus said, will cause people, instead of converting, to curse God. People will get more angry, instead of getting closer to God, and get deeper into sin.

Q. Is there anything you can tell us now that you have not previously said or revealed?

A. Yes. I was shown a parable, by Jesus, regarding the Church. I received this in 1993. In this experience, I found myself looking at this huge field with thousands of priests in this field. They were shaking seeds. After a short time, some of the priests began to sweat and some were sweating blood. Other priests didn't sweat anything. Then the seeds seemed to sprout up and come to flourish very swiftly—at least as quickly as they were shaking them. The priests who were sweating, especially those who were sweating blood—their seeds sprouted into a very thick cane and were very full where the grain is at the top. The ones that didn't sweat at all had nothing but big ugly weeds. They were very large weeds. This was something I have never seen around here. They continued along this way. Then when Jesus appeared, He was illuminated in light. Jesus came to the people and to the priests who had not sweated. All they had around them were weeds. Jesus said to them, "What have you to give me?" Those priests trembled and begged forgiveness. The priests just turned and looked at Jesus, and you could hear them all repeating, "Jesus, forgive us." Jesus didn't reply. Immediately the angel came and I knew it was the Angel of Wrath. He came from behind Jesus and he had a sword. He drew the sword and he went as I thought he would to cut down the weeds. As he touched them, the weeds automatically burst into flames. At that, the priests began to drop and disappear. Then Jesus went over to where the priests were who were sweating blood. Jesus was crying, but He seemed to be crying with joy. He said, "My brothers, to you

I give all this." At that point, He threw back His hand to where the weeds and the priests were and then they were all gone. In their place I found myself looking at a very rich beautiful soil, with no weeds, priests, or anything. The priests and the weeds were both gone, and all that was in place of it was beautiful rich soil.

Q. What did the rich soil indicate?

A. Jesus was rewarding them for their fruitfulness and offering them opportunity to bear even greater fruit as in Scripture Jesus Himself says, "To him who has more, more will be given and from him who has nothing, even what he has will be taken away."

Q. What did all this mean to you?

A. It was very clearly showing me the error of some of the priests. The seed to me represented Jesus' Word. Those who were spreading His Word, but spreading it in error, had no fruit, only weeds. Those who worked hard had obviously sweated in blood. This will come when Jesus will burn the discrepancies that are set by man.

PART V

A Victim for Christ

CHAPTER THIRTY-ONE

A Little Soul

I HAVE BEEN CRUCIFIED WITH CHRIST AND THE LIFE I LIVE NOW IS NOT MY OWN.

—GAL. 2:20

Michael Freze, S.F.O., in his book *They Bore the Wounds of Christ,* seems to sum up very well one of the most incredible mysteries of the Christian faith—the stigmata. Freze writes, "Despite the rich deposit Sacred Tradition has left to us, some mysteries of the faith continue to fascinate and even baffle the best of minds, be they theologians or laypersons.

"Such is the case with a mystical phenomenon known as the Sacred Stigmata. Those imprinted with Our Lord's wounds upon their bodies become transformed into living crucifixes by sharing in His Passion for the redemption of the world. They are His most chosen souls."[1]

The rich legacy of the stigmata is said to have begun with Saint Paul, while Saint Francis of Assisi was probably the most well known. According to the renowned Parisian scholar Dr. Imbert-Gourbeyre, there have been 321 authentic stigmatists (also known as stigmatics) in Church history. This list was composed in his monumental two-volume work *La Stigmatization* in 1984. Dr. Gourbeyre identifies 62 of those stigmatists who have been canonized or beatified by the Church.[2]

According to Freze, the twentieth century might rightly be called the "era of the stigmatist," since more than two dozen cases of stigmatization have been reported and investigated. However, few have been authenticated by the proper Church authorities. "Unlike past centuries, we now have thoroughly documented cases of many living and recently deceased stigmatists who have undergone extensive investigations by both medical experts and theologians."[3]

Freze also points out that we have significant evidence from the world of photography, anatomy, biology, and chemistry to help substantiate these claims.

Because of this evidence, says Freze, the question of authentic stigmatization is now more than a theological curiosity. It is an observable fact. "Understandably a rare phenomenon, considering that there are over 1 billion Christians in the world, the Sacred Stigmata is truly one of the greatest miracles that Christendom has ever known. And it is perhaps the greatest visible sign of Christ's presence among us today. It's as though Our Lord still shows Mercy to the 'Doubting Thomases' of our world by allowing them to be witnesses to the Reality of God in our midst. 'Put your finger here and see My Hands, and put out your hand and place it in My Side. Do not be faithless, but believe.' (John, 20:27)

"Without a doubt, God has gifted us today with a sign of the times. A sign displayed through victim souls known as stigmatists. These souls share in the sufferings of Our Lord's Passion to redeem the world. These are extraordinary souls, holy and pure. By imitating Christ so intensely, they have been invited to become one with Him. They are His beloved. He demands much from their example and from their sacrifice."[4]

Indeed, as Jesus told Christina Gallagher, "I thirst for little souls who will abandon themselves to Me. I thirst for souls out of love."

Christina Gallagher is such a soul. She has received the wounds of Christ, which are not always visible, in her body. She has suffered from the five wounds, including the crown of thorns, and the scourging. Worse than these wounds are the sufferings she has experienced through the inner torments of Christ, meaning His abandonment and His anguish at the sin of the world. This suffering, says Christina, has been the most difficult for her. Yet it is the heart of her sacrifice.

From her experiences Christina describes the sufferings of Jesus in Gethsemane as worse than His sufferings of His final day. This was because, she says, "The isolation, loneliness, and inner wrenching of the Heart of Jesus were actually sufferings more intolerable than the physical tortures."

She wrote Father McGinnity, "Father, more and more I want to live for God alone. It's like being hungry for food and thirsty for drink. Truly only God can give me what I desire most—suffering for souls."

In retrospect, these are fascinating writings coming from someone who, prior to the apparitions, described herself of average prayerfulness.

Like most people, Christina had endured her share of difficulties in life. Inevitable hardships and the usual troubles of everyday living did not spare her. She never considered herself spiritually special.

Christina first began to experience the stigmata when as she says: "I first experienced pain in my wrists, my feet, and my forehead, and then red marks appeared."

In actuality, this partaking of the suffering of Christ came to her by invitation. Christ's invitation. She knew not what it implied. Christ first asked her if she wished her will to be joined with His. "Will you allow Me to suffer in you?" Jesus inquired of her in 1989. Afterward, she began to receive the Stigmata of the Passion.

Like Mother Teresa, whose self-imposed life of hardship parallels the poor and homeless with whom the famous nun works, Christina no longer sees any use for this world's many charms and pleasures. Those cravings are gone forever. Through total abandonment, God's will for her to suffer is all she now hungers for. It is a constant hunger.

It is in this way, says Christina, "I can strip myself of my weakness. The closer I come to Jesus the more my weakness disappears." To her spiritual director she confided more:

Today, Tuesday, I am suffering even more than Thursday night, but I try and try to surrender all, even though it is only in words. Father, I am weak and feel lost, but if that is the only way on the narrow road of the Cross to Jesus and Our Holy Mother, than that is the way I want.

Jesus is my way, my truth, and my life, even though I feel no progress nor see any light. I live, not because I want to, but because I must, to let my flesh become dust. Out of my weakness may the Good Lord have Mercy on me and purify me and draw souls to Himself.

I feel as if I'm just breaking up in mind and body and soul. It's not just one suffering at a time, but many at the same time. I think of God. He is the living spring in our souls and when we do something, whether it be our prayer or sacrifice, unless it is from the heart and out of love for God alone, then we allow that pure spring of Divine life within us to be clouded and it is of little value. It is of no value to get our reward in this world—the clap on the back, as it were. The only reward I desire now is that of Heaven. I do understand now, when Jesus said in the Gospel that people will see and yet not see, hear and yet not hear.

Putting on her best face to explain about her sacrifice and suffering, Christina reluctantly exposes her inner self to us. This is hard for her, because her spiritual aspirations reveal the depth of her response, and the way she gives God total freedom to do as He wishes with her.

"It is an awful deep suffering inside, not of mind or body, but of soul. I don't know how to describe it, only to throw myself at the Mercy of God and surrender. 'Lord make me surrender, I am nothing. Use me like a mat, if that is what pleases you.' "

Surrender, embrace, abandon—the words of the life of a victim soul.

In yet another remarkable letter, Christina permits us an even deeper glimpse of the weight of her cross, and teaches us more about how to suffer, sacrifice, and pray. Like seeing through the eyes of a prophet, we are asked to feel through the body of a victim soul. "It is not easy. But this in a way," says Christina, "is what we all must strive to do to truly live in union with God.

This morning I went to Holy Mass to receive Jesus. . . . I only had the normal pains in my wrists and head, now and then. Then after Holy Mass, at about eleven o'clock, I found not only a weight in my heart but in my body. Such weight I don't understand. I felt it was the weight of sin which Jesus permitted me to experience, but then at the same time, there was a love that was so great . . . the love was so great it was also pain. It was the love of God Triumphant through the Cross. I felt like a cup that God was filling with the Divine Love that was flowing from the Heart of Jesus. In my nothingness, I felt that it was nearly unbearable and to die would be easy, for it would lead to eternal union with Him.

This went on for a long time. I had an awareness that it was truly the Love of God as if Jesus or God wanted to reach out to all. I was aware of how little love there was in the hearts of all people. I was not able to contain it in my heart, soul, or body. I don't know any other way to express myself.

This is a prayer inspired in Christina by the Spirit of God, as she shared Christ's suffering.

O God, Our Father in Jesus, consume me into the wounds of Jesus and hide me therein for the Holy Mercy of God, to save souls. That is my submission to Thy Holy Will. You will draw souls to Yourself through the Passion of Jesus. Look, Holy Father, upon the Holy Wounds of Jesus and the tears of Mary, His mother, and embrace with Thy Love my poor nothingness, hidden in the shelter of the deep wounds of Jesus. As I embrace in my heart, soul, and body Your Holy Will, grant Mercy to the souls, which Jesus Your Son thirsts for more.

> O Holy Father, my only Father, in life or death, let the golden Light of Your Love in the Holy Spirit fly forth and draw all to the Holy Wounds of Jesus. Through His deep wounds draw souls and in those wounds they will find life in the love of the Most Sacred Heart of Jesus

God's will! Here is the answer. From her suffering, Christina's soul has come to understand God's will in her life. With this knowledge and acceptance, she has learned through the spirit of fortitude, to surrender all fear. Fear holds us back, but not Christina.

She now has peace, real peace; the peace she hungered for. It is a peace especially noted by experts who have seriously examined the mystical events surrounding her life.

Her spiritual director, Father Gerard McGinnity, who studied Spirituality at the Gregorian in Rome, has marveled at times at what he beheld God doing in her soul. Again, only textbook accounts of the lives of some of the saints could compare with what he was observing.

Father McGinnity wrote, ". . . I saw that Christina was being led more and more deeply into the plan of God, in being asked to suffer. This is not something she speaks much about, because Our Lady so requested, but I can say that her sufferings have been incredible. She has suffered the Passion of Jesus, and worse than the physical sufferings, which are almost constantly with her, and which I have witnessed—is the abandonment or desolation of Christ in His Agony. She has been given the impact of the sin of the world on Jesus' Heart. Jesus has invited her to atone, through her sufferings, not just for Ireland—though she suffers mainly for Ireland—but for the whole world."

But perhaps we must return to Christina's own words, once again, to comprehend how this victim soul has come to totally understand and embrace God's will in her life. In her words we see how it is only through complete abandonment that one can come to total peace. God's peace.

Overwhelmed with pain and plagued by attacks from Satan,

Christina tells us more than just the account of a victim soul. Her words dig deeper.

In reality, they offer us a moment of reflection to examine our own souls to see whether or not we are even scratching the surface in our response to God's will for our lives. We all are called in some way to expiate in union with the Lord, whether we're aware of it or not, whether we want to or not. The suffering in our lives is meant to have meaning.

Pope Pius XI, wrote of this necessity:

> It is entirely proper that Christ, Who is still suffering in His Mystical Body, should want to have us as His companions in the work of expiation. This is required of us also by our close union with Him, since we are "The body of Christ and individual members of it" (1 Cor. 12:27), and all the members ought to suffer with the Head anything that the Head suffers. (1 Cor. 12:26)
>
> (Pope Pius XI, *Miserentissiumus Redemptor,* 1928)

Somehow the Popes always seem to say it right. As if God dictates to them the words of truth the flock so desperately needs to hear.

And what a confusing world it is! Misery shadows the world like fallout from a cosmic collision. Like the flood waters from Noah's day, sorrow has now submerged the planet.

As we head into the twenty-first century, the world is filled with entire nations of people in constant suffering. It is a suffering the secular world denies has any purpose or significance. Thus, to most, because the world defies understanding, this suffering is ironically pointed to as a primary reason for the denial of the existence of God.

But Jesus told Christina that the world, like herself, will only enter into peace through this suffering. In fact, visionaries tell us the entire world will be massively suffering to the point of surrender. Then, like Christina's soul, it will have no place else to turn but to God. From the dense darkness will come forth the great light. All will be renewed, especially the Church. Indeed, Christ has promised this to Christina and other victims of His love.

Christina's "yes" to a life of suffering, in union with Christ, has blessed her with extraordinary graces not fully comprehensible.

On two occasions, she received mystical gifts that illustrate her special union with Christ. These gifts were in the form of invisible rings which Jesus placed on her fingers. Surrounded in mystery, these rings are meant to be symbols of her powerful spiritual union as a victim with the Savior.

On May 2, 1992, she wrote to her spiritual director concerning the second of these gifts and then recalled how she received them both:

I was feeling so helpless, and I sat down and offered all I felt to Jesus and Our Holy Mother, that in some way to let my tears be of consolation to the Heart of Jesus and His mother Mary. At some point through this I then could see Saint Thérèse, then Saint Bernadette. Saint Bernadette was dressed in brown with the gray hood as I have seen her before and Saint Thérèse as normal, with the cream cloak, brown dress, etc. They both went into a kneeling position, and then came behind them Our Holy Mother. She was smiling and said, "My daughter be at peace."

At that, Our Holy Mother came forward, as if through Saint Thérèse and Saint Bernadette. Then Our Holy Mother looked toward my right hand and asked me to give her my hand. I gave Our Holy Mother my hand, as it was my right hand she was looking at. I could see this wedding ring just sparkling. Our Holy Mother held the ring in her hand for a little while as she asked me, "My daughter, will you accept to be truly one in union with my Divine Son Jesus?" I did not know what she meant, but I said "yes."

Our Holy Mother then took the ring finger of my right hand and put the ring on my hand to the knuckle. Then our Holy Mother turned to her left-hand side, and I could see Jesus and His Face was so bright and so full of love. He was dressed in white, as was Our Holy Mother. Then Jesus said something about it being our mystical union in marriage. With that, Jesus looked upward and said, "Nothing in Heaven or on Earth will break this union." At that, Jesus looked at me with such love and then Jesus bent down and kissed my forehead.

I felt as if I was in Heaven! I felt a warm heat coming from the area from my forehead where Jesus kissed me and it got a heat going through my head and I felt so at peace, and I loved Jesus and Our Holy Mother so much, words cannot express. Our Holy Mother said that her anointed Son will be of consolation to me. What all this means I do not know.

Some time ago Jesus said the same, and put a golden ring on my left-hand ring finger and there was a diamond countersunk in the wedding ring. Jesus did not say anything then about the ring, only about the diamond stone. The stone was His gift to me, of the virtue of His Love. Jesus then said, that as time went by, the ring would be encircled with diamonds.

I have seen that ring a few times. The last time there were three stones in the ring, but I don't know what the other two mean. About the ring today Jesus said it will become visible on my finger when I suffer, and later His heart and the Heart of His Immaculate Mother will come on the ring and I will suffer in complete union with their hearts.

Much more has happened to her since then. The Lord has gotten closer to His victim.

On October 5, 1992, Jesus again sought to console her. This time helping her to better understand this mystical union of suffering.

"Little flower, be not afraid, it is I, Jesus."

Upon hearing these words, Christina recalls, "I got a fright. Jesus' voice was so real and alive. I said a few words to Jesus in resonance to His Words. Then Jesus said to me . . .

"You are a victim in union in My Love. You give Me a drink of souls. There are few this day willing to give Me a drink of love, little flower. The Blood of the Lamb is being desecrated, trampled upon. How can My little ones give glory to their Lord God? The blind try to lead the blind. I am Love. I am Unity. I am Peace. Few come to drink of Me."

After hearing this declaration, Christina still didn't fully understand, but in her total spirit of abandonment and trust, she concluded, "It doesn't matter."

So in faith, she marches forward. It is this way with all victim souls. They are to be blind to their own needs and sufferings, trusting all to the Lord.

In 1992, Christina Gallagher was even shown her death. This caused her to respond in the only way she knew how. She pleaded for a more painful form of death to save souls.

This was not unusual, because victim souls constantly hunger for more suffering. Never do they have enough, like Padre Pio, whom Our Lady said is with Christina at all times. Padre Pio wrote to his spiritual director:

"This desire has been growing continually in my heart so that it has now become what I would call a strong passion. I, in fact, have made this offering to the Lord several times, beseeching Him to pour out upon me the punishments prepared for sinners and for the souls in purgation, even increase them a hundredfold for me, as long as He converts and saves sinners and quickly admits to Paradise the souls in Purgatory."[5]

Like Padre Pio, Christina says it must be like this because "Only in this way can I be of any value."

In death the Lord has promised a crown awaits the faithful. This crown was symbolically shown to Christina. On one occasion, Our Lady appeared to her with a crown. Christina insists this crown was, to her, "as physical and material and real as the Blessed Virgin Mary before her."

On this occasion, she tried to grasp the crown from Our Lady, but the Queen of Peace withdrew it saying, "Later, my child."

Afterward, Jesus offered her a second crown. This crown was larger and more beautiful. The Savior then explained, "The more you abandon yourself to me the bigger your crown becomes."

This indicated, according to the Lord's words, her glory was increasing with her suffering. This is true not just for her, reminds Christina, "but for all of us."

So Christina's total abandonment to the Lord is all she focuses upon. All that is left for her to live for, is the Lord alone, causing one to ponder the words of Saint Louis de Montfort:

What ill or evil, Lord, can harm this joyous heart
that You alone can charm?
I love You more with every breath
So how can I fear life or death?
To love You, Father, is to live and sing
The song the angels sing their King.
God alone in every cell of me!
God alone! For all eternity![6]

NOTES

Chapter 1: *From Genesis to the Triumph*

1. Mary Purcell, "Our Lady of Silence," in *A Woman Clothed with the Sun,* ed. John J. Delaney (New York: Doubleday Dell Publishing Group, 1990), p. 147.
2. Author's interview with visionary Christina Gallagher, February 1992.

Chapter 3: *"My Son Has Chosen Christina"*

1. René Laurentin, *The Apparitions of the Blessed Virgin Mary Today* (Paris: Veritas Publications, 1990), pp. 171–172.
2. Michael H. Brown, *The Final Hour* (Milford, Ohio: Faith Publishing Company, 1992), p. 281.
3. William Thomas Walsh, *Saint Teresa of Avila* (Rockford, Illinois: TAN Books and Publishers, 1944), p. 286.

Chapter 4: *A Pure Conversion*

1. Sandra L. Zimdars-Swartz, *Encountering Mary* (Princeton, New Jersey: Princeton University Press, 1991), p. 5.

2. Ibid. p. 5.
3. Ibid.

CHAPTER 7: *Beautiful Beyond Imagination*

1. Father Joseph Dirvin, C.M., *Saint Catherine Labouré of the Miraculous Medal* (Rockford, Illinois: TAN Books and Publishers, 1994), p. 87.
2. Josye Terelya with Michael H. Brown, *Witness* (Milford, Ohio: Faith Publishing Company, 1991), p. 121.
3. Catherine M. Odell, *Those Who Saw Her* (Huntington, Indiana: Our Sunday Visitor Publishing Division, 1986), p. 78.
4. Ibid. p. 132.
5. Francis Johnston, *The Wonder of Guadalupe* (Rockford, Illinois: TAN Books and Publishers, 1981), pp. 26–27.
6. Fiscar Marison, *The Mystical City of God* (Rockford, Illinois: Ave Maria Institute, 1978), pp. 68–69.

CHAPTER 8: *Through the Eyes of a Prophet*

1. Father René Laurentin, op. cit. pp. 16–17.

CHAPTER 10: *One with Christ*

1. Father Joseph Vann, O.F.M., ed., *Lives of Saints* (New York: John J. Crawley & Company, 1954), p. 429.
2. John Beevors, *The Autobiography of Saint Thérèse of Lisieux* (New York: Bantam Doubleday Dell Publishing Group, 1989), p. 143.

CHAPTER 12: *I, Your Father, Yahweh*

1. Vann, op. cit. pp. 289–298.
2. Ibid. p. 290.
3. Ibid.

CHAPTER 13: *Where Angels Tread*

1. Father Pascale P. Parente, *Beyond Space* (Rockford, Illinois: TAN Books and Publishers, 1973), p. 43.
2. Ibid. p. 18.

CHAPTER 14: *The Church Triumphant*

1. Vann, op. cit. p. ix.
2. Ibid.

CHAPTER 15: *The Abyss of Sin*

1. Father F. X. Schouppe, S.J., *Hell* (Rockford, Illinois: TAN Books and Publishers, 1989), p. 152.
2. Ibid. p. xxviii.
3. Ibid. p. xxvii.
4. Father Louis Kondor, S.V.C., *Fatima in Lucia's Own Words* (Still River, Massachusetts: 1989, The Ravengate Press), p. 104.

CHAPTER 17: *The Chamber of Suffering*

1. Father F. X. Schouppe, S.J., *Purgatory* (Rockford, Illinois: TAN Books and Publishers, 1986), p. 16.
2. Ibid. p. xvii.
3. Ibid. p. 21.

CHAPTER 18: *The Sign of the Power of the Antichrist*

1. Rev. P. Huchede, *History of Antichrist* (Rockford, Illinois: TAN Books and Publishers, 1976), p. 10.
2. Ibid. p. 10.
3. Ibid.
4. Ibid. p. 11.
5. Ibid. p. 12.
6. Ibid.
7. Ibid. p. 13.

CHAPTER 19: *Searching for Meaning in the Revelations*

1. Sister M. Faustina Kowalska, *Divine Mercy in My Soul* (Stockbridge, Massachusetts: Marion Press, 1987), p. 148.
2. Ibid. p. 282.

CHAPTER 20: *Heart to Heart Prayer*

1. Vann, op. cit. p. ix.
2. Ibid. p. x.

CHAPTER 22: *"Arm Yourself with My Rosary"*

1. St. Louis de Montfort, *The Secret of the Rosary* (Bay Shore, N.Y.: Montfort Publications, 1984), pp. 44–45.

CHAPTER 25: *From Mercy to Justice*

1. Kowalska, op. cit. p. 100.
2. George W. Kosicki C.S.B., *Special Urgency of Mercy: Why Sister Faustina?* (Steubenville, Ohio: Franciscan University Press, 1990), p. 21.
3. Kowalska, op. cit. p. 11.
4. Ibid. pp. 149, 198.

CHAPTER 27: *"My Beloved Children of Ireland"*

1. Brown, op. cit. p. 280.

CHAPTER 31: *A Little Soul*

1. Father Michael Freze, S.F.O., *They Bore the Wounds of Christ—The Mystery of the Stigmata* (Huntington, Indiana: Our Sunday Visitor Publishing Division, 1989), p. 11.
2. Dr. Imbert-Gourbeyre, *La Stigmatization,* 1894 (cited in ibid. p. 11).
3. Freze, op cit. p. 11.
4. Ibid. p. 12.
5. Padre Pio, *Epistolario* [Letters, vol. 1], November 29, 1910 (cited in ibid. p. 64).
6. Eddie Doherty, *Wisdom's Fool* (Bay Shore, New York: Montfort Publications, 1987), p. 14.

Selected Bibliography

Beevors, John. *The Autobiography of Saint Thérèse of Lisieux*. New York: Bantam Doubleday Dell Publishing Group, 1989.

Brown, Michael H. *The Final Hour*. Milford, Ohio: Faith Publishing Company, 1992.

Croiset, Father John, S.J. *The Devotion to the Sacred Heart of Jesus*. Rockford, Illinois: TAN Books and Publishers, 1988.

Delaney, John J., ed. *A Woman Clothed with the Sun*. New York: Doubleday Dell Publishing Group, 1990.

De Montfort, Saint Louis. *The Secret of the Rosary*. Bay Shore, New York: Montfort Publications, 1984.

Dirvin, Father Joseph I., C.M. *Saint Catherine Labouré of the Miraculous Medal*. Rockford, Illinois: TAN Books and Publishers, 1984.

Freze, Father Michael, S.F.O. *They Bore the Wounds of Christ—The Mystery of the Sacred Stigmata*. Huntington, Indiana: Our Sunday Visitor Publishing Division, 1989.

The Holy Bible: Translated from the Latin Vulgate. 1899. Reprint, Rockford, Illinois: TAN Books and Publishers, 1971.

Huchede, Rev. P. *History of AntiChrist*. Rockford, Illinois: TAN Books and Publishers, 1976.

Jesus and Mary Speak in Ireland—Messages to Christina Gallagher. Ireland: 1991.

Johnston, Francis. *The Wonder of Guadalupe*. Rockford, Illinois: TAN Books and Publishers, 1981.

Kondor, Father Louis. *Fatima in Lucia's Own Words.* Still River, Massachusetts: The Ravengate Press, 1989.

Kosicki, George W., C.S.B. *Special Urgency of Mercy: Why Sister Faustina?* Steubenville, Ohio: Franciscan University Press, 1990.

Kowalska, Sister M. Faustina. *Divine Mercy in My Soul.* Stockbridge, Massachusetts: Marian Press, 1987.

Laurentin, Father René. *The Apparitions of the Blessed Virgin Mary Today.* Paris: Veritas Publications, 1990.

Marison, Fiscar. *The Mystical City of God.* Rockford, Illinois: TAN Books and Publishers, 1978.

The New American Bible: Translated from the Original Languages with Critical Use of All the Ancient Sources by Members of the Catholic Biblical Association of America. Wichita, Kansas: Catholic Bible Publishers, 1970.

Saint Catherine of Siena. *The Dialogue of Saint Catherine of Siena.* Translated by Algar Thorold. Rockford, Illinois: TAN Books and Publishers, 1974.

St. Michael and the Angels. Compiled from approved sources; no author listed. Rockford, Illinois: TAN Books and Publishers, 1983.

Tanquerey, Adolphe, S.S.D.D. *The Spiritual Life—A Treatise on Ascetical and Mystical Theology.* Westminster, Maryland: The Newman Press.

Terelya, Josyp, with Michael H. Brown. *Witness.* Milford, Ohio: Faith Publishing Company, 1991.

Vincent, R. *Please Come Back to Me and My Son.* Milford County, Armagh, Ireland: Milford House, 1992.

Walsh, William Thomas. *Saint Teresa of Avila.* Milwaukee, Wisconsin: Bruce Publishing Company, 1944.

Zimdars-Swartz, Sandra. *Encountering Mary.* Princeton, New Jersey: Princeton University Press, 1991.